HOW MAINE DECIDES

AN INSIDER'S GUIDE TO HOW BALLOT MEASURES ARE WON AND LOST

CHRISTIAN P. POTHOLM

With an All-Star cast featuring
Dave Emery, Dennis Bailey,
Edie Smith, Erik Potholm, Kay Rand

Down East Books

CAMDEN, MAINE

Published by Down East Books
An imprint of Globe Pequot
Trade division of The Rowman & Littlefield Publishing Group, Inc.
4501 Forbes Blvd., Ste. 200
Lanham, MD 20706
www.rowman.com
www.downeastbooks.com

Distributed by NATIONAL BOOK NETWORK

ISBN 978-1-68475-206-5 (Paperback)
ISBN 978-1-68475-207-2 (e-book)

∞™ The paper used in this publication meets the minimum requirements of American National Standard for Information Sciences—Permanence of Paper for Printed Library Materials, ANSI/NISO Z39.48-1992.

To all the Political Consultants of the Pine Tree State
Those who got things done and made things
happen along a multiplicity of campaign trails.
What would they do without us?
What would we do without them?

CONTENTS

"It's not how far the buffalo flew, it's that the buffalo flew at all."

"You can fool some of the people all the time, and all the people some of the time. And those ain't bad odds."

"It was fabulous, just like the OK Corral. They brought their guys, and we brought our guys, and we gunned them down some good, something like 60–40. I felt bad seeing them lying there in the dust. Not too bad though."

"Great. Count me in. Give me the gun and the bullets. Say, whose side are we on anyway? Not that it matters."

"They're saying that? Hell, without me they would have lost a lot worse."

"Let's just have a little fun and make a little money. Maybe both. We're done with campaigns with neither. They're not worth it."

"Aye me hearties, the treasure fleet of the Dons has entered the Straits of Florida. We will strike them there and rob them of their gold and silver and jewels and send them to the bottom of the sea. Look lively now, lads. Ye can rest all this winter."

"A camel is a horse designed by a steering committee." —Dave Emery

"Him? He's one of those consultants who knows a hundred ways to make love but doesn't know any women—or men—to practice on." —Dennis Bailey

"For this campaign, we want a nice quiet little war and a quick one." —Joe Cowie

"When it's time to circle the wagons, be sure all of your weapons are not pointed at each other." —Phil Harriman

"There's nothing better than a scared, rich candidate or client." —Molly Ball

"A campaign that won't listen to its consultants is destined to become nothing but a goat rodeo." —Dave Emery

"Sweat the small stuff and the big stuff will take care of itself." —Mary McAleney

And one more time, the best:

"Living well is the best revenge." —George Herbert

IN MEMORIAM

All those who have gone to the great "C Street" in the sky, where all the clients are appreciative, generous, and docile.

George Smith, Abby Holman, Peter Burr, John Christie, Maureen Sullivan, Charlie and Marlene Petersen, Dale "Boy" Geary, Jack Havey, Link Linkovitch, Lil Caron, Neil Rolde, Sid Watson, Georgette Berube, Charlie Butt, Nate Kendrick, Hattie Bickmore, Alex Ray, Clyde McDonald, Nate Dane, Charlie Moreshead, Roger Putnam, Harry Richardson, Marshall Stern, Bud Leavitt, Jane Johnson, Chris Duval, Gayle Corey, Joy O'Brien, Mert Henry, Jim Brunelle, John Cole, Ted Curtis, Steve Tremblay, Rod Quinn, Fred Nutter, Robin Lambert, Mal Leary, Fran Quinn, Davis Rawson, Peter Damborg, Don Hansen, King Harvey, Don Larrabee, Glenn Adams, Nancy Grape, Bob Cummings, Peter Cox, Jack Linnell, Greg Stevens, Davey Redmond, Dan Paradis, John Jenkins, Dale "Girl" Geary, Mark Harroff, Chuck Winner, John Donovan, Haz Hazelton, Paul Hawthorne, Shep Lee, John Rensenbrink, Frank Coffin, Roger Mallar, Arthur Stilphen, Harold Jones, Ken Hayes, Ed Kelleher, Dick Morrell, and Dan Payne.

Note: any possible omissions or faulty inclusions are unintentional.

PREFACE

I have been authoring books since I was twenty-three, and almost sixty years later I am still writing them. In fact, I don't know how to live without writing a book. I've tried it once or twice, but I didn't like the feeling I got. Writing even got me through COVID with my sanity intact. As David Cornwell (John le Carré) says in *A Private Spy*, "When I'm writing properly, I still feel 23."

So here comes another one! Why this particular one?

This one has been percolating for a long time. I spent forty years in politics and met many, many very interesting people and watched them interact on the political trail, making and breaking candidates and public policy. They all had stories to tell and incidents to relate. Many were inspiring and praise-worthy. I also spent fifty years teaching about politics, and over those years I refined and distilled what I thought was important about politics in general and Maine politics in particular into fourteen axioms. Then I asked a lot of political insiders to respond, positively or negatively to them.

Although I have been fortunate to be able to work on campaigns in a wide variety of other places—New Hampshire, Florida, Texas, New Mexico, Nevada, Idaho, Oregon, Minnesota, Ohio, Pennsylvania, Rhode Island, and New York—this one is primarily about patterns of political campaigns in Maine, but I'm sure most any of the axioms work elsewhere as well.

This book isn't really about the specifics and evaluations of candidates and causes; it's more about the various consultants—polling, strategy, media, press, grassroots, GOTV, and all the rest—who play such important roles in political campaigns in Maine. It is, in many ways, "An Ode to Consultants" (with apologies to Robert Browning). The general public often undervalues the role so many play.

But this work is more than that. While there are many books about Maine's political figures like Ed Muskie and Margaret Chase Smith and the Republican and Democratic campaigns, there is no major work on Maine's ballot measures and ballots. Certainly, none that provides an overview of what they are, what they are meant to accomplish, who gets them on the ballot, and who passes them or shoots them down as they fly overhead.

This is thus the story of the men and women who, working outside the legislature and with the help of, or in spite of, elected officials, make public policy for the Pine Tree State.

My fellow principal writers—Dave Emery, Dennis Bailey, Edie Smith, Kay Rand, and Erik Potholm made vital contributions to this work. Their sparkling remembrances of both ballot measures and candidate campaigns give it depth and meaning far beyond what I could have provided on my own. They had very valuable input on my own material as well, and I thank them deeply for the pleasure of having worked with them on various enterprises before this one as well. In victory or in defeat, they were steadfast.

I want to give a most special shout-out to Dave Emery and Dennis Bailey whose professional copyediting job on the entire manuscript was a gift from the publishing gods. They were a terrifically positive influence in the writing of this book: careful, consistent, and patient. They have a whole new career in front of them should they wish to pursue it. And Dave was extremely helpful in digging out difficult to find material, polling and otherwise. His database and work ethic are truly outstanding.

Many others have contributed—by thought, word, action, and deed—to this work and to my ongoing political education, including all the contributors, by being and especially doing "in the Maine political arena."

These include Keith Brown, Tommy Davidson, Betsy Sweet, Angus King, Larry Benoit, Bruce Chalmers, Jean Carbral, Ralph Coffman, Cory Haskell, Pat Peard, Rosemary Baldacci, Shenna Bellows, Bruce Davis, Severin Beliveau, Susan Longley, John Diamond, Dick Barringer, Paul Dillaway, Tony Corrado, Willis Johnson, Carolyn Cosby, Dick Davies, John Delahanty, Ed Kane, Peter O'Donnell, John Orestis, Allen Philbrick, Seth Berry, Chuck Cianchette, Jimmy Betts, Vinny O'Malley, Ed Gorham, Charlie O'Leary, Robyn Merrill, Ted O'Meara, Kaileigh Tara, Jerry Plante, Les Otten, Bill "B.J." Johnson, Barb Kovach, Hal Gosselin, Al Gamache, Jamie Firth, Amos Eno, Shep Lee, Sandy Faucher, Phil Harriman, Will Gardner, Seth Kurzman, Dave Kerry, Dick Morrell, Rod Quinn, Joe Pietroski, Jim Ward, Linwood Ross, Dan Coyne, Charlie Jacobs, Rick Barton, John Kerry, Dave Ault, Peter Chandler, Lucille Burr, Ken Burrill, Jeff Romano, Hal Pachios, Dave Vail, Jim Mitchell, Bill Haggett, Robin Lambert, Julie L'Heureux, Jed Lyons, Paul Jacques, Barry Hobbins, Maria Fuentes, Peter Cutler, Dana Connors, John Oliver, Gerry Talbot, Joe Mackey, George Campbell, Joe Cowie, Bob Turner, Brownie Carson, Pat McGowan, Tony Buxton, Matt McTighe, Jonathan Carter, Greg Nadeau, Paul Mills, Alan Caron, Karin Tilberg, Bob Deis, Sandy Potholm, Ann Mitchell, Phil Merrill, Dave Sparks, Pat Eltman, George Isaacson, Ethan Strimling, Bobby Reynolds, Lance Tapley, David Farmer, Betsy Smith, Anna Lidman, Newell Augur, Lance Dutson, Justin Alfond, David Lemoine, Tony Armstrong, Jim Wilfong, Mary McAleney, Jerry Conley Jr., and John Hathaway. Note: A list of some of Maine's top campaign managers appear in chapter 6 as well.

Some have shared their experiences directly and admit to being role models but have chosen, even begged, to remain anonymous.

In the process of putting this collection together, I also learned that in the interest of Maine's reading public I should next try to get Barry Hobbins to sit still long enough to write his own book. Give me a dinner with Tip O'Neill, Ronald Reagan, and Barry, and I bet Barry wins the storytelling contests without breaking a sweat. Writing this book and checking out campaigns and the stories that go with them, I cannot tell you how many times I laughed out loud getting Barry's take on the Maine political scene over the last forty years. His stories are unvarnished, extremely funny, and very illuminating.

A special, special thanks to the Bowdoin Special Collections staff in general, and Ann Sauer in particular, for all their assistance in finding support (or even more helpful dissuasion) for my many wild claims and faulty memories. Carmen Greely also was a great help in researching these various campaigns. Thanks also to Elise Hocking who always gets hard-to-find materials and to Libby Hunt whose careful perusal of the manuscript was most helpful and illuminating. A special kudo and thanks to Senator Angus King for his careful and insightful reading of the manuscript and his numerous observations, corrections, and suggestions.

To Mike Steere of Down East Books and Jed Lyons and Elaine McGarraugh of the Rowman & Littlefield Publishing Group Inc., many, many thanks. Mike encouraged the creation of this work and was very helpful through the production process. Elaine was a joy to work with and her copyediting skills are truly renowned. Jed is the most outstanding publisher going today and publishes under so many imprints that they cannot all be listed here. He remains an author's best friend, in or out of academia. Try out both of them for your next book!

Finally, as always, to Sandy Quinlan Potholm, muse, model, and inspiration, and recent author of her own inspiring book, *In Those Days*. She simply makes my every day on earth a true, blessed treasure.

Harpswell, Maine
2023

INTRODUCTION

Descriptions of campaigns usually devote 95 percent of their coverage to the candidate or the cause. This is probably how it should be because candidates and cause leaders put themselves out there. They are risking the most, and many causes transcend any given election cycle.

But this book seeks to redress the balance a bit by focusing on the consultants who serve those candidates and those causes and, on the campaign, "axioms" or patterns that offer ongoing insights into the nature of all, both candidate and ballot measure campaigns. These axioms can also apply to image enhancement and revenue generation campaigns by companies and philanthropic organizations, although these aspects are not covered here.

Campaigns are, at base, interactions that occur over a fixed period of time and represent a relationship between one side and another. This yin/yang relationship is central to our understanding of how campaigns really work. You and your cause may have a perfectly sound plan for winning your ballot measure, but as war planners are fond of saying (but seldom follow their own advice), "The enemy gets a vote."

Thus, your campaign's chances of success are related to a considerable extent by what your opponent does or does not do. The mistakes the opponent makes or doesn't make. Thus you should always be aware of Napoleon's dictum, "Never interrupt your enemy when she or he is making a mistake." Or the reverse, "Interrupt your enemy" when she or he isn't making one.

Readers may also note here that "targeting" in elections has changed dramatically over the last forty years. The playing field has shrunk substantially. Previously, while working for Republicans, Democrats, and Independents in Maine, I never heard anyone wish for a smaller turnout, let alone wanting to "suppress" any segment of the electorate. We always thought the more voters, the better. The more we could persuade. The more we could convert. "Politics is addition," went the refrain, and we lived it!

As Bobby Reynolds, an important Maine operative who has played a significant role on a variety of ballot measures as well as the campaigns of Senator Susan Collins and Representative Jared Golden, agrees, "The most important and impactful lesson I learned from the people who taught me the business of electoral politics is that winning is about addition."

I always thought we had the better or best candidate or the better or best cause and/or the better campaign. We always wanted the maximum number of voters out and about and hearing our messages. We always favored a November vote over a June one. We favored a large turnout over a small one.

And we always felt we could convert many on the other side. We always felt that getting one of their voters was the same as getting two more of ours out. Today, almost the entire focus goes the other way. It is reduced to getting out your base while keeping down the turnout of your opponents. Subtracting instead of adding and then trying to reduce the opponent's access further? Madness for democracy. Again, in forty years in Maine politics, with all types of political groups, I can't ever remember anyone talking about suppressing the opponent's turnout. That line of thinking today is most antidemocratic and very corrosive to the body politic. It's a shame, and those currently advocating it should be ashamed.

To test the validity of my own experiences, I asked Mary "She was a Splendid Waitress" McAleney if she had ever heard talk of suppressing voters. Mary's amazing career in politics spans fifty years, including at all levels (beginning with Ed Muskie) of managing campaigns (Phil Merrill for congress and Joe Brennan for governor), serving as chief of staff for George Mitchell and working in the US Small Business Administration, as well as being an entrepreneur in her own right, even building the Maine Irish Heritage Center.

Her answer was unequivocal: "NEVER. NEVER. NEVER. NEVER. You reach out. You persuade. You educate. You find common ground. You aim to solve problems. You don't suppress."

For his part, Barry Hobbins, an insider's insider in Maine politics for fifty years, likewise says, "No. No. No" to having seen voter suppression being advocated in the Pine Tree State. Instead, he maintains that in Maine "Election Day is a Holy Day of Obligation."

To illustrate the imperatives of broad targeting as opposed to suppression, here is but one example of the operational significance of this conversional approach. It is a set of actual instructions given to the NO side during the Palesky Tax Cap referendum of 2004. At that time, many Republicans and those favoring it wanted the referendum held in June. We and Governor John Baldacci wanted it in November in order to maximize our time to convert opponents and have a larger pool of voters susceptible to education and persuasion. The more people who would vote, we thought, the better our chances to convince a majority to vote our way.

For this "Quiet Period," that is, before we went on the air with TV, here were my targeting values for *this specific campaign* (Palesky Tax Cap) and *this particular ballot measure* as conveyed to the campaign ground game coordinator, specific goals based on our polling that reflect this effort:

1 business person = 10 other voters
1 Franco = 2 Irish
1 Republican = 2 Democrats
1 small town R = 2 urban Ds
1 conservative = 2 liberals

That was our mindset *before* we went on TV and radio. Broaden the playing field, target our opponent's voters, convert, educate, persuade—not subvert or suppress.

Assumptions about turnout and targeting approaches can determine overall strategy as well. For example, in 2009, advocates of gay marriage suffered a loss in an off-year, concentrate-on-turning-out-your-own-supporters effort. After that defeat, they adopted a much more ambitious, holistic targeting strategy. They fought the next gay marriage referendum in a presidential election year and continued their most impressive outreach/conversion effort.

This resulted in a victory in 2012.

The axioms depicted in this book represent years of political engagement on all levels, and taken together I hope they will give readers a much richer and in-depth look at the political process so critical to our rich national heritage. In Maine, our state motto is *Dirigo* ("I Lead"); accordingly, we seek to educate, enlighten, and hopefully amuse as we do.

This is thus the story of the men and women who, often working outside the legislature and with the help of, or in spite of, elected officials, make public policy for the Pine Tree State.

As you read this, especially if you didn't like one of the ballot measure outcomes, always remember the words of more than one political operative: "If the legislature does its job, we wouldn't need any of these referenda."

AXIOM #1

"All the Big Mistakes Are Made Early"

Act in haste, repent in leisure.
—WILLIAM CONGREVE

The first rule of Maine politics is "All the Big Mistakes Are Made Early." So much political lore and history focuses on "October Surprises" and last-minute endorsements, game-changing events, and mistakes made at the end of an election cycle that it is very easy to lose sight of this fundamental rule.

In this regard, we owe a great debt to Chuck Winner of Winner Wagner (later Winner and Mandabach Campaigns) who first taught us this axiom in 1980 during the Maine Yankee Nuclear Shutdown referendum. When the Save Maine Yankee committee hired his firm to do the advertising and strategic management that year, the campaign manager John Menario and I initially proposed a traditional big Maine rollout, with flying visits to Presque Isle, Bangor, and Portland, and with heavily covered press conferences in all three to kick off the campaign.

The first thing Chuck did was to cancel all our plans. "If we do this," he said, "the opponents will get equal time in the press, the reporters will be gunning for us, and we will not control the message. Remember, all the big mistakes in politics are made early." Then he added, "We'll own the airwaves with our advertising and tell our own story."

He was so right, although as Erik Potholm points out, "The axiom is always strategically true, but only tactically true if you have the money to own the airwaves or at least more money than your opponent. If you don't have the money to tell your story, then you have to use free media to get it told because you have no choice. But if you do have the money and the other side not so much, you don't want to have press conferences to give them free airtime, the oxygen of campaigns."

Looking back on forty years of political activity, this axiom shines through with sharp clarity.

To illustrate, let's take the example of Tom Andrews, state senator from Portland and successful congressman, but subsequently unsuccessful candidate for the US Senate. To really understand his situation, you can go farther back in history to the story of the Greek boy Icarus who thought he could fly up to the sun, so he made some nice, feathered wings and attached them to his back with wax.

Icarus started off in the cool morning air and actually got off the ground. In fact, he managed to get far up into the clouds but then, as he got closer to the sun, the sun took its revenge for his hubris and melted the wax that held the wings in place.

Off came the wings.

Down, down, down plunged young Icarus, finally falling into the sea and into oblivion, much to the chagrin of himself and his family, including those who had encouraged him with this early example of the "audacity of hope."

Tom Andrews was a very likable, capable, bright guy who had gotten elected to Congress in 1990. A Bowdoin graduate, he had beaten cancer as a young man and found his niche in politics. Cool and shrewd, smart, and resolute, he was also very, very liberal and had been elected as the state senator from probably the most liberal district in the state before running for Congress.

In that small urban universe, his dedication to organization, going door to door and concentrating on get out the vote (GOTV) efforts as well as the ideological makeup of the voting population made a substantial difference. The force of his personality and smiling demeanor, along with his progressive, urban stances on most issues, carried the day. Now he was an up-and-coming liberal Democratic star in Washington, and since Maine has only two congressional seats, he was seen as a major actor in the whole state.

In the heady afterglow of his victories, however, like Icarus, he began to make mistakes, including some real doozies—at least if he had any realistic statewide ambitions. First, he rather glibly agreed when the Pentagon called for the closure of the Loring Air Force Base in northern Maine—a base about as far away from his Portland political base as could be and still be in the Pine Tree State. All the other members of the Maine congressional delegation vigorously opposed the Pentagon's decision to close it.

Whatever the merits of its closing from a military point of view, the base was regarded in northern Maine as an irreplaceable economic engine, and he outraged political figures, Democrat and Republican alike, by agreeing too readily to its closure. "It's not even in his district, for God's sake," some said.

Next, in a state with 250,000 hunters and other assorted sportsmen and sportswomen, he talked loud and long about gun control and for good measure, even voted against a bow hunting season in Maryland just to show folks who hunted that he wasn't afraid of thumbing his nose at them. Finally, and to put the icing on the cake, as people in Maine used to say, he even picked a fight with the then most important Democratic power broker, John Martin, who happened to live up north, even farther north than Loring Air Force Base!

Speaker Martin was—and remains—not a man to take criticisms lightly in general and certainly not from young whippersnappers from Portland in particular. Young Tom ended up not having a lot of friends in the establishment wing of the Maine Democratic Party before he ran for the US Senate, and he had fewer after.

Now all of this would have been irrelevant (as Icarus and his wax-fastened wings would have been, if he hadn't tried to fly with them), if he'd only stayed in his safe, small 1st CD. But one fine day, Senator George Mitchell, the Democratic majority leader of the US Senate who was supposed to run for reelection, decided enough was enough. Perhaps because being a Supreme Court justice or commissioner of baseball or making a lot of money in private life would be much more fun than continuing to try to manage the many, many supremely grandiose egos in the US Senate.

After all, he'd won his previous Senate race by a Maine record 81 percent to 19 percent, so some of *that* electoral challenge was gone. Retiring, Mitchell generously donated his not insignificant war chest to set up a college scholarship fund for Maine students and headed off into the proverbial sunset, a very happy camper, indeed.

Mitchell, of course, didn't want to leave a bad taste in President Bill Clinton's and the national Democratic mouths, so as he bowed out, someone seems to have convinced President Clinton that Congressman Tom Andrews, this loveable little lefty munchkin, could beat Republican Congresswoman Olympia Snowe who was already firmly dug in the Maine 2nd CD, a great advantage if she decided to run for the Senate in 1994. The 2nd CD is the largest CD east of the Mississippi and a candidate killer in those days—and still is—due to the difficulty in getting around to meet all the voters. She had been to every bean-hole supper in the North Country and knew all the important locals. Voted in their interests too, all these many years.

So here was young Andrews, and one fine day he got what must have seemed magical calls from Senator Mitchell and President Clinton, encouraging him to run for the US Senate. Pretty heady stuff. Tom didn't hesitate.

Icarus II glued on those beautiful wings and started flapping away. Perhaps he thought he could "organize" the whole state (which of course can't be organized—ever—by anybody).

Perhaps he also thought the president and Senator Mitchell would get him enough money so he could win on TV. Perhaps he thought he could beat Olympia Snowe one on one. Certainly he would be able to handle her in debates. Certainly his drive and personality would prevail. Etcetera, etcetera.

But those assumptional mistakes flew in the face of the existing realities—big time.

While Andrews jumped in on the spur of the heady moment, Snowe had been waiting sixteen years to run for the US Senate, and she was very, very ready. She had a strong staff and key advisers such as Dave Sparks and Jock McKernan. Snowe was very knowledgeable politically herself. Her eventual electoral record of twelve wins and zero losses speaks to her political sagacity and drive. She even knew enough to organize Maine motorcyclists who donated "toys for tots" every Christmas. She always got an A+ rating from the Sportsman's Alliance of Maine, probably the most important statewide interest group throughout Maine at that time. Young Andrews, of course, had an F rating, if they bothered to rate him at all.

Snowe had wanted to run against Mitchell in 1982 but dropped out of the Republican primary race when Congressman Dave Emery claimed the inside track. A lot of Republican State Committee people urged her to "wait her turn." It turned out they were correct, albeit perhaps for the wrong reasons. Once Emery was decisively defeated by Mitchell (61–39 percent), however, she had been waiting patiently for her chance. Whether or not she ever thanked Congressman Emery for taking that initial Mitchell fusillade head on and thought it was "better to be safe than sorry," is unclear. But ready she was when, subsequently, her next big chance arrived.

In any case, this smart, tough, and motivated woman raised a ton of money and began campaigning as if her life depended on it and ran some great TV commercials. Put simply, she blasted Icarus II out of the sky and tore him apart with interest groups such as veterans and hunters and fishermen and women as well as snowmobile and motorcycle riders.

With barely concealed glee, she seared off the wings of Icarus II with the heat of her TV commercials. She eventually won 60–36 percent with 4 percent going to the Independent candidate Plato "Two Great Names, One Great Man" Truman (see chapter 13). Andrews never recovered politically in Maine, although he eventually carved out a nice living for himself on the national stage with MoveOn.org and "Win Without War."

Writing this chapter, I remembered I received a call from Tom one day when he was plummeting headlong back to Earth that fine October. He knew what was happening and candidly said he wished he'd paid more attention to his political science classes, especially the lecture about the law of large numbers. I asked him why he had gone off on such a suicide mission. He said simply, "Professor, everybody said I could beat her, and I thought so too."

"But what about the polling, what did it say?" I asked.

"I didn't do any," he replied. "I wish I had."

Yes, even if you're on top of the world and the president of the United States is telling you, "You can do something very important, no problem," it's probably a prudent idea to get a second opinion or two—or in this case the opinions of six hundred randomly selected registered voters. Big mistake not to. There was way, way too much hubris with Tom and his top staff, and a high-quality poll might have punctured some of it.

Ethan Strimling also makes an extremely important point concerning early mistaken assumptions: "Tom's team mistakenly interpreted Olympia's close wins in her last two elections against Pat McGowan against his winning easily in his two. The assumption was that all he had to do was hold close to McGowan numbers in CD2 and simply maintain his margin in CD1. Without polling, of course, he didn't realize that Olympia was way more liked in CD1 than Linda Bean, and that he was way more disliked in CD2 than Pat McGowan."

I thought this would conclude our initial example of "All the big mistakes are made early" if I simply added another personal adage: "Poll early, poll well." But I am indebted to Dennis Bailey, who pointed out another horrendous mistake made very early in the Andrews campaign. During the whole NAFTA debate, Tom had sworn off PAC money for his campaign in order to demonstrate his independence on the issue.

But that, of course, was before Mitchell urged him to run for the Senate, and Tom did not want to reverse course and look hypocritical by now being willing to take PAC money. But, and it's a huge *but,* in retrospect, he effectively turned his back on millions and millions in PAC money that would have at least made him competitive in the subsequent election. Also another huge early mistake.

On reflection, though, it wasn't just Tom who made a lot of mistakes early. I don't know but that there may be something in the Portland area water supply that promotes this kind of Icarian suicide mission because a few years later in 2002, 1st CD Congresswoman Chellie Pingree, as liberal and antigun as Tom Andrews, decided *she* could beat Senator Susan Collins.

Now I know Pingree is actually from North Haven, but she drinks the very liberal Portland water in prodigious quantities.

Many Portland wags labeled Collins "Uzi Suzi," as if that were a negative moniker statewide. It certainly wasn't in the 2nd CD and vast swatches of the western part of the 1st CD or along the Maine coast. Collins would win that one 58.4–41.6 percent, as Icarus III had her wings blown off just like Young Tom. Chellie, though, had wisely kept her 1st CD parachute with her the whole time, so she survived and even prospered when she returned to familiar home territory.

Wait a minute. Hold the phone.

There *is* something in the Portland water that prompts continuing huge political mistakes by liberal Democrats from that fair city. In 2008, another Bowdoin-educated liberal Democratic congressman, Tom Allen (Icarus IV), sortied out of that by now-infamous incubator of Icaruses, the 1st CD, and got himself slaughtered by the by now proudly Uzi Suzi Susan Collins, garnering only 38.6 percent of the vote to her 61.4 percent in the process.

All the big mistakes are made early!

By contrast, when Olympia Snowe left the US Senate in 2012, Angus King was well positioned to run for the open seat. A very popular two-term governor, King never had a "north-south Maine" problem as he enjoyed widespread support statewide and was positively regarded by the hunting, fishing, and outdoors communities. When he first ran in 1994, he reached out to sportsmen and sportswomen. George Smith, the head of Sportsman's Alliance of Maine (SAM), even did King's direct mail advertising in that campaign. Subsequent polling showed voters held him in high regard, so King could move forward knowing he had a viable option to run.

A quick note here on George Smith. He was a most amazing and engaging guy, from being Bill Cohen's driver and Dave Emery's campaign manager, from doing fundraising to direct mail, as head of SAM, and as a major, major behind the scenes operator in dozens of ballot measures and candidate elections, to major columnist and conservative-turned-moderate-turned-Independent. His long, varied, and impactful career is truly astonishing.

For over four decades he would shape Maine's political and environmental future, reinventing himself again and again and always having impact. His weekly column in the *Kennebec Journal* and several books read as lively and timely today as when they were written, and his courage and fortitude under the ravages of ALS (amyotropic lateral sclerosis—better known as Lou Gehrig's disease) are legendary. In his final incarnation, he and his lovely and astute wife, Linda, toured the state as food and travel guides. He was also a hunter and fisherman of the highest professional caliber.

Also most unusual among the political consultants of Maine, in all the years I knew him, I never saw him lose his temper or drop an F-bomb. He was and remains one of a kind—a truly magnificent Son of Maine who had an outsized impact on the Pine Tree State.

While King could have moved slowly, accepting a "draft" from supporters all over the state, he instead moved quickly and decisively to head off two potential rivals. He called Icarian survivor III, Chellie Pingree, and told her he was running and wanted her support, thereby eliminating one candidate who might have gotten substantial national support from the Democratic Senatorial Campaign Committee (DSCC). Since the head of that committee, Senator Chuck Schumer, knew King was likely to vote with the Democrats on all major issues, it would be easy for him to justify doing very little to support any other Democratic senatorial candidate in Maine.

Next, King called Eliot Cutler, who was then the most formidable possible Independent candidate (hard as that may be to imagine today) and asked for his support, cutting any potential Cutler candidacy off at the pass. King had endorsed Cutler when he ran for governor as an Independent in 2010 (when he received 35.9 percent of the vote) and again in 2014 (when he received 8.4 percent of the vote), so this request had some impact. Cutler did not run for the US Senate in 2012.

But perhaps the best example—or set of examples, more precisely—for our illustrative purposes occurred in the Maine election cycle of 2002.

In 2002 we were approached by Donald Soctomah and representatives of the Passamaquoddy Nation. They wanted to pass a referendum allowing them to have a small casino on tribal land in Washington County.

By now so much metaphorical water has flowed under the casino/no casino bridge in Maine over the last thirty years that readers may need to be reminded this initial polling occurred before all the pro and con millions had been spent in almost a dozen state and local referenda on casinos.

Back then, options were still very plentiful and varied and open to consideration at this juncture. There was strong support for a casino in Maine, albeit of a *very particular* type. There were no existing casinos at that time, either, to oppose any new ones. The world of gaming in Maine was new. The waters, as they say, were clear. The subject was open for true discussion. Most people in Maine still had open minds on the subject or liked the idea, at least in the abstract.

Now some backstory may be of relevance to understanding everything that happened. When I was ten or eleven and living in Niantic, Connecticut,

Livy Huntly, a Nehantic Indian (the term *he* used and was proud of), befriended me and taught me about hunting and fishing. I still remember the day he got me out of my seventh-grade class so I could go scalloping with him on opening day. Niantic Bay scallops were highly prized, and it was such a thrill to be out on the bay with him that glorious day. I also got five dollars for my trouble and wore my fishing boots to class when I arrived suitably late. It was a high point of my seventh-grade year.

More to the point of this story, I've never forgotten the poignancy I felt when he gestured toward the whole shoreline while we were scalloping and said, "Just think, my people once owned all that land."

He didn't hold that against me personally since all four of my grandparents had come to the United States in the 1890s.

Much later when our family visited the newly constructed Mashantucket Pequot Museum & Research Center near their Foxwoods Resort Casino and hotel in Connecticut and saw its Native American casino with its $160 million Native American museum, it was quite a revelation. How happy Livy would have been to see it, I thought. It was hard to miss the pride and dedication of the Native Americans who ran the facilities and headed up the police force and fire department, both firemen and women. We were all very impressed.

So I was enthusiastic about the possibility of helping to bring this casino to Passamaquoddies. The elders let me do my own, very instrumental poll, one that was exploratory and very free-ranging. Could it be done? Would the voters of Maine accept a Native American casino on their land in Washington County? How could it be done? I checked it all out from beginning to end. The issue. The influence vectors. The authority figures. The swing voters. All of it.

The results were fantastically positive. At that time, there was very widespread support statewide in Maine for (1) a small casino (2) on Native American land (3) in Washington County—which at the time had the highest unemployment in the state and (4) in a county with a substantial Native American population. Unusually, in my experience, Maine conservatives and liberals also agreed in supporting such a ballot measure package!

Why? Basically, the liberals wanted the casino because the Native Americans wanted it. Lots of other folks wanted it so they could gamble all they wanted in their own state. At the same time, conservatives salivated over the influence vectors we tossed at them, vectors such as "so they could get off welfare and pay taxes." Regardless of party affiliation, the economic development/jobs-inclined portion of the Maine electorate loved the idea of luring

Canadian tourists south and east to take their money. "Vacationland" still had promotional magic for a lot of different projects.

Voters also liked the fact that the gaming facility would have to have the approval of the residents of Washington County as well as the whole state, so both of those bases were covered. And all four of the Maine Native American peoples—the Passamaquoddies, the Penobscots, the Mi'kmaqs, and the Maliseets—would all share in the proceeds. The terms of the payoffs from the Passamaquoddy facility to the state were very generous and included profits from all the games. To get the Passamaquoddies over the 60 percent threshold for successful ballot measures, we even threw in a provision that by law a special portion of the profits were to pay to provide for prescription drugs for the elderly poor statewide.

Support for *this specific, generous* Passamaquoddy proposal was thus firm and widespread: 65 percent favored it, only 19 percent opposed it statewide. If only "most likely voters" showed up, the margin went to 68–21 percent. Most important to me, support ran very high among all the largest ethnic "tribes" in the state: the Irish (71 percent), the Francos (70 percent), and the English-Yankees (65 percent). It looked like a slam dunk. I was very excited.

I was quite sure they would win if we could get adequate funding to run a quality campaign. Driving home after presenting my findings, I called Livy Huntly, and *he* was very happy. I even constructed potential commercials in my head: one had a young Native American woman asking for voter support so she "could take herself and her child off welfare" and "start paying taxes. I'll feel good about that," she said to close out the commercial.

I also thought I had a good source of funding. For the previous ten years I had done the state and national polling for the Nature Conservancy (TNC), and we'd won ballot measures and bonds in places as disparate as Nevada, New Mexico, Florida, Rhode Island, Minnesota, Idaho, and Montana, as well as two or three in Maine. I'd learned that TNC prized ongoing revenue sources (as opposed to one-time bonds) like a small tax on cement in Colorado. Note: for a remarkable history of the Nature Conservancy and how it became the largest environmental organization in the world, see Bill Birchard, *Nature's Keepers*.

So I went to Kent Womack of the Maine TNC and proposed they put up $1 million and the Passamaquoddy Nation would give them a small percentage of the take. The Passamaquoddies at the meeting thought that was a fine idea as it would free them from fundraising concerns up front. Eventually TNC decided not to do it, but by then I could see money would not be much of a hurdle.

But there *was* one problem, a big one.

There was already an ongoing, small-scale bingo gambling operation in Maine on Indian Island (as it was called then) in the Penobscot Nation. I was afraid the Penobscots, with a bigger population, being better organized and already in something of the gambling business, would look askance at their "little brothers" and take over their project. From their point of view, I thought they would feel there was simply too much at stake to leave it stuck way out in Washington County.

Thus followed this advice: "The one thing you must not do is take this to the Penobscots, or anybody else for that matter; they will hijack it. If you lose control over the project, you won't get it back."

Well, Native American solidarity apparently triumphed over such gratuitous advice, and the Passamaquoddies soon tried to bring the Penobscots and other Indigenous nations into the process and sought their assistance. Early Mistake #1.

Of course, doubling the early error rate, the Penobscots then took the project over; perhaps THEY wanted it on THEIR tribal land. Early Mistake #2 from the Passmaquoddies and from the eventual electoral point of view.

Once the project left Passamaquoddy land, the lovely small, generous casino in Washington County and I were quickly, summarily, and permanently thrown off that potato truck together and left as roadkill, so I'm guessing a little about what happened next.

But I think the end results underscore the dangers one's "friends" can pose early in a campaign cycle. I know I felt very bad for Donald Soctomah and Richard Stevens because they had such a good idea that could have become law at that time and would have helped their nation and those of the other Native Americans in Maine as well as providing needed revenues for the state of Maine. Unfortunately, their fine vision was doomed the moment they lost control over the project (see chapter 8 on rules for successful ballot measure campaigns).

By the time they got the idea back and finally were able to put a Washington County casino on the ballot in 2007, a variety of other casino proposals had failed and one, cleverly sold as a "local" "dog track," "Racino," had passed (the same year the Sanford casino failed to pass muster), so public opinion had been hardened by a half dozen previous anti-casino campaign efforts.

Equally important, there was now a casino already operating in Bangor, their principal market being Canada and northern Maine, so Bangor interests were naturally opposed to their plan. The Passamaquoddies would eventually lose the 2007 effort by a margin of 52–48 percent. By then it was just too late for their good idea.

We now need to turn back to the earlier process, however, to see the axiom in full flower as its lethality spread. Apparently after it was brought to their attention, the Penobscots then took the project down to the Mashantucket Pequots in Connecticut because the latter knew a lot more about all of this as their own casino had been up and running very successfully for quite a while. This resulted in Early Mistake #3 because, of course, the Pequots told them they would help them run the eventual facility and would even show them how to pass it.

Now I have no idea how or why the Pequots and Maine Native Americans then took the idea of the project out to the money and gaming crowd in Las Vegas to get those heavy hitters involved. But they seem to have done just that. Out to Vegas the project traveled, at least metaphorically. Early Mistake #4.

Regardless of whoever then put together the actual ballot measure and gaming proposition, unchecked and untethered from the Maine realities as it was, they proceeded to change many of the most important internals and moved the entire project to York County (!) as visions of tens of millions of sugarplums from Massachusetts, Rhode Island, and New Hampshire undoubtedly danced in their heads. I'm quite sure they never tested all the new, discordant elements or they would have taken the worst ones out. Or maybe they did test them and thought they could win anyway. Either way, Early Mistake #5.

So now, instead of a small casino with generous payouts on tribal land way up north where there was high unemployment and numerous Native Americans with their own tribal land and where it would be in a place where even many people statewide who didn't like gambling could justify it since it would be stuck way up there by the Canadian border, there was now a proposal before the electorate for a huge, stingy casino on non-tribal land in a county with the lowest unemployment and one of the highest per-capita incomes in Maine. It was also to be built in a county with few, if any, Native Americans with no Native American land. So most of the many positive influence vectors were stripped away at the very beginning—by its very proponents! Early Mistake #6. Huge error.

And just for good measure, the now entirely misplaced and misguided new project was filled with amazingly marvelous benefits for the prospective owners and operators of the facility. Whereas the original Passamaquoddy proposal had been generous in giving the state of Maine a percentage of all the gambling, not just the slots but the table and roulette operations as well, the new mega casino gave the state only a percentage of the slots. Miserly indeed, and soon to come back to haunt them. Early Mistake #7.

Then the architects actually went further in handicapping their own proposal by their including what would turn out to be a true kill switch when they added the idea of a "kiddy casino" inside the adult one. The idea behind the kiddy casino was like a Chuck E. Cheese to babysit and seemingly to introduce restless teenagers to the proper ways to gamble. And if they were twelve, they could even work there! What backroom wizard in Las Vegas added that? One can only wonder. Early Mistake #8 aka "the Death Star" had now been made.

Note: Dave Emery even once saw the "kiddy casino" menace playing out in real time:

A few years ago, we visited a brand-new casino in Mississippi with friends who wanted to see what it was like. As we were leaving, we witnessed a kiddy casino meltdown firsthand. A nine-year-old youngster had been playing the kiddy games and refused to leave when his parents needed to go. "But I can't leave now!" he bellowed. "I won't! I want to win the prize! I've almost won! I'm not leaving until I win!" Whereupon his very chagrinned father grabbed him by the shirt collar and marched him off to the car.

Quite a metamorphosis.

The campaign for the York County facility was not without its humorous moments, however. After the new architects had loaded up the Sanford casino with all its many negative facets, the Casinos *NO!* campaign led by Dennis Bailey did a focus group in Lewiston to test some of the arguments on both sides. When the moderator gave all the reasons for the proposed casino, the fifteen members of the focus group were unanimously for it, led in part to that conclusion by a very handsome, poised, and articulate Native American. He was a very effective and knowledgeable proponent.

After a short break, the negative elements were introduced to the panel. These included all the elements that later led Leon Gorman of L.L. Bean to label the Sanford proposal "the heist of the century" along with its truly ill-advised proposal to have a "kiddy casino" located inside the facility.

This latter notion initially horrified the group. One woman kept saying over and over, "But that's just awful. It'll just brainwash them to become gamblers." But the Native American effectively countered with "No, we'd never do that; we'd put in safeguards." Once they heard that the casino would be getting "safeguards," the group flipped back to favoring the casino.

So it was clear that while the "kiddy casino" could be the final nail in the coffin of the proposal (*a concept killer,* the focus group moderator called it!), the other side would have several months to try to rectify it if it were spotlighted early. Thus if Casinos *NO!* brought this element to the public's attention too early, the other side would be able to introduce some "remedies" and take away the NO side's best argument.

Luckily, Dennis Bailey, the astute press secretary and public face of Casinos *NO!* as well as other leaders of the Casinos *NO!* effort, and others had recently been told of the blessed axiom "All the big mistakes are made early," so they were prepared to act accordingly.

Because, of course, once the findings of the focus group were presented, many friends of Casinos *NO!* wanted to get that idea out there right away. "It's too good to sit on. Lead with that!" said many supporters. Thus one of the hardest aspects of the campaign turned out to be getting the supporters not to use their best argument too soon! Dennis Bailey and others spent a great deal of time dissuading those supporters who could hardly restrain themselves.

That Casinos *NO!* team had many other noteworthy members, led by campaign manager Edie Smith and including Val Landry, Tim Hussey, John Oliver, Leon and Lisa Gorman, George Isaacson, Chris Harte, Mo Bisson, and Phil Harriman. They ran the entire campaign with skill and dispatch, using tight control to take maximum advantage of the YES side's many early mistakes.

They also used very effective messaging by Erik Potholm and Greg Stevens of Stevens, Reed, Curcio and found outstanding, believable authority figures (ranging from the Attorney General Janet Mills to Governor Angus King to police officials to outraged mothers). John Baldacci, despite major pressure from the Maine AFL-CIO, stood firmly against the Sanford casino.

In November 2003, the Sanford casino proposal would go down to defeat 67–33 percent. Casinos *NO!* avoided an early, disastrous mistake or two, ran to daylight and won going away.

Yes, when it comes to Maine politics, "all the big mistakes are indeed made early."

Chuck Winner certainly knew what he was doing when he coined that axiom for political campaigns, both candidate and ballot ones.

Chuck and the 1980 Maine Yankee Shutdown referendum would also usher in a new era of Maine politics in terms of ballot measures. National groups with national agendas would find Maine an inexpensive state in which to operate. For a million dollars or so they could attempt to score "wins" for their causes and over the coming decades, more and more state and national public policies would be put out to Maine voters as referenda. This newfound status would, to the state's hungry consultants, became manna from heaven and, as of 2023, the gift that keeps on giving.

And Chuck's axiom "All the big mistakes are made early" would be forever enshrined in Maine political lore. At least among its consiglieri.

AXIOM #2

"Your Friends Will Do You More Harm Than Your Enemies—If You Let Them"

The dogs bark but the caravan moves on.
—TUAREG SAYING

O f course when you run for office or push for a cause, you want as many supporters as you can get. That's just common sense. But what many people don't realize is that your supporters often want other things that you do not, often giving you very bad advice on how to win your campaign. They usually want you to win it doing it their way, and some even would rather see you lose than see you do it your way.

One of the axioms I came to accept is that when it comes to political campaigns, "your friends will always cause you more harm than your enemies—if you let them." Certainly, they will give you more heartburn because that complication should be unnecessary. This may seem like something of an exaggeration, but as we saw in the last chapter, the "friends" of the Passamaquoddies caused them immeasurable harm while "helping" them. As we will see in this chapter, there is, in fact, a lot of persistent truth to it. Other examples follow.

Take the Maine Nuclear Shutdown referendum of 1980. Antinuclear activists wanted to shut down the plant in Wiscasset, Maine. Naturally, most of their supporters were also opponents of nuclear power in general. Many of those who were against the shutdown of the Wiscasset plant *specifically* were not for nuclear power more generally. Others who supported the plant were also strong advocates for nuclear power in general. So it wasn't surprising that many of those supporters of the plant *and* nuclear power more generally wanted to make this a referendum not just on the Wiscasset plant, but on nuclear power itself. Many felt strongly about this point. But in 1980, it was much, much harder to sell the benefits of nuclear power *generally* than to sell the idea of keeping this one particular small plant at Wiscasset open, so that multiplicity was a major impediment to victory in the election of 1980. Many

19

supporters of the Wiscasset plant wanted to make it a referendum on *more* nuclear plants. Some insisted. Many even wanted to make it a referendum on nuclear power all over the country. But remember that this referendum was being held in the aftermath of the biggest US nuclear disaster (at Three Mile Island), which had upped the ante considerably.

Believe it or not, still others wanted to make the campaign about a chance to promote the next generation of nuclear fusion plants, a technology that, even now in 2023, is still decades away from commercialization! They wanted to make it a referendum on nuclear fusion at the very time nuclear power was facing its biggest electoral challenges. This was true of some of the financial backers.

Imagine the heartburn this caused within the campaign.

Luckily for the Save Maine Yankee campaign, Chuck Winner and his firm had been through all this before in numerous successful referenda on nuclear power. So he was able to short-circuit many of the rabid pro nuclear voices in general, impulses of some of the biggest financial backers of the plant. Chuck got Westinghouse and General Electric to donate money but not "donate" strategy. Skip Thurlow, the head of Central Maine Power Company (CMP) at the time, wisely deferred to the professionals such as Chuck and our campaign manager, John Menario, and sidetracked many of the pro-nuclear activists. But it was not easy.

I say luckily because, in fact, it is fair to say that had the campaign been fought on the broader issues of nuclear—let alone fusion—power and had used influence vectors and themes pushed hardest by our supporters, we would have lost.

In addition, even if we were able to convince our supporters to fight the battle on our strategic best behavior, that is, focusing on just the single running plant in Wiscasset, many of our supporters still wanted to fight that battle using arguments about the issue of health and safety of the plant. There were economic arguments for or against the plant, and there were health and safety arguments for or against its continuing operations. The polling showed conclusively that one argument (the economic) worked for us while the other (health and safety) did not.

The dynamics of the campaign qua campaign thus played out amid strategic disagreement on both sides. Initially the antinuclear side constantly focused on the dangers of nuclear power, so our strongest supporters wanted—sometimes desperately wanted—to meet this cluster of issues head on. "Talk about health and safety. We must convince people of the truth of how safe they are," they urged.

Yet the polling was very clear. The more we talked about health and safety issues, the more people thought about them and said, "Why take the chance? We don't know who's right." Many of our very own supporters would simply drift away from us if we even *talked* about health and safety. That's right; the very focus on the issue dragged down our voter support among people initially on our side. The health and safety of nuclear power was exactly the debate our opponents wanted.

Some of the engineers at the plant were actually indignant that we weren't talking all the time about safety and health and how superior nuclear power was in this regard. Whether they were right or wrong, this dimension was a loser for us and despite continuing pressure we focused not on health and safety but on economic issues.

Interestingly enough, of course, the other side had the same (albeit reverse) problem, and for them it would prove fatal. They could not get their supporters and ultimately their campaign to stay on the health and safety message whenever we raised the economic arguments. Their supporters kept insisting they talk about the economics, how renewable energy like small-scale hydro power, wind, and solar power could replace the plant and actually save money over time. They could not win on that argument, and when the costs to individual households were illuminated, support for the shutdown diminished week by week.

Chuck Winner produced a powerful set of ads that focused on the economic and common-sense arguments for keeping the plant open: "It's open and running and saving millions of dollars." Interestingly, the polling showed that the most effective authority figure to deliver our message in ads was "a foreign-born scientist." We didn't have any of those, but a Bowdoin professor of physics, Will Hughes, "looked the part" with a Van Dyke beard and a Germanic, forceful delivery. Ninety thousand voters changed their minds during the campaign, most driven by the projected high costs of replacing Maine Yankee. The key Franco-American demographic also flipped into opposition.

Not that there weren't hiccups along the way. On a lovely summer day I woke to the early morning news to see pictures of a huge truck lugging a giant generator north on the Maine Turnpike. The announcer said that said generator was coming from the wrecked plant at Three Mile Island. That's right, Maine Yankee was bringing machinery from the very place we were bound and determined to never mention!

I was stunned. Stupefied. Alarmed.

My first call that morning was, of course, to Skip Thurlow. Skip, being a calm and knowledgeable engineer, gave a sensible, scientific answer: "Oh, the generator was from the non-nuclear portion of the plant. It's fine. We got a great bargain on it."

My second call (immediately afterward) was to a sleeping Chuck Winner in California. Once he was fully awake, Chuck said with pith and candor, "Remember, in ballot measures, your friends will always do you more harm than your opponents. We'll have to put another 1000 GRPs (gross rating points, a measure of audience frequency and reach on TV) behind our economic ads this week. Don't get into a battle on this issue in the press. We can't win. We've already paid the campaign price for that machinery. We can't put that genie back in the bottle."

He was proven right. There was a negative blip in our position for a week or so after, and then the tracking settled back to where it had been before as the proponents of the shutdown went back to the economic argument. But the Save Maine Yankee example illuminates the axiom in spades.

Another fine example of the axiom is taken from 1983. Thanks to the good offices and leadership of John Cole, then editor of the *Maine Times*, and his organization SMOOSA (Save Maine's Only Official State Animal), enough people signed petitions to repeal the hunting season on moose. Moose hunting had been outlawed in 1935 because of a dwindling herd, but by 1979 biologists agreed that the Maine moose population had recovered to the point that an annual limited moose hunt would help to maintain the herd at a healthy and sustainable level. The legislature agreed, and the annual Maine moose hunt became legal once again.

In my memory, John was a most interesting figure on the Maine scene: a Yale graduate who made a living for some years digging clams and gillnetting fish, and a decorated war hero who spent thirty-five missions in combat and was proudly a man of peace. He was a longtime avid hunter who hung up his guns, but never became anti-hunting. As editor of the *Maine Times*, he was honest and poignant, gruff and provoking, but he was also a messenger who could soothe and calm. For decades he was at the center of outdoor and political debate in Maine. A transplant from Long Island, he loved the state of Maine and its people with a fierce and enduring pride, and he had a profound appreciation for the durability and strength of those who live in rural settings, especially those who lived by Ralph Waldo Emerson's "the dignity of honest toil."

There had been very good reasons to ban moose hunting earlier in 1935. But in recent years, the herd had once again grown large enough so that the Department of Inland Fisheries and Wildlife got the legislature to institute a limited Maine moose hunt (only in September and only in a northern zone). The newness of the proposal, the existence of the animal as an icon of the state of Maine, and the widely held perceptions that moose were semi-tame and quite stupid as well, all seemed to tip the electorate in favor of eliminating the newly enacted hunt.

Maine sportsmen and women (and the state's game biologists) faced an uphill battle. The Sportsman's Alliance of Maine and its executive director, George Smith, led the opposition to the repeal and turned to then vice president of the National Rifle Association (NRA), Gus "Doc" Garcelon of Augusta. Garcelon, a longtime champion of hunters and gun rights, and a sometime hunting companion of Maine Senator Ed Muskie, was confident that the NRA's national leadership would support the effort financially.

Imagine our surprise—and horror—when the national NRA guy showed up. "Lots of money. Lots of it up front," he said. "But we want to make this a referendum on automatic rifles as well. That's a huge issue for us."

George Smith looked incredulous. "Are you serious?"

"Dead serious," said our "friend," the Washington apparatchik.

I shook my head. "But the polling says we're going to have a very difficult time keeping the hunt at all, even without that burden."

"Look," I added, "I have ten or eleven guns, and I'd fight like hell if you tried to take them away from me, but there is no earthly reason for hunters or any other civilians to have an assault rifle in their closet. We are not selling that."

"Sorry," he said, "then there's no money."

"Well then we'll do it on our own," George said firmly and bravely. "That's just crazy."

Can you imagine? I suppose now forty years later since the NRA has pushed for, among other things, armor piercing bullets and students packing heat on college campuses and has opposed every gun control measure in every state and nationally since then, even background checks for all, you can.

As soon as the guy left, George turned to Doc and said with some feeling, "I thought you were still vice president of the NRA?" Gus assured him that was not the end of the matter. I don't know what Doc said to the national, but the money eventually came, and no more minions were ever dispatched to the Pine Tree State that year to try and screw up our campaign. There was no more talk of assault rifles in that cycle.

The campaign had many other interesting and humorous dimensions as well. At that time, Maine had the first state woman game warden in the whole country named Debra Palman. George and I marveled at what she must have gone through to attain that position in those days. Debra subsequently did a fabulous job and eventually became the head game warden of the whole Maine Warden Service. The polling showed that the game wardens were the best authority figures in the polling and ideally would be used to carry our messages: there were now too many moose for the existing habitat, the herd was growing, not shrinking, and Maine biologists needed access to more moose carcasses in order to test for the many diseases they faced.

In our naivete, we thought having a female game warden as an authority figure would help us with our worst demographic group: women in Maine's 1st CD. We were getting slaughtered with that cohort. Jack Havey had provided very effective and well-done commercials such as Jim Longley's for governor and subsequently would again in campaigns such as Maine Yankee II and the Elected Public Utilities Commission referenda.

During the moose hunt campaign, he really outdid himself creating some marvelous commercials featuring Debra and another game warden, this one a male named Chuck. On the day of the shoot, Governor Joe Brennan (quite rightly, I thought) refused to let them wear their uniforms in the commercial. But after outfitting them in civilian clothes at L.L. Bean, they were great on camera, and the campaign rushed the ads on the air, Chuck's up north and Debra's down south.

After several weeks, the numbers changed, positively up north, but stayed the same down south where we had used the female authority figure more extensively. The campaign decided to do a focus group. Focus groups, which put twelve to fifteen voters in a room for an hour or more, rely on two things: skill in choosing the demographic being tested and the actual conduct of the session. Although a poll is mostly science with some art, a focus group is really more art than science.

Its successful operation depends on the moderator's ability to introduce positive and negative vectors and facilitate good flow and openness (and also preventing some "know-it-alls" from dominating the discussions). Focus groups enable pollsters and other campaign operatives to select target audiences based on previous polling for maximum utility.

In this case, because of the problems suggested by the tracking polls, it was done exclusively with female voters from the 1st CD. In it, we showed both commercials. The women overwhelmingly preferred the male authority figure Chuck. So much for women's liberation. Or at least for our misperceptions of women's liberation anyway. In fact, after the session, two women came up to the moderator and asked for Chuck's telephone number!

We switched the rotation and used additional commercials highlighting the size of the herd and featured the game biologists.

At the end of the day, Maine voters rejected the SMOOSA petition 60–40 percent.

After the vote, we had some very fine NRA money left over and so did another focus group to post-test the messages and senders who had worked the best. The moderator asked the all-women panel what the best messages were. Most of them alluded to the science behind the season. One in particular offered that game wardens really knew their moose dung ("They really get down into the moose shit"). But when asked why they voted NO, many spontaneously offered, "Because Chuck told us to." One lady was even convinced Chuck was not a "real" game warden but an actor in a daytime soap opera. "I've seen him a lot." Please don't share this anecdote with the League of Women Voters; it doesn't fit their citizenship model.

Another amusing moment during the moose-hunting campaign came on live TV. We had been running the ads statewide and in them the game wardens and state biologists had been trying to counter "the slander" that moose were dumb and tame. When I appeared on a WCBB statewide discussion of the debate, I went merrily off on this theme. The moderator, Jean Meserve, smiled as she put up on the screen while I was talking—a picture from the St. John Valley of an adult moose in harness pulling a Christmas sled. I began laughing and could hardly hold it together. John Cole did have a point. At least for some moose.

One final example for this axiom.

Although the question of gay rights had been before the Maine legislature numerous times, it was not on the statewide ballot until 1995. At that time a coalition of Concerned Maine Families (CMF) led by Carolyn Cosby, the Christian Civic League led by Michael Heath, and the Coalition to End Special Rights (CESPR) led by Paul Madore put a referendum on the ballot "limiting protected classifications." Their efforts were designed to prevent the legislature from expanding those classifications to include sexual orientation.

The measure was opposed by a broad coalition called Maine Won't Discriminate (MWD) led by Jesse Connelly, Patricia Peard, and Mark Sullivan. Peard would prove to be a dynamic leader and always kept the big picture in mind, and Sullivan would do a very good job with the press and keeping the campaign in motion. Glen Richards did yeoman service as treasurer of the group. Connelly would go on to service as John Baldacci's campaign manager in 2006.

While initially the statewide sentiment was considerably in favor of the referendum opposing gay rights, the MWD launched a vigorous campaign with highly effective ads arguing against it.

Amy Pritchard was the campaign manager. Will Robinson was tasked with doing the paid media and created a number of very good ads. One, featuring Governor Angus King, was launched and played for a week or so. I then got a call from King from Yokohama, Japan. He was concerned about the "harsh" colors in his ads. Angus knew a ton about TV and was a perfectionist when it came to his commercials. Some of the Dan Payne thirty- and sixty-second ads in 1994 took twenty or more takes before passing muster.

But I told him that our nightly tracking showed he was having a very positive effect on women who worked at home, suburbanites, and Independents, so regardless of the lighting or the colors, the ad was doing just fine with these target groups we had to convert in order to be competitive. I think Amy even upped the buy at that point.

His and the other ads were not, however, having their desired effect on Francos, especially Franco males. In fact, I was quite worried, writing to Amy on October 13, "Francos always predict the future, and right now they are saying we will lose." Amy and Will responded by being willing to produce a "blocking spot" that would at least blunt the impact with those groups. At least so we didn't lose 3–1 with them. The campaign's internal tracking polling showed that the issue was still winning by a margin of 60–40 percent along Maine's coastal counties, especially Sagadahoc, Knox, Lincoln, Waldo, Hancock, and Washington, and was thus poised to prevail statewide.

Not to put too fine a point on it, but when it came down to crunch time in 1995, Will Robinson, Amy Pritchard, and Jesse Connelly won the election for their clients. I believe if Robinson hadn't created that ad, if Pritchard and Connelly hadn't resisted the supporters' calls to take it off the air, and if they had not been backed up by the leadership of MWD, the YES side would have won.

The ad "It's Just Not Maine" (dubbed "Lobster Boy" by insiders) was stunning in its simplicity and power, and remarkable for the skill with which it took some of the YES side's rhetoric and used it against them. A strong, young lobsterman told the audience he didn't like the government telling him what to do and couldn't see how new regulations would do anything good. Then he delivered the punch line urging voters "to tell the outsiders to go home by voting No." "Vote No on 2. It's Just Not Maine." It was a dynamite commercial, one of those ads when you first see it you say, "Home run!" and "Double the GRPs behind that one."

Luckily, the ad was not presented to many supporters beforehand because literally overnight when the ad went up, there were furious calls from our supporters from all over the state directed to Pritchard. Some supporters, thinking it had come from the YES side, were devastated by the efficacy of "Lobster Boy."

"It's killing us. It's awful," they said.

Pritchard was consistently able to respond, "But what does it tell people to do?"

"It tells them to vote NO."

"Well, isn't that what we want voters to do?"

"Well, yes, but I still don't like it."

Other supporters, hearing some of the dog whistles from the other side such as "outsiders" and "from away" said, "but it doesn't mention us at all." Again, Pritchard faithfully calmed them down, saying, "Listen carefully. Our ad is all about personal freedom and choice. We're the good guys. Lobster Boy is on our side."

As the commercial ran more and more, the tracking numbers changed in those coastal counties, and on October 23 I reported to Amy that our tracking was now showing more and more positive results along the coast and with the Franco males, concluding, "We can win this thing."

By Election Day the coastal numbers had flipped around just enough to ensure that the NO side could win, which it did by a margin of 53–47 percent statewide. Many, many people had made a heroic effort to defeat it, and it was a group win for certain. But perhaps nobody deserves more credit than Will, Amy, and Jesse for the eventual victory. Many, many others had helped make the NO side competitive, but they put it over the top. Thanks to them Lobster Boy had done his part—and then some! This was one of the first times in American history that gay rights had been upheld in a statewide vote.

But even after the exhilarating victory, some "friends" continued to rail against the most effective commercial of that cycle. The editor of the *Portland Press Herald*, for example, a staunch advocate of gay rights, called it a "jujitsu ad" (as if that were a bad thing!) and said he would rather have lost than to have used it.

Fortunately, his position was a minority one within the Maine Won't Discriminate coalition, and Maine ended up taking a very important step toward enshrining equality under the law.

Of course, when it comes to "friends" being less than "helpful," we can't forget the national parties—in my experience Republican, Democrat, and Green Parties are famous for sending legions of field people from Washington into the state to tell us local yokels what to do. How irritating to have these worthies periodically coming up and telling us how to do things in Maine. At best, their advice was banal, at worst seriously off-point, although we all liked hearing their inside Washington gossip. I will admit today that I wish I'd paid more attention to one of those "sent from heaven" guys, a young Paul

Manafort. I don't remember anything he said, but I do remember he wore a very, very expensive-looking suit. Smiled a lot then, too.

Anyway, while we had to listen to these people early on, we soon developed a very effective coping strategy with these advice-givers from away.

We soon realized they were coming to Maine because (1) it was summer, (2) they liked lobster, and (3) they had to be somewhere to justify their salaries. We found it worked out much better to take them sailing or fishing and get them all the lobster rolls they could eat rather than meet them at campaign headquarters where they would only upset and confuse the local staff. In exchange, they had to keep their (spoiler alert: Maine vernacular coming) pieholes shut and report back to DC that all was well Down East.

Occasionally, though, we got some "helper" from a national organization or random trade association who had been primed by his bosses to come to Maine and show us potato heads how to do things. I remember one began sending one and all his "thoughts" based on whatever weirdly inappropriate screed they'd sent with him. In this case, for example, a strong memo instead of a lobster roll was required:

> Dear xxxxxx,
>
> I want to make it very clear that I do not want any more of your stream of consciousness memos. I was irritated enough at what you sent me re the polling, and I hoped you would not repeat that pattern. The one I saw today was completely off target and off the reservation as far as I am concerned. These stream of consciousness memos are not welcome in this campaign.
>
> First, they are unprofessional.
>
> Second, they can give off the odor of panic to those not familiar with campaign dynamics.

(Note: Not all wording from items Three through Seven are suitable for family-friendly publications and are therefore not included here.)

> Eighth, the steering committee is not to be burdened with tactical matters. I thought I made that crystal clear to everybody at our initial meeting. I do not want them bothered with day-to-day tactical stuff. Anything you want considered by this campaign is to be sent to—and me and —. The steering committee has delegated all strategic and operational responsibility and authority for this campaign to me and I am the ultimate arbiter of what we will and will not do.
>
> I want to welcome your positive input on this campaign, but I must ask you to reconsider both your situation and the process of the coming campaign. If you do not feel that you can play a constructive albeit subordinate role as outlined by—and me, please let me know.
>
> I hope you will join with me in moving forward positively.

Fortunately, there was no need to have a subsequent "Come to Jesus Meeting" with the young man, and from then on lobster rolls sufficed.

Of course, sometimes the "friends" can turn out to be consultants or friends or family who either make significant and costly mistakes or allow the candidate to make them. I have a vivid memory of a long-forgotten thirty-second ad I would put in this category.

In 2002, John Baldacci was giving up his congressional seat to run for governor, and there was a six-way race for the Democratic nomination for it, including state Senator Susan Longley, daughter of the famous Independent Maine governor.

While my personal favorite in that race was Mike Michaud, I thought John Nutting had a good chance. He was a standout legislator, had a great story to tell being "the only working farmer in the race," seemed like just the type of conservative Democrat who would fit with the district, had raised enough money to have a considerable TV presence (enough to buy both Bangor and Portland TV or I wouldn't have seen it), and had a talented team.

But Nutting's closing TV commercial turned out to be stunning in its mysteries. Here was Farmer Nutting dressed up in an ill-fitting, black Sunday-go-to-meeting suit awkwardly standing in a schoolyard with a waiting school bus with children on it. I don't remember what anybody was saying or what he was trying to do because the image of the female bus driver shutting the door of the bus and keeping the who-knows-what guy off the bus was startling. And off-putting. I concluded that many viewers would say simply, "I don't think I'll vote for a guy she won't even let on the bus to discuss crosswalk safety."

Talk about "live by the thirty-second ad, die by the thirty-second ad." It could have been an attack ad by one of his opponents. In any case, it was not an ideal closer ad, whatever its inherent (and still mysterious) intentions, its true purpose, or even its genesis. The ad certainly didn't seem to help Nutting very much as he finished fourth with 12 percent of the vote as Michaud won and Longley finished second.

Edie Smith recalls a similar "vendor acting as friend,"

In the beginning stages of the Les Otten campaign for governor, we paid a firm to design a shiny new logo and design a shiny new website in which to place that shiny new logo. The headlines the next day said something like "Otten campaign copies Obama logo and website." Friend, yes. Helpful? No. We had to hire another firm that actually searched other logos and websites to make sure ours was unique.

Still, when you think that the friends of Sarah Gideon spent $60 million (that's right, millions!) and still lost so badly to an initially wounded Susan Collins in 2020, you could probably write a whole book about who did what, or didn't do what, or how is that even possible? And examine a campaign that never got around to targeting Franco-Americans. Or women who work at home. Or scruffy gents who live in the Great North Woods. There's a lot more to this axiom to reflect on. PS—They *didn't even spend* the other $15 million they had in the bank at the end. As Larry Benoit points out, this was the most expensive election in Maine history by far. Counting dark money, something like $115 million was spent to elect Gideon, $88 million to elect Collins. Gruesome. Worst of all, perhaps, neither Larry nor I ever got our paws on any of it.

Lance Dutson, one of Maine's premier Republican strategists and messaging experts, agrees on the importance of careful initial selection of staff and consultants. "Hiring the wrong people at the beginning of any campaign" is one of the more persistent dimensions of "all the big mistakes are made early." His broad experience spans fifteen years of public policy work and campaigns, such as Senator Susan Collins and Georgia's Secretary of State Brad Raffensperger, so it is wise to listen to his advice when it comes to campaign staff and consultants, "Better wait and get it right." Avoid those early mistakes like the plague.

Another excellent example for this axiom of "friends" being unhelpful occurred in Lewiston in 1993. Alan Caron was the astute and effective campaign manager for the anti-Turnpike widening effort in 1991 who also would help steer the Gay Rights coalition in Portland to their first ever victory in 1992. He was then asked to organize the effort to overturn the antigay proposition the following year in Lewiston. Our polling showed a very tough, very difficult hill to climb, but the campaign was making excellent progress until the end when the Lesbian Avengers from New York City showed up, uninvited and electorally unwelcome.

As Caron remembers, "We had that campaign trending up, on a message against discrimination—which Catholics and Francos understood well—until the final days, when the Avengers sent a busload up from New York, which made them the center of attention and front-page news on the final weekend of the campaign, as they chanted, "We're here, we're queer, get used to it!" Needless to say, it was not the message you run in conservative Catholic Lewiston, and we lost badly."

Talk about "friends" torpedoing your best interests!

Refreshingly, not all clients in ballot measures insist on trying to do things their way. George Isaacson, a prominent member of the Casinos *NO!* board, underscores this pleasant reality when it occurs:

Asked about why we were against the referendum, we went around the table giving high-toned (and self-righteous) explanations, such as gambling being morally objectionable, leads to addiction, invites criminal elements and government corruption, and was contrary to the culture of Maine.

The strategist listened patiently and then stated flatly, "OK, but if those are the reasons you plan to lay out in newspaper and television ads, you are definitely going to lose this referendum."

Talk about being stunned! He then went on to explain that most people in Maine were not fundamentally opposed to casino gambling. They viewed it as a form of entertainment, a personal choice, not sinful, and a welcome source of additional revenue for the state. A majority of Maine citizens, he declared, simply did not share the committee members' moralistic opposition to gambling.

Instead, he went on to explain that "to win" it would be necessary to exploit flaws in the casino proposal, flaws that would trigger opposition. We simply couldn't win with just what we wanted to say. We deferred to his professional advice, although I'm sure some members had doubts until later.

Matt McTighe, the experienced and savvy campaign director of Gay Marriage and other important referenda as well as Mike Michaud's 2014 campaign for governor, is a firm advocate of an operationally tight buy-in at the beginning of any campaign with the disparate groups of supporters (in this case EqualityMaine, the Maine ACLU, GLAAD [Gay & Lesbian Alliance Against Defamation], and other LGBTQ groups). That initial buy-in at the beginning and subsequent control of the messaging by campaign central allowed Mainers United for Marriage to adopt the non-confrontational approach which ultimately produced a historic win in 2012.

As he put it, "Right after the loss in 2009, we knew we would be going for it. In 2010, there was no winning playbook. We created it. We insisted at the very beginning there be unity and one cohesive center that all our partners accepted. We didn't want any rogue messaging . . . we never deviated from our basic strategy." McTighe had the campaign chops and force of personality to make that strategy work. Not all campaign managers can manage their supporters as well.

We could give here many other examples of friends and allies wanting to derail campaigns such as the "Sand and Gravel Boys" who wanted to widen the entire Maine Turnpike into three lanes all the way to the end, or some of the big box stores in the Sunday Sales referendum wanting to be open all night long, or the Maine Christian Civic League wanting to become important message senders in the assisted suicide referendum when they would have turned off more voters than they had converted.

But we won't.

Besides, we like ending on a positive note.

If you haven't got the message from the above examples, you never will. But perhaps you'll understand some of these dimensions even more when you check out the rest of the chapters, such as the one on authority figures, and see all the misery and heartburn one's friends can bring you on the campaign trail.

Or why consultants wish they only had to deal with their opponents during campaigns.

Of course, just as we were about to go to press with this version of this chapter, Larry Benoit provided us with the absolute best contemporary example. Let's say you are a progressive or a liberal or a Democrat or a moderate Republican or an Independent, and you are trying to put together a winning strategy. You are anxious to reach out and build a coalition to prevent the Trumpkanoids from ever winning again. Quite a challenge. But don't worry; your strongest supporters and "friends" have already come up with a great, can't miss slogan *guaranteed* to convert the hearts and minds of America. They want you to use the slogan, "Defund the Police."

We re-rest our case, Your Honor.

AXIOM #3

"The Wild Wild East Lives"

The wilderness is near as well as dear to every man.
The very uprightness of the pines and maples asserts the ancient
rectitude and vigor of nature. Our lives need the relief of such
a background, where the pine flourishes and the jay still screams.
—HENRY DAVID THOREAU

The 2022 2nd CD congressional race featured a close contest between the incumbent Jared Golden, a Democrat, and Bruce Poliquin, the Republican who had held the seat previously, only to lose with ranked choice voting in 2018. Tiffany Bond also ran as an Independent in that race. For some useful background on the earlier struggle between Golden and Poliquin, see Michael Norton's *Chasing Maine's Second*.

Sometime during the 2022 campaign, someone must have said that Jared Golden hadn't done enough for lobstermen. Of course, my remembrance of politics—and life for that matter—in Maine, is that it's impossible to do enough for lobstermen. But that aside, some wag must have decided that Jared should address the issue by making a commercial of him eating a lobster on camera.

Now in fairness, nobody, and I mean nobody, looks cool tearing apart a lobster, at least if they are sober and in a restaurant and not out on a beach by a roaring fire with a cold one in their hand. It just never happens—because it cannot happen.

So the sheer awkwardness of Jared tackling one in broad daylight, not on a beach, but in a tiny luncheon place, was not only surprising, but it was more than a tad off-putting when the commercial tried, somehow—bizarrely—to connect Golden tearing apart a lobster to standing up to Biden's national agenda. Weird stuff.

But leaving aside the overall utility of such an odd commercial and the resulting mirth it generated statewide, it led to what can only be called "the campaign of the dueling lobstermen."

Fine gentlemen of the sea held forth in Golden and Poliquin commercials bemoaning Golden's poor performance re the keepers of the coast, or was it Poliquin's lack of interest in their problems? Hard to remember. Other equally fine lads, seemingly authentically smelling of bait, were then enlisted to say how great Poliquin had been for them. Just a bunch of lobstermen yakking away for one or the other. On and on. Several rounds worth.

During the last week of the campaign, I even saw another lobsterman, this one a fine-looking fellow named "Billy Bob" used as a closer. Boy, did he look authoritative and big and bold. I sure would have believed him if he told me pogies fish are better than red fish or said that using roadkill like opossum will draw those bugs for days. But here he was saying the exact opposite of some of the other lobstermen. It was all very confusing. It turned out "Billy Bob" was actually Billy Bob Faulkingham from Winter Harbor, and he was a *Republican* state representative. Imagine the shock value of that when it got out—a *Republican* endorsing another *Republican*.

Startling.

"I'm sure going to vote for Poliquin now."

Think about this, however: why would lobstermen be thought of as authority figures? I'd bet nobody on either campaign asked six hundred 2nd CD voters how believable they were in a congressional race, especially when both sides had them. One tiny lily pad, two big lobster men, what could possibly go wrong?

And why in the world would anybody in Lewiston or Ashland or Milo, Maine, let alone Presque Isle, care what a person who catches lobsters for a living thinks about a congressional candidate?

To many, in the largest CD east of the Mississippi, it would seem there would be other more germane authority figures than dueling lobstermen.

But that would not be considering the Wild Wild East mindscape of Maine. How to explain the use of these authority figures? Lobstermen are iconic figures in our state, just like Maine game wardens. They are part of that mindscape we hold so dear. The problem in this case was that with two of the same authority figures, lobstermen, arguing for two different candidates, they more or less cancelled each other out on that little lily pad.

But over the last four decades doing dozens of ballot measures, I have found a consistent pattern that ties believable authority figures to the Wild Wild East of Maine. Maine guides, Maine game wardens, game biologists, spokespeople from conservation, and sportsmen and sportswomen's groups such as the Sportsman's Alliance of Maine, strong advocates for environmental health such as Maine Audubon, the Nature Conservancy, and yes, lobstermen, all have high believability quotients because they represent that world in some fashion or other, and the public believes in the messages they bring.

One of my favorites is the figure of the timber cruiser, a mythic figure from olden times who went out on snowshoes in the middle of winter and marked individual trees for future harvest. Still a good look. Still carrying symbolic weight in the twenty-first century. The cruiser certainly helped improve the image of a number of Maine paper companies back when they cared about things like that. Good stuff, those cruisers, going out in the woods and carefully selecting individual trees rather than clearcutting by the square mile!

The mystique of the Wild Wild East lives as surely as it did centuries ago. The great northern forest still casts a magic, mythic spell as does the wild, untamed granite-bound coast of the state.

Do you doubt the efficacy of the mindscape of the Wild Wild East and its iconic figures, hunters, fishermen and women, lobstermen, and Indigenous men and women?

Why did Ed Muskie in the 1950s feature himself hunting pheasants? Why was Angus King filmed fishing for salmon in the Allagash in the 1990s? Why, when facing defeat in 2020, did Senator Susan Collins turn to Bill Green, the longtime TV host of *Bill Green's Maine* and legendary outdoorsman to cut her very effective closer TV commercial? Why was Janet Mills filmed fly fishing in 2022? To show their solidarity with the Wild Wild East and its tradition of hunting and fishing and the Great North Woods. And we need always to be reminded by Mary McAleney of Vanceboro, that the Wild Wild East lies "East of the Kennebec" as well in the "Great North Woods."

Remember, too, how effective the Maine lobsterman was in the Gay Rights referendum of 1995. Quite a last-minute surprise, and the other side certainly never considered using one.

Remember what happened when the Congresspeople Andrews, Pingree, and Allen journeyed to the Great North Woods without being properly armed and acting as if it wasn't a special place at all.

Part of this fascination with the outdoors is explained by psychographics and the use of psychographics in Maine political campaigns. Originally used in advertising and marketing to denote lifestyle and consumer preferences, psychographics have become a valuable and useful tool in understanding Maine politics.

"Psychographic" refers primarily to the psychic imagery around which voters make decisions. It is a shorthand way of describing the "inner landscape" of the voters of Maine, the images they hold in their heads as they make public policy decisions in many ballot measures. The use of psychographics turns out to be a highly valuable concept in determining why voters vote a certain way on certain issues at certain times and then vote another way at other times.

Part of this has to do with the basic and existing mindset of the voters— that is, what imagery do they bring to a particular referendum or issue? And part of it has to do with the ability of various campaigns to reinforce, change, or obliterate the existing imagery by substituting new images and new connotations to older cognitive maps.

For all these reasons, the Wild Wild East continues to intrigue and demand our psychographic attention, and we ignore its rhythms at our peril. I believe the Wild Wild East mystique is in part responsible for Mainers' pride of place and contentment with their state. In forty years of polling Maine people, I have always been aware of their love of their state. Even with all the contentions about the environment, and our conflicting views about which directions we should voyage, I have very seldom heard anyone say, "I wish Maine was more like —." Even when Maine people wish Maine had x or y or z or wish we could do a or b or c, they almost never couple that with an alternative state as a model.

Our sense of place is deeply embedded in our wilderness as well as in our imagined sense of that wildness.

"Maine is triumph," say many because that is what Maine people do when faced with adversity.

I think Maine history offers some insights as to why the Wild Wild East mindscape endures and controls.

From the early days of European settlement, Maine has always been a frontier society, "a place apart." It is the only state on the eastern seaboard to be settled from the west to the east and the south to the north. Caught between French Canada and English Massachusetts, Maine was a battleground as well as a lightly populated, heavily wooded place, "a wild place in between."

As Lew Dietz in *Night Train at Wiscasset Station* writes, "Maine was and still is a frontier. Maine people continue to be engaged in a battle with nature and an austere environment."

So it is not surprising that our culture and our politics and our societies have been mixed in character, pulled this way and that by countervailing influences. Maine is thus many things to many people, and over the last four or five decades more and more people from away have arrived, many—although not all—bringing with them a sense of suburbia and a desire to "tame" and make more user-friendly their portions of that wildness.

But there is widespread and consistent opposition to "taming" the Wild Wild East. Anti-hunting efforts fail along with gun limitation laws; in fact, "open carry" of firearms is now the law of the land in the state of Maine.

Even in our quite gentrified town of Harpswell with the longest coastline in the state, people rose up as one to oppose some do-gooder from away who started to circulate a petition banning the storage of lobster pots on front lawns. "Get real, lady, we've been doing it for four hundred years, and we ain't about to stop doing it now," became the refrain. Think of the hubris of that woman for a moment and understand the pushback from the Wild Wild East.

There has been a real-life struggle of economic forces and environmental concern. A while back, the Wilderness Society produced a very powerful film of the industrial forest at the end of the twentieth century. It showed a massive, three-story-high machine clumping through the woods, literally picking up trees by the roots and shaking off the dirt and cutting them up. Very off-putting.

The response of Champion International and other paper companies was to show commercials of single foresters carefully marking trees in the old "cruiser" tradition, when in the middle of winter their snowshoe-clad scouts cruised the forest and carefully marked the trees to be harvested. Others showed a single worker with a single horse "twitching" a fallen tree out of the woods, slowly, carefully. Not surprisingly, the public sided with the paper companies' sense of place.

This ambiguity is found elsewhere. Many of his readers find it hard to grasp that Henry David Thoreau was frightened by the sheer wildness of the Katahdin wilderness at the same time he enjoyed it and happily went back to his small pond and his weekly Sunday dinners with his mother. That's part of the Great North Woods' appeal. It is awesome.

Or that contemporaneously, a semi-industrial forest harvesting system was in place in many parts of the state, using a narrow gauge rail system to take out the logs, a process that led to millions of board feet of lumber being exported yearly, crowding, and eventually suffocating, whole river systems with bark and wood in mammoth log drives and the effluent from a dozen paper mills.

For a first-rate analysis of the struggles over the wild forest and the industrial one, see Thomas Urquhart's illuminating *Up for Grabs: Timber Pirates, Lumber Barons, and the Battles over Maine's Public Lands*.

There is thus necessary ambiguity in our appreciation of our Wild Wild East heritage, for that heritage is chockfull of paradoxes and ironies. For example, those bemoaning the cutting of trees seldom mention that 90 percent of the state is still covered in trees. There are more trees standing now than during the Civil War. There are also more deer (over 320,000 in 2022), at least in the southern part of the state—certainly more deer than when the Indigenous peoples hunted for a living. Deer are not really creatures of the deep woods like moose and bears as much as they are of the fringes of that woods. Suburbia, it turns out, is great deer country.

And where those deer are may surprise you as well.

Do you want to be guaranteed of getting "your" deer today in 2023? Hunt around York, Maine, down in York County, not where Thoreau wandered up north in the shadow of Katahdin. There are forty deer per mile in the former, two to three per square mile in the latter. Over the last ten years more deer have been tagged in York than in any other town in Maine. Or check out deer hunting in Cape Elizabeth. Ignore the majestic "cottages" and McMansions. There are so many deer hanging around, they even let you shoot an extra deer there for good measure.

But always, despite these pesky realities, it has been the mindscape, not the actuality of the Big Woods of Maine, with its myriad trees and hundreds of rivers and lakes and a wilderness sense of place that makes us, and many hunters from away, think of the mystic allure of those Great North Woods and would not stop in York County to get "their" deer if you paid them real money

It was the moose hunt in 1983 that first showed me the potential of marshalling the mystic of the Wild Wild East to win battles over its dimensions. But the 1986 Wildlife Bond that would prove to be seminal in providing a blueprint for carrying the day statewide by bringing together disparate groups, groups that were often in opposition to each other on other issues. To this day, I call it "The Eureka Bond" because it showed me that combining those who hunt and fish with environmentalists would give you a 65 percent bulletproof majority on virtually any issue connected with the out of doors.

George Smith and SAM enabled us to do polling that would change forever the way we looked at the possible alliance between the hunting and fishing community and environmentalists. One important person who hunted, fished, and was the executive director of Maine Audubon Society from 1969–1977 was Richard "Dick" Anderson. He would later serve as commissioner of the Maine Department of Conservation (1981–1987). He helped us to look at the overlap between the hunting and fishing community and those who more vigorously carried the environmental banner.

It was in that election cycle that we discovered the underlying realities of Maine politics tied to the Wild Wild East. When you totaled up the people who hunted and fished and snowmobiled and added the people who cross-country skied and birdwatched and hiked or camped, you got to 80 percent of the population. That is quite a constituency, if it could be harnessed together for the public good.

Likewise when it came to authority figures who could carry important messages concerning the out of doors, if you took those who believed SAM and those who believed environmental groups such as Audubon and the Nature Conservancy, you arrived at a quite surprising 65 percent of the voting population. Although many saw—and continue to see—these two groups as separate and often at odds, when you combined them on an issue concerning the out of doors you got a solid majority—even an unassailable total—of the voting population of the state.

Parenthetically, it is worth noting that when I polled for the national Nature Conservancy in other states, wherever I checked—Texas, New Mexico, Pennsylvania, Colorado, Rhode Island, Florida, Idaho, Montana, Minnesota, and New York—the same unbeatable coalition could be formed and would be successful at the ballot box. Often the most difficult task in any ballot measure or even legislative effort would thus be getting "the hook and bullet crowd" and "the tree huggers" (to use their favorite names for each other) together in the first place.

In Montana, for example, it took three days to get the cowboys and the environmentalists to agree on a package. It came down to pointing out—in exasperation—that the cowboys wanted to shoot more elk and the enviros wanted to save the black-footed ferret. Since the black-footed ferret ate the prairie dogs into whose holes the cowboys' horses fell and broke their legs, it would be a win–win. Kill a few more elk and let the black-footed ferret population thrive, and only the prairie dogs would suffer.

There was some interesting and, to some, startlingly ironic data found in Maine people's attitudes toward the environment. We consistently found as well that quite a few more Republicans than Democrats belonged to or donated to environmental or conservation groups. While this is not the public's perception since virtually all the major environment groups in Maine are headed by Democrats, in poll after poll I found this reality verified.

In this regard, it should be noted that in the 1970s, Republican political figures were at the forefront of fighting for what today most environmentalists would revere as "Bible" issues, while Democratic politicians were fighting for large projects that placed employment over place.

For example, in the 1970s and 1980s, Democratic Governor Ken Curtis proposed that Maine allow an oil refinery to be built Down East, while Senators Ed Muskie and Hathaway and various Democratic congressmen strongly advocated the damming of the Allagash Wilderness Waterway with the mammoth Dickey-Lincoln Dam.

These projects were not only opposed by all the major environmental groups, but also by Republican political figures such as state Representatives Harry Richardson and David Huber and state Senators Sam Collins and Bennett Katz, as well as US Senators and congressmen and governors such as Bill Cohen, David Emery, Olympia Snowe, Jock McKernan, and Susan Collins. Cumberland's Harry Richardson, for example, was also at the head of the political effort to retrieve Maine's public lots from the paper companies that controlled them. He made it a centerpiece of his run for governor in 1974.

It was following the successful referendum on the out of doors in 1986 when Carol Baudler of the national Nature Conservancy and the local chapter led by Kent Womack and Mason Morfit joined with Sherry Huber and the Maine Audubon Society to put together a holistic bond package, that I knew there was adequate opportunity to win if earlier errors could be avoided.

I remember going to the first meeting of the group and being shown an Audubon-proposed poster to kick off the campaign. It was a lovely, exquisite pen wash drawing of a mountain, looking like a Japanese print. Absolutely beautiful. You'd love to have it framed in your living room. There was only one problem I could see: there were no people in the drawing. When I asked, "Where are the people?" I was told, "Our members don't like to see people in the woods."

The seminal warning "all the big mistakes are made early" came to my mind, but I contented myself with saying, "But we are asking people to set aside tens of millions of *their* tax dollars for the purpose of saving views like that. They will want to go there."

In fact, it was by combining access (by people!) to public lands and water *and* including deer yards and working farms that we came to a saleable package, one that tapped into the Wild Wild East ethos and at the same time also provided the hope that one could go to these special places. Interestingly, in addition, we found that 12 percent of Maine people would sign on to the bond, but they wanted to be able to drive to the locations.

Yes, in the aggregate, we the people of Maine wanted to save "virgin" land. Yes, we wanted to save hunting areas and wild deer yards, but we also wanted to save views we could drive to and enjoy if we were old or infirm or simply used to driving around. The resulting Land for Maine's Future bond in 1987 changed history and led to a series of landmark ballot measures and bond issues.

The campaign dynamics of this effort are covered in chapter 9, "Fear Drives Out Favor," and chapter 11 on "Authority Figures and Influence Vectors." But suffice it here to mention that the hybrid bond received 65 percent of the vote as the overlapping constituencies of the Sportsman's Alliance of Maine and the Nature Conservancy and Audubon Society held firm.

For a final look at the mindscape of the Wild Wild East and its impact (real, imagined, and possible) on our way of looking at political issues, we turn, no doubt surprisingly, to the Same Sex Marriage referendum of 2012.

In 2009 Maine voters were asked to repeal a state law passed by the Maine legislature and signed into law by Governor Baldacci. Called "An Act to End Discrimination in Civil Marriage and Affirm Religious Freedom," the new law had been immediately challenged by the Maine Christian Civic League, the Catholic Church, and the Stand for Marriage Maine Coalition with national support from the National Organization for Marriage (NOM). Enough signatures to put the vote to repeal the new law on the November ballot were gathered, and the group wisely chose to use an off-year election to make their case. Marc Mutty was the ultimately successful campaign manager for Stand for Marriage.

Gay Rights advocates formed No on 1/Protect Maine Equality with a powerful board made up of EqualityMaine (Betsy Smith), the Maine Civil Liberties Union (Shenna Bellows), the Gay and Lesbian Advocates and Defenders (Mary Bonauto), and the LGBTQ community in Maine (Pat Peard), along with Peter Chandler, Ben Dudley, Jim Mitchell, and others. They hired Jesse Connelly, who had been the successful campaign manager of the NO side in 2005, had been John Baldacci's campaign manager and had served as Chellie Pingree's chief of staff.

During the campaign, several newspaper polls by Pan Atlantic, Research 2000, and Democracy Corps showed the NO side either ahead or within the margin of error. The No on 1/Protect Maine Equality's own internal polling also showed them ahead. As Betsy Smith put it, "We had 47 percent with 12 percent undecided. We thought for sure we could pick up 3 percent out of that 12 percent. We really expected to win."

But on election night, though, the YES side prevailed 52.9–47.1 percent.

The gay marriage advocates were disappointed but not dissuaded from their mission, as gay marriage referenda had previously been defeated over twenty times all across the country. In Maine, they vowed to press ahead and continued their impressive outreach and on-the-ground conversation conversion efforts for the next several years. They thought they would have a better chance in the larger turnout election such as a presidential year in 2012.

Betsy Smith, longtime executive director of EqualityMaine, agrees, describing the process that involved a major "Go–No Go" meeting with all the stakeholders—national and state—who would decide Maine should be the only state to bring marriage equality directly to the voters: "It was a strategic decision, ultimately made by advocates who believed that in the presidential election of 2012, Mainers would turn out in large numbers and would embrace the message of 'love and commitment' for same-sex couples. This message would blunt the other side's attacks."

The Catholic Church, Christian Civic League, and others, and spokesperson Bob Emerich again opposed the referendum while EqualityMaine and Mainers United for Marriage supported the measure, which read: "Do you want to allow the state of Maine to issue marriage licenses to same-sex couples?"

Matt McTighe, the perceptive and very effective leader of numerous ballot measures in Maine and elsewhere, outlines the strategy: "We wanted to diffuse the attacks we knew would come, and we coalesced around the broader positive messages of love and commitment. We incorporated these in all our messages, going beyond those of our strongest supporters. We didn't believe that the core messages of our supporters alone would accomplish our goals."

After considerable research and collaborative discussion, Mainers United for Marriage decided on a nonconfrontational effort, a soft-sell, disarming outreach. The goal was to covert voters by blurring, deflecting, and isolating the hardest-core opponents of gay marriage.

"Marriage is love and commitment" was the focus on persuading those who could be moved either in person or with TV. In many ways this had been going on since 2005 and was now amped up. By Election Day 2012, over 250,000 conversations, in person and by phone, would take place with Maine voters.

In the process, Mainers United for Marriage put together a formidable team with McTighe as campaign manager. Amy Simon was the pollster, and the preparation for the GOTV was done internally based on research imported into EqualityMaine's database through NGP VAN (a leading technology provider to Democratic and progressive political campaigns and organizations, nonprofits, municipalities, and other groups). David Farmer was a senior strategist and the principal spokesperson for Mainers United for Marriage. Betsy Smith was the primary spokesperson for EqualityMaine.

Their media campaign was very ably run by David Loughran of Frame Strategies and ended up producing some truly outstanding TV ads. One included a Franco mother and her gay son and his partner, another featured a firefighter, another a service man in Iraq, and a final closer called "Why Marriage Matters Maine" featuring four generations of a Machias, Maine, family led by Harlan Gardner, a World War II vet, wanting love and inclusion for their granddaughter and her partner.

In April 2011, Ethan Strimling, former state senator from Portland, subsequently mayor of that city and member of the board of EqualityMaine (along with Timothy Diehl, Barb Wood, Shawn Legrega, and others), asked me to meet with Betsy Smith, the executive director of EqualityMaine and a decade-long, very powerful force for equal rights. Eventually they had me do a poll analyzing the previous defeat and suggesting strategies for dealing with the significant losses the group had suffered in the northern portion of the state.

This effort was a very peripheral, specific (and probably a courtesy) effort since their entire polling, media, and GOTV team was already in place, and had what would prove to be a successful campaign strategy ongoing on a statewide basis.

At the time in 2011, he and Betsy simply wanted another point of view on the people who had voted against their cause. The hope was to identify some possible ways to reduce their margin of losses in the north.

Looking first at the 2009 data, I was amazed. While the NO side had successfully carried the Portland Designated Market Area (DMA, or TV market reach), it had handily lost both the Bangor DMA and the Presque Isle DMA. And the NO side had been slaughtered in the heart of the Great North Woods of the Wild Wild East. More importantly, overall they had lost the statewide Franco-American vote as well.

Going forward, I attempted to look at the psychographics of the opposition and test influence vectors and authority figures for converting the previous antigay marriage voters to supporting the subsequent referendum in its favor. The resulting 2011 cognitive map was designed "for detaching significant numbers of antigay marriage voters from the opposition's current coalition."

There were many worthwhile targets. For example, the gay marriage advocates were still ahead in the Portland DMA 56–32 percent, but behind in Bangor 32–44 percent, and in Presque Isle from 20–66 percent. They were losing with a number of specific groups:

1. Women who worked at home were against gay marriage by a margin of 50–30 percent.
2. Franco-Americans were against it by a margin of 51–36 percent.
3. The Great North Woods population (the counties of Aroostook, Piscataquis, Washington, Somerset, Franklin, and northern Penobscot taken together) was over 60 percent against it. Indeed, a special oversample of the small predictor towns from the Great North Woods region showed an astonishing 72–22 percent opposition. I wrote, "the losses in and around the GNW (Great North Woods) psychographic are truly mindboggling."
4. There was a huge cohort of voters who said they "didn't like the idea of gay marriage and were afraid of it." This seemed to me to be a huge opportunity based on what I knew about the Wild Wild East. The "I'm afraid of gay marriage" group made up almost 40 percent of the antigay marriage coalition!

With relish, I thought of all the opportunities to change even a small percentage of minds of that cohort. I thought item (4) was tailormade for Maine's Wild Wild East ethos. My Wild Wild East fixation kicked in big time, and I wanted to shoehorn it into this campaign by stressing the mindscape of "Maine as a frontier." "Live and let live." "Do your own thing, I'll do mine." "Freedom on the frontier."

I thought they could pick up votes in the North Country (the Bangor and Presque Isle DMAs) if they would embed gay marriage into that environment by striking the familiar historical cords of the Wild Wild East mindscape and using its usual symbolic referents. They could tie gay marriage to freedom for one and all in a way that would resonate across the north.

What first popped into my head when I saw this data were the words—and sentiments—of a longtime registered Maine guide, "If you don't like gay marriage, don't marry a gay." Period. End of story. "Let personal freedom reign." "Don't constrain the rights of others. You don't like anyone to constrain yours." That's the true Maine.

As usual I leapt wildly ahead with what I imagined would be a strong closing commercial for the Bangor and Presque Isle DMAs. I envisioned a rugged-looking game warden or registered Maine guide, standing tall and confident in front of the kind of huge, dark woods of the type that scared Henry David Thoreau. The guide was saying, "Look, I'm not afraid of the dark. I'm not afraid of wolves, I'm not afraid of the great Maine woods, and I'm certainly not afraid of gay marriage. And you shouldn't be, either."

I thought about that image for weeks. Challenge these North Woods voters to "Prove you aren't afraid. Vote YES." I was pretty excited, and it probably showed when I subsequently presented my findings to the EqualityMaine board. I told them I thought if they focused on the categories outlined above, I believed they could change enough minds so that a 55–45 percent victory was possible.

After all these years of teaching, polling, and consulting, I'm pretty good at reading a room quickly and readily. The EqualityMaine members present that night were polite and seemed mildly interested in my findings. But it was soon very clear to me that while they wanted to win this referendum—and they really wanted to win it—they also wanted to win it their way. They didn't need to win it "my" way or anybody else's. I could see that for them the Great North Woods were a distant and unwanted mirage.

This time around, these advocates didn't want another Lobster Boy *deus ex machina* or jujitsu-type commercial. They didn't want to be "saved" by some game warden dude from the north, no matter what. They wanted, indeed needed, to win it on their own and on their own terms. They themselves wanted to be accepted along with the civil unions by the people of Maine. How they won was almost as important as winning it.

Besides, as stated above, EqualityMaine was already a part of the broader coalition that had a very high-caliber, full-court press team already in place and getting ready for the final struggle. They had a strong game plan and viable strategy, and it was working for them. They certainly didn't need this diversion into the woods.

Driving home that night, I understood. Sure, I was disappointed. What consultant doesn't want to be even a small part of a win of this moral and historical significance, one he or she cares about. But to EqualityMaine, to members of the gay community and the principals of Mainers United for Marriage more generally, I thought this was more than just a referendum on an issue affecting them. It was a recognition of selfhood, a need to be acknowledged properly by the people of their state. Plus, they believed in their initial strategy and expected to win with it. Why deviate just because someone was excited about challenging the population of the Great North Woods?

I respected them for that then, and I still do today.

So, I was doubly proud for them in November when they won by doing it their way.

In this regard, I thought their eventual closing spot was a pitch-perfect end to their efforts. It was a deeply moving commercial about four generations of Mainers from Machias. It spoke of how hard it was to be gay and featured a Maine military veteran, Harlan Gardiner, wanting to see his gay granddaughter married in Maine. It closed with Harlan delivering a key message: "It isn't about politics. It's about people and how we treat each other." It was very powerful. And very influential. Dave Farmer wrote after the campaign about Harlan that fittingly "he was made the grand marshal of the Pride Parade in Portland."

Ethan Strimling also correctly gives maximum credit to the two-year outreach effort conducted by EqualityMaine and the Coalition all over the state:

> The field campaign was over two years long. From almost the day we lost in 2009, work began on identifying tens of thousands of possible swing households and armies of volunteers and paid field staff were sent out to knock on every one of those doors.
>
> The conversations at the doors were not persuasion in the classic sense of "Vote for gay marriage!" They were just that, conversations. Conversations by and for those most affected by the lack of legal protections. These conversations were absolutely instrumental in turning the 2009 five-point defeat into the 2012 five-point victory.

This time Gay Marriage advocates would win 52.6–47.4 percent, and Maine would become the first state in the Union to approve gay marriage in a referendum. It was a historic win for gay women and men, and for our state and country. And, like Frank Sinatra, they had done it their way with their own strategy. Of course, the consultant part of me was also happy to see that statewide the Franco towns in the aggregate had finally voted 51.3–48.7 percent for it as well. But the Great North Woods towns again came in over 70 percent NO.

Ethan also captures that this whole effort had been more than just about winning an election:

> What I saw was one of the smartest, most strategic campaigns I had ever been part of. From micro-targeting households that could be swung our way, to macro-messaging that motivated and strengthened our base, to a fundraising machine that capitalized on every opportunity and created ones we never imagined.
>
> But mostly I saw an incredibly committed board who always focused on one thing—how do we win equal marriage in a sustainable and affirming way. Unbelievable hours, stress, excitement and intelligence. It changed my understanding for life of how you make change in America.

We conclude this chapter where we began—with the Wild Wild East still firmly back in our frame and with its coastal icons firmly in place as the 2022 race for Congress in Maine's 2nd CD continues. Ads featured some of its iconic symbolic referents, with both sides using lobstermen as authority figures at the end.

It would appear they canceled each other out, for despite the best efforts of Billy Bob as closer, Golden won by a larger margin than the time before, getting 53.1 percent to Poliquin's 46.9 percent in the ranked choice run-off, while Tiffany Bond upped her previous total to 6.8 percent. Perhaps her movement was the result of a hidden anti-lobsterman vote up north. But *that* I do not know.

I'm sure, if asked, bemused voters in the 2nd CD sitting in Jay or Patten would say at the end game with the dueling lobster dudes, "Ah well, when did lobstermen ever agree on anything?"

To which those of us living on the coast could reply, "But they *always* agree on a couple of things: the cost of bait and fuel are too high, and the price they get for their bugs is too low."

"That they do, dearie, don't you know. That they do." But highlanders wouldn't necessarily know that. Especially highlanders away from the coast.

AXIOM #4

"Ethnicity Matters—The Francos Rule" with Dave Emery

Long live the Francos.
—TERESA McCANN-TUMIDAJSKI

During Christmas week 2021, I got a call from a good and longtime friend. This person was concerned about the reelection of Janet Mills and did me the honor of asking me what I thought she should do to be reelected. As it happens, I long had a high opinion of Janet and, having dealt with her on various referenda, agreed with political insiders' designation of her from many years ago: "As tough as any man and twice as smart."

I thought she was an excellent attorney general, and as governor she very deftly guided Maine through the pandemic. When you think Maine has the highest percentage of elderly in the nation and we ended up having the highest rate for vaccinations and one of the very lowest rates of COVID, that's quite an accomplishment. Like many others, I was surprised to see in the middle of the pandemic signs saying, "Impeach Mills," often on the same lawns as ones saying, "Stamp out Child Sex Trafficking, Vote Republican." So in the Twilight Zone of today's Crazy Town politics, I understood the caller's concern.

Being governor is so much harder than being a congressperson or a senator, and being under constant, hour-by-hour challenges is a huge burden. I told the caller I thought there were three things she should do to be reelected. The first was to try and get the progressives in Portland and elsewhere *not* to run an Independent candidate, regardless of how much they might like to do so and cost mainline Democrats the election. Very important.

The second was to make sure that the suburban women (especially Independents and Republicans) in the "Gold Coast" ring around Portland—Cape Elizabeth, Falmouth, Cumberland, Yarmouth, Freeport, and Scarborough—did not blunt what would be her big margins coming out of Portland (as happened to Mike Michaud when he ran against Paul LePage in 2016). Note: For an introduction to the rise of LePage in Maine politics, see Mike Tipping's *As Maine Went.*

Third, and most important, I said that if she ran her campaign so that she split the Franco-American vote in Maine (20 percent + of the total statewide) with former Governor Paul LePage, he could not win no matter what his strategy would be, which I guessed would be to try to blunt her progress in the Gold Coast and thus keep down her Portland margins as the vote moved north to the land of the Trumpkanoids. Although as the campaign developed, I had to admit I didn't see *any* election strategy except "Have Paul be *not quite Paul*." Pretty strange when all was said and done. I honestly never figured out what LePage's campaign was trying to accomplish strategically.

Back to Francos. In the forty years I was in active politics, from 1972 to 2012, I *always* made the Francos the center of my election focus, whether in candidate elections or referenda and ballot measures.

So that last assertion for the Mills campaign was old, old news.

But still very, very relevant. Just look at the US Senate race in Maine in 2020.

For me, an appreciation of the Franco-American role in Maine elections has not been simply an academic enterprise to be taught to students, it has had a real-world grounding with numerous practical electoral payoffs.

Ever since I was the campaign manager for Bill Cohen in 1972 when he first ran for Congress, I have been fascinated by the Franco-American voter in Maine. In 1972, fully two-thirds of all Franco-Americans were registered Democrats and most voted a straight Democratic ticket. The Franco-American strongholds such as Biddeford/Saco, Lewiston/Auburn, and the St. John Valley brought in huge majorities for Democratic candidates.

But from the earliest polling and personal interactions, I always noted that while the Francos were registered Democrat and usually voted that way, many of them shared "Republican" values such as distrust of government and emphasis on small business concerns. They also exhibited a pattern of seeing the government as more often the problem than the solution (which has been generally less true for Maine's English and Irish cohorts).

The Francos displayed a much different profile than the other pillar of the Democratic Party in Maine, the Irish Americans. Over half of them were registered Democrats as well, but they had a far different psychographic profile. Irish Americans more often saw government as a solution, not a problem, welcomed expanded government employment, and were far less likely than their Franco compatriots to be sympathetic to the needs of small business.

I believed then, as I do now, that the key to any Republican and Independent success in Maine depends on appealing to the Franco-American swing vote (20 percent + statewide) because even a near split in the voting pattern often means the Democrat cannot win, no matter what else they do if that key element is lost.

Some background is probably in order.

In terms of the law of large numbers, Maine has only three major "tribes." There is the English/Yankee tribe, about one-third of the voting total in any given election cycle; there is the Irish American tribe, with about 20 percent; and the Franco-American tribe, with 20 percent of the vote. While there are lots of nice people of Swedish and Russian and Greek and Italian heritage, they can all be lumped together as "other" for polling purposes.

PS—I'm of Swedish and Danish extraction. Nobody cares.

There are some fine books for readers interested in the history of the Irish and the Franco-Americans in Maine for those interested in these two groups. Among the ones most helpful to my understanding their history are James Muncy, *Hard Times, Hard Men: Maine and the Irish*; Michael Connolly, *They Change Their Sky: The Irish in Maine*; Dyke Hendrickson, *Quiet Prescence: Franco-Americans in Maine*; Mark Richard, *Loyal But French*; Maurice Violette, *The Franco-Americans*; and Nelson Madore and Barry Rodrigue (eds.), *Voyages: A Maine Franco American Reader.*

Why did the Franco-Americans end up being such a swing vote in Maine's elections?

I think I know why. When the second wave of French immigrants came down from Quebec after the American Civil War (the first wave came earlier from Atlantic Canada and settled in the St. John Valley), many found work in the shoe and textile factories and paper mills of Biddeford, Saco, Sanford, Westbrook, Lewiston, Auburn, Brunswick, Rumford, Mexico, Waterville, Old Town, and Winslow.

Many of their basic societal and governmental values should have made them "small government, low taxes" Republicans but for the fact that the mill owners were Republicans. That coupled with discrimination against them as well as the Irish and other minority groups by the descendants of the English settlers made the Democratic Party a more natural fit for them for the first one hundred years they were in Maine.

Initially, Francos were overwhelmingly Democratic and could be counted on to vote that way from the time of their enfranchisement until 1972. Part of it was habit: they were Democrats and voted that way. Part of it was institutional: there was a big box at the top of the ballot that easily enabled anyone who wished to vote a straight ticket. Many Franco-Americans did so.

Finally, part of the ongoing Democratic success among Francos was also the result of a self-fulfilling prophecy.

Republican candidates "knew" that the Franco-Americans were going to vote Democrat, so they didn't bother to campaign among them very much or to find out what they wanted.

All this changed in 1972. Democrats in Maine had actually long thought that the so-called Big Box favored Republicans, and when they commissioned a study under the direction of George Mitchell, they fully expected to find that to be true. But their report proved the opposite—the Big Box actually favored the Democrats precisely because so many Franco-Americans chose to use it. All Democratic efforts (by then well under way) to get the Big Box removed now had to be stopped in midstream. But now it was the Republicans who wanted reform.

Thanks largely to the efforts of Bob Monks, who led the fight to eliminate the "Big Box," by the time of the general election in November 1972, Franco-Americans would theoretically come "into play." Despite the vigorous objections of Bill Hathaway ("I'd never heard two grown men yell like that," said one staffer), Democrat Governor Ken Curtis held the vote on the Big Box at the June primary election, rather than in the November general election.

Thus, the Franco-Americans *actually* came into play when Bill Cohen campaigned extensively in the Franco-American communities and walked across Maine. From a working-class background—his father was a baker who got up at 2 A.M. every morning to bake the bread and rolls—Cohen not only projected an image different from that of previous Republican candidates, but he also spent enough time in and among the Franco communities so they could appreciate how many values he and they shared.

Cohen was elected in 1972 precisely because the Franco-American vote split significantly. For example, previously the Republican candidate for Congress in the 2nd CD came out of Androscoggin County down 23,000 votes, but in 1972 Cohen lost the Androscoggin Valley by only 6,000 votes. His small business orientation, his blue-collar background, and his basic distrust of government for all political solutions resonated with Franco-Americans. It also helped that his opponent, Elmer Violette, while a Franco-American, was an Acadian from the St. John Valley while many other Franco-Americans were originally from Quebec and many in Lewiston did not want to see someone from the Valley get the seat.

In subsequent elections, Cohen would actually carry Lewiston, Auburn, and the Androscoggin Valley on his way to eight straight elections without a loss. Adopting Cohen's Franco-centric outreach, Dave Emery, Jock McKernan, Olympia Snowe, and Susan Collins, along with Independent Angus King, who campaigned as a small businessman in 1994, all put and kept the Franco communities in play.

Dave Emery also tells of his interaction with the Franco-Americans in the 1st CD, first in his initial congressional run of 1974 and his subsequent races of 1976, 1978, and 1980. Here he shares with us some of his insights:

I grew up in Rockland, and consequently did not know many Franco-Americans as a youngster; although Rockland had a surprisingly diverse population, it has never had a significant Franco-American community. I was, of course, very much aware of the French heritage and culture in such places as Lewiston and Biddeford, but I had not experienced it during my formative years.

My first close association with Franco-Americans was as a freshman state representative in 1971, when I got to know several as colleagues in Augusta. It became readily apparent to me that, even though they were strong Democrats, their values and views on many issues were virtually indistinguishable from my own. I was also becoming aware that among legislative Republicans, there were those whose views, interests and priorities diverged from mine more than did the views of my Franco-American colleagues.

One of the Democrats I particularly respected was Roland Gauthier of Sanford, who, as it happened, was my seatmate in the Legal Affairs Committee. In those days, seating was not by party, so this was not at all unusual. He was friendly and helpful to me as I was learning the ropes, and from our casual discussions, I learned quite a bit about the Sanford-Springvale area, a community that I had never visited at that time.

We did, however, have a common acquaintance—Ralph Lovell, a well-respected pharmacist whose business was located on the east side of town, in the Franco-American neighborhoods where Gauthier lived. Lovell, a Republican, represented heavily Democratic Sanford in both the House and Senate at various times, and it was apparent that his electoral success was due to his being an active and involved member of that community.

Building upon my contacts there, I focused on the Sanford Area throughout the 1974 campaign and established my York County congressional district office there after my election victory over Peter Kyros. I rented the office space from Emile Roy, who provided a small room adjacent to his barber shop. Before long, Emile became an enthusiastic supporter and eventually became an active Republican, so much so that any campaign stop in Sanford by any Republican candidate included a photo in Emile's barber chair. There is even a photo of Emile Roy cutting Vice President George H. W. Bush's hair.

Although I lost Sanford in 1974 and again narrowly in 1976, I did much better than expected, and I carried Sanford comfortably in both 1978 and 1980. The extra effort I made there and in other Franco-American communities provided my razor-thin margin of victory in 1974 and virtually guaranteed my electoral successes during my subsequent reelection campaigns.

Another Franco-American member of the Legal Affairs Committee was Albert Cote of Lewiston, one of six Democratic House members representing the Spindle City. During my first term in the legislature, I really didn't get to know him too well beyond our occasional interactions during Committee hearings. But I became House Chairman of Legal Affairs during my second term, and in that capacity, Albert came to me one day requesting help with a bill he had introduced on behalf of the Lewiston snowshoe clubs.

The snowshoe clubs, as I later learned, were a cultural phenomenon throughout the greater Franco-American community. There were, at one point, as many as two dozen such clubs in and around Lewiston, and many others around the state wherever Franco-Americans lived. These were primarily social clubs, less about winter sports than about partying and boisterously celebrating their unique culture. They became a political force to be reckoned with; any candidate hoping to represent Lewiston would have to work the Lewiston snowshoe clubs hard.

Albert's bill amended the law to allow a scratch-off game known as "lucky sevens," similar to today's scratch-off lottery tickets; the snowshoe clubs would be able to sell the tickets as a fund-raiser and some lucky participant would win a small pot of cash. Without his input, I would have probably been inclined to oppose this bill, but after hearing Albert's arguments and seeing that it would be helpful to him and his constituents, I agreed to support it. And it passed!

After I was elected to Congress in 1974, I ran into Albert Cote only occasionally; the First District did not include Lewiston. But in the fall of 1981 while in Lewiston for a meeting regarding a possible run for the US Senate, I ran into him by chance at a local restaurant and joined him for a cup of coffee.

"You helped me once when I asked, and you've always been friendly and respectful to me," he said. "Now, I'm going to help you!"

Albert was as good as his word. He took me through parts of Lewiston where Republican candidates were never seen, and that included snowshoe club facilities on Lisbon Street. That year, 1982, was a bad year for Republicans in Maine and nationally, and I lost the Senate race to George Mitchell. Campaigning with Albert Cote was one of the few highlights of that particular campaign, and I very much appreciated his friendship and support.

Probably the most difficult place in the First District for Republicans was the City of Biddeford. Like Lewiston, it was a bastion of Democratic electoral strength, yielding no more than 15% to 18% or so to Republican candidates. I knew I had to work it hard if I hoped to cut into that usual Democratic advantage. Most Republican activists thought that it was a waste of my time to campaign in Biddeford, but my instincts told me otherwise, so I snaked through Biddeford on my campaign walking tour, stayed with a Democrat family in Biddeford Pool, campaigned at Biddeford High School football games, and regularly ate at local restaurants, the Wonderbar Restaurant in particular.

My 1974 opponent, Peter Kyros, was of Greek ancestry, and the owners of the Wonderbar were also Greek, so I was very surprised when one of the brothers introduced himself to me, offered the opinion that I would do much better than expected in Biddeford, and took me around to meet his customers and employees. Needless to say, I became a regular customer there whenever I was in the area.

His instincts proved correct; hard work in Biddeford had paid off. I carried 31.5 percent of the Biddeford vote that year, nearly double that of the previous Republican candidate for Congress, and well above the vote of any Republican in recent memory at that time.

But it was during my reelection campaign in 1976, however, that I really understood the impact of the groundwork I had laid, and of subsequent constituent service. During that campaign, I was knocking on doors in Biddeford one afternoon when I was greeted at the door by a late middle-aged Franco-American woman. She recognized me immediately and excitedly invited me in for a visit. Upon entering her modest second-floor apartment, I noticed three framed objects on her TV; in the center, displayed with great reverence, was a picture of the Sacred Heart of Jesus; on the right was a photo of her son in his Coast Guard uniform; and there on the left was a framed letter from the office of Congressman David F. Emery!

Not bad company for a candidate seeking reelection!

Apparently, the Union had encouraged its members to write their congressman and senators to urge limits on textile imports, and I had responded favorably. The signature on the letter was real. Some members used an automated signature device, but I always personally signed all correspondence that came from my office. To this day, I am humbled and amazed that a routine answer to a constituent letter should have been so greatly valued.

"If Biddeford was the toughest Franco-American community, Waterville was definitely the most fun. Waterville has long been a Democratic stronghold, the home and political launching pad that has produced any number of Democratic officeholders and activists, including US Senators Edmund Muskie and George Mitchell.

But in the 1970s and 1980s, Waterville was home to a group of popular and successful Republicans including Mayor Paul Laverdiere, state Senator Dick Pierce, and state Representatives Paul Boudreau and Lee Conary. Conary actually lived in Oakland but ran a doughnut shop in Waterville and represented a section of the city as well as the Town of Oakland.

Campaigning with this crew was a hoot! It usually included stops at various Waterville restaurants, clubs, bars and similar hangouts, unannounced drop-ins at various homes and businesses and attending any number of Waterville social events such as the annual Hafli, a celebration of Lebanese heritage; in addition to the Franco-American community, there is a strong Lebanese presence in Waterville. One Fourth of July afternoon, I found myself with the Waterville crew tubing behind a speedboat on Messalonskee Lake (better known locally as Snow Pond).

We must have stopped at dozens of camps along the lake, to the great surprise and entertainment of our unsuspecting hosts. One stop that afternoon was at a small country store near the lake. Standing at the counter was a very attractive young woman with her boyfriend; naturally, we all introduced ourselves, whereupon she asked, "Where do you stand on nuclear power?"

Conary jumped right in. "I'm all for it!" "But what are you going to do about all that nuclear waste?" Whereupon a heated argument ensued, neither Conary nor his young female debating foe yielding an inch. Finally someone in the store shouted out, "I think we should have a nuclear waste dump right here in Snow Pond. That way, we can go swimming all year round!"

With that, we ran for the door as quickly as possible, very relieved to notice the couple driving off in a sports car with Massachusetts plates.

And so it went. I did very well in Waterville, much better than expected in 1974, and winning comfortably there in each of my three House reelection campaigns. George Mitchell beat me badly there in the 1982 US Senate race, but that was always to be expected, since he was part of the Waterville Lebanese community.

As much as I would have liked to serve Maine as a US Senator, Mitchell was always a class act and served with distinction. But in retrospect, I can always take comfort in the fact that I came in *second*, and George Mitchell came in *next to last*!

The fundamental lesson I learned from these experiences is straightforward: if you want people to be interested in *you*, you have to express interest in *them*. This should be no revelation to anyone. So my advice to any candidate running for office is never to assume that any group is beyond reach if you are willing to put in the time to listen and learn about their concerns, and particularly to respect their heritage and culture.

Note that Emery has tracked that the registration profile for Franco-American voters has shifted rather continuously from that time. Emery and his firm Scientific Marketing recently ran an analysis of the standard voting blocs of Maine politics—the English, the Irish and the Franco-Americans—and cross tabulated them against party enrollments.

As we will see in chapter 5, "Polling Rules the Roost," Emery currently has the best data bank in Maine when it comes to operational polling results and parameters.

What follows is his assessment based on 2,100 interviews and has a margin of error of plus or minus 2 percent at the ninety-ninth level of confidence. Bear in mind also that these are real voters who have self-identified themselves as to which ethnic heritage they choose for themselves.

Currently in Maine, there are about 30 percent Republicans, 37 percent Democrats, and 28 percent Independents registered to vote with a smattering of Greens and Libertarians. Of these, 35–36 percent are of English or British heritage (self-defined), 18–19 percent are of Franco heritage and 13–14 percent are of Irish heritage.

The Franco-Americans remain the most important swing group, but their party affiliation has changed dramatically as more and more have become deracinated. Thirty years ago, approximately two-thirds of Francos were Democrats. Today, that number is down substantially to 45 percent. Twenty-two percent of Francos self-identify as Republicans (up from about 12 percent earlier) and 33 percent are Independent (a number just about double what it once was).

So the Francos have not only become more deracinated and independent behaviorally—that is, how they vote—they have also become more "Independent" in terms of their actual registration. This represents a significant sea change in Maine politics.

The Republicans have lost some of their English cohorts to the Democrats (think of the suburban belt around Portland with upscale Democratic voters) and to Independents (think of the rural vote for Ross Perot in the 2nd CD). But they have gained in the St. John Valley, where in 2022, *all* the state representative seats were held by Republicans.

The Irish, too, have moved, with 25 percent of them registered as Republicans, 37 percent as Democrats, and 37 percent as Independents.

And Franco-American voters in Maine were the swing voters in electing both Independent governors in Maine history, James Longley in 1974 and Angus King twenty years later in 1994. Both men were elected by broad coalitions of urban Francos and small-town Republicans. The first coalition seems to have come together by both purpose and accident, and the second was a conscious effort by the King team to target the exact similar coalition.

As the Longley campaign slogan (actually invented by Jack Havey of Ad Media) goes, "Think About It." In the forty-eight years from 1974 to 2022, other than Longley and King, twenty-four people have run for governor as something other than Republican or Democrat. The two who were elected were elected because of their much larger shares of Franco voting cohort than the others in their losing campaigns.

In terms of partisan races, Francos are not only still the most important swing voting group both demographically and psychographically (lifestyle and value orientation), they are now essential to Republican success in general elections, but they are also twice as important in statewide Republican primaries as they were when Bill Cohen first ran for office.

For those planning campaigns in Maine in ballot measures, targeting Franco-American voters for the past fifty has been very fruitful. For instrumental politics, the Franco-Americans continue to be a vital swing vote in Maine politics. They have the power to determine who will be the next senator, governor, or representative. As a group, they also indicate which influence vectors will work statewide, and thus can help determine which ballot measures and bonds will win, and which will lose.

I found them critical, not only in candidate races but in ballot measures as well. Targeting Franco-Americans and paying attention to their influence vectors and authority figures could result in success in not just candidate races, but also in many ballot measures as well.

For example, when Chuck Winner of Winner/Wagner came from California to do the Maine Yankee Nuclear Shutdown referendum in 1980, he was surprised to see no Hispanic voters in the mix and also amazed at our focusing on the Franco-American group. "They're both a target and a bulwark" was the response.

In the first Maine Yankee campaign, for example, the Franco-Americans were narrowly split in the early polling cuts, but they were more concerned, by an almost 2–1 margin, in focusing on the importance of the economic implications of the shutdown. They placed the costs of turning off Maine Yankee far ahead of the perceived dangers of nuclear power in terms of health and safety.

Generally on this issue they were voting with the statewide Republican numbers (initially Democrats and Independents were more likely to support the shutdown than Republicans), although the nightly tracking produced a number of Republican areas—Sebago, Bar Harbor, Kennebunk—inclined to vote YES and shut down the plant.

These outliers were dubbed psychographically "rich Republicans with sailboats" after the respondent who, upon hearing of the extra three hundred dollars a year shutting down Maine Yankee would cost the average consumer, said with some vehemence, "Why, I pay more than that for my mooring. I'm voting to shut the damn thing down."

As the 1980 election campaign proceeded, there were fluctuations here and there, but the movement toward a NO vote was consistent over time, especially after the Professor Hugh's summer ad, which changed ninety thousand minds statewide. The Francos were showing the way, both in terms of messaging and in terms of where the balloting could eventually go.

So on election night, Chuck was rightly expecting a considerable victory and was therefore quite quizzical about the early returns. This was especially true since Peter Burr, the mathematical genius who was steering the nightly tracking results, had already predicted at least a 55–45 percent victory, both off the tracking and again as a result of the Election Day exit polling.

But the TV stations were all showing the YES side winning, first by hundreds, then by thousands of votes. "Where are those votes coming from?" a concerned Chuck asked, beginning to wonder what we local yokels had gotten him into. "Just the back to the earth crowd in Waldo County, the flat-earth people," responded Peter, who was checking on some of the key precincts across the state. "No problem. Wait for the Franco votes. We're going to hit 60 to 40 percent. It's over." Sure enough, once Biddeford and Saco, Lewiston and Auburn, Fort Kent and Van Buren were in, the result was 59 percent NO to 41 percent YES for the Franco communities as well as for statewide overall. The Francos had shown and led the way to a statewide victory for the Maine Yankee nuclear plant.

Chuck, who had the smile of an angel, showed a most beatific smile that night. Far from home and with a lot of responsibility on his shoulders, he was, in fact, jubilant.

And more good news—luckily, Peter Burr wasn't working for Fox News in these troubled times, or he would have been fired for *accurately* predicting the outcome, as happened to those poor chaps who called Arizona correctly for Joe Biden in 2020! Crazy Town politics and Crazy Town "news."

Perhaps the least known and surprising situation in which Francos were decisive was the 1990 vote on Sunday Sales. It may seem almost impossible to comprehend today, but in 1989 stores larger than five thousand square feet like Hannaford and Shaw's were prohibited from opening on Sundays or holidays. Amazingly, Bob Reny, a very influential businessman from Damariscotta, the founder and owner of the Reny's chain of department stores, managed to kill every previous effort in the legislature to end this "blue law." It seemed a holdover from the time when the Puritans insisted everybody go to church all Sunday long and even had deacons in the back of the church with a long pole to nudge awake anybody who had fallen asleep.

Bob was very effective at lobbying the legislature, but he did so without being a registered lobbyist. He could legally take this approach because he did not accept any kind of a fee for his efforts and argued only as a private citizen, not as an industry representative.

His motivation, however, was not a religious argument, although the Maine Christian Civic League undoubtedly supported his position; his primary motivation was business. Bob obviously did not want the substantial competition that the growth of "big box" stores would generate.

Bob masterfully pleaded for the rights of his workers not to have to work on Sundays, and even offered the specter of social rot if stores were to open.

The Maine legislature went along with him and his arguments year after year. He was supported by a broad coalition of church and business interest groups.

Remember also that Maine's blue laws had a long and durable history. For example, it was not until 1966 that a referendum passed that allowed the sale of liquor in hotels and restaurants on Sunday—and that by a very thin margin of 50.3–49.7 percent.

Equally surprising to us today was how many people initially opposed the referendum to open big stores on Sunday. The referendum was way behind when the campaign started. One of the principal voting groups against opening the stores were the Franco-Americans, especially Franco-American women. The polling showed that the only wedge issue for them really was "choice," but of course that word was often associated with abortion rights.

Enormous credit in the effort to repeal the law and permit Sunday Sales should be given to Reet Sterns who headed up the effort, to George Smith and his sister Edie who got enough signatures to put it on the ballot, and to Bob Cott of Creative Design and Marketing who designed a series of ads with the theme of individual choice presented by four people. An older Franco-American woman said forcefully, "If we go to church in the morning and want to go shopping in the afternoon, it should be our choice."

Several young women spoke directly to the camera saying earnestly, "I work all week long. Sunday is the only day I can go to the store. It should be my choice." Finally an older man spoke authoritatively, "It's about choice." A layperson might look at that ad and say, "A bunch of people talking about an issue . . . pretty ordinary." But in fact, the ad was pitch perfect and its tagline, "Yes on 1: The Real Issue is the Right to Choose" changed the nature of the whole campaign. Bob Cott deserves high marks for successfully capturing the essence of what the polling showed was the only path to victory.

"Choice," not particular store openings or people going to church, became the central focus of the campaign, the issue on which we wanted people to vote. As Edie remembers, "The Sunday Shopping ballot question talked about choice, pointing out that stores weren't being forced to open on Sunday—just that those who wanted to now could, if this new law went into effect."

If the referendum question had mandated that all stores in Maine *must* be open on Sundays, it would not have passed.

Because of the ads and the Franco-American authority figures, the opposition among that community was softened considerably, and election night provided a very narrow 52–48 percent victory for the YES side.

The next time you go shopping on Sunday at a big box store or pick up a six-pack of beer at the supermarket, thank Reet Sterns who led the fight,

Bob Cott who did the ads, and the Franco-American women who shifted the debate away from church on Sunday to be church *and* shopping on Sunday, and by accenting how important individual choice should be in modern society.

To show the importance of Franco-American voters in ballot measures as well as partisan contests, Dave Emery has now developed some key precinct predictors for the Franco-American towns in Maine and combined them into manageable groups: all "Franco" towns statewide, 1st CD Franco towns, 2nd Franco towns, St. John Valley Franco-American towns, and Franco-American Towns over 10,000 and Franco-American Towns under 10,000.

Here we will simply note the initial polling for all Francos and then at least the statewide totals for each of a number of ballot measures to show the importance of Franco-Americans in Maine both for targeting and swing voter purposes.

Save Maine Yankee (1980), where 30 percent of the Franco-American voters were initially undecided but became strong NO proponents (63 percent); this was followed by the Widening of the Maine Turnpike in 1997 where 40 percent of Francos were initially undecided but 64 percent later voted to widen it.

While initially a majority of Franco-Americans supported the proposed Native American gaming facility, when the election was held in 2003—and as late as early October 2003, 40 percent were undecided—only 38 percent voted YES when the final vote was held. Note that in 2010—when they were *not* targeted—55 percent of Franco-Americans would approve the Oxford Casino.

Also, look at this swing: in 2009, Franco-American communities across the state voted YES on the banning of Gay Marriage with 54.6 percent of the Franco community statewide voting for the ban. But after a strong ground effort and very effective TV commercials including one featuring a Franco grandmother, in 2012, 52 percent of those same communities approved Gay Marriage.

Also note the bifurcation of the Franco vote on bear-hunting limits as the Bear Hunting Ban of 2014 saw the Franco-American towns statewide divided by geography: 53.9 percent of 1st CD Francos, more deracinated, voted for the ban, but only 43.8 percent of 2nd CD towns did so.

All in all, Francos remain extremely important to the winning of any statewide races in Maine. Yes, I suppose there are other ways to win elections without concentrating on the swing Franco-American voters. And perhaps they go along with the flow in some instances. But in my experience what you have to do to get Franco-American voters will get you other voters as well. After forty years of successfully targeting them and listening to their wants and wishes and knowing they deliver, why try some other way?

As Teresa McCann-Tumidajski, the Portland Roman Catholic Diocese manager, put it after the assisted suicide referendum, "Long live the Francos." They had made a difference in that race, just as they had in the ultimately successful passage of Gay Marriage. Counterintuitive perhaps, but true.

One ignores the Franco vote at one's peril.

In 2022, not only did Mills win a majority of Franco voters in traditionally Franco areas, but she also won a huge majority of them statewide, and thus for the first time in history, a non-Franco candidate beat a Franco-American among that total statewide community as she crushed Paul LePage. There had been previous Franco-American winners in CD and statewide races, but this was the first time a non-Franco ever beat a Franco candidate among purely Franco voters. A truly impressive feat.

In the 2022 election when the votes for governor were counted among the traditional Franco-American cities and towns (from Sanford, Biddeford, and Saco, through Lewiston and Auburn to Madawaska, Fort Kent, Saint Agatha, and Van Buren), Mills got an astonishing 58.3–39.7 percent win against LePage in the head-to-head within that cohort. She beat him in the 2nd CD in the Franco areas and slaughtered him in the 1st CD with the same cohort. Analysis of the vote shows that Mills carried the CD1 Francos by 2–1 (66–33 percent), but only edged LePage in CD2 by a 51–46 percent margin. Mills easily carried the more-deracinated southern Maine Franco communities having populations of ten thousand or more by 63–35 percent, but LePage edged her 49–48 percent in the small Franco towns statewide, including those in the St. John Valley, which he carried 52 percent to Mills's 47 percent.

This is truly amazing. In fact, I do not believe that any other non-Franco has ever beaten a Franco candidate running in this cohort either in a statewide or CD-wide Maine election in all of Maine history.

Previous non-Franco winners over Franco-Americans in state- or CD-wide as provided by Paul Mills include: Daniel F. Davis over Alonzo Garcelon in 1879 for governor; Frederick Hale over Harold Dubord in 1934 for US Senate; Lewis Barrows over Dubord for governor in 1936; Clyde Smith over Dubord for Congress in 1938; Margaret Chase Smith over Ed Beauchamp for Congress in 1940 and 1946; Fred Payne over Louis Lausier for governor in 1948; Fred Payne over Roger Dube for US Senate in 1952; Margaret Chase Smith over Lucia Cormier for US Senate in 1960; and Bill Cohen over Elmer Violette for Congress in 1972.

But none of these, I believe, won the aggregate of just the traditional Franco cities and towns in their races. Janet Mills won the aggregate of Franco populations across the state in the head-to-head with LePage.

This was thus truly a historical and a very most impressive achievement. And more than enough to guarantee her victory statewide.

Additionally, and adding to her margin of victory, among the Gold Coast towns (Falmouth, Yarmouth, Cape Elizabeth, Scarborough, Cumberland, Freeport), moreover, Mills ran up an even higher aggregate percentage, 69–31 percent. As when he ran against Mike Michaud, the Portland suburbs were supposed to be LePage's way to begin to blunt the traditional Portland Democratic margins. After that was accomplished, he would then win with the northern small Republican towns (with any concomitant Independent and Democrat Trumpkanoids).

In 2014, Barbara Bush's very effective last several weeks' endorsement commercial in the Portland DMA gave LePage a big boost against the Democrat Mike Michaud, also a Franco, all across the Gold Coast. But instead of helping LePage in the 2022 vote, the Gold Coast numbers helped to run up the score against him statewide. No Barbara, no barrier, no buffer to the tsunami of defeat.

And the apparently expected Trumpkanoid wave up north for LePage was far less than expected. Brett Littlefield, the effective Republican senior strategist (for Governor Paul LePage and Bruce Poliquin) told the BDN that the Republican losses in 2022 gave him a "gut ache," stating he thought that "many conservative voters did not come out during that cycle because they thought the election was rigged."

Gosh, rigged elections in Maine? Who could have spread such a foul tale? Gog and Magog perhaps?

In any case, Mills's combined margins within the Franco community and the "Gold Coast" would deliver to her what would turn out to be the *highest total of votes* for any governor in the history of the state.

AXIOM #5

"Polling Rules the Roost—But Only If You Do It Correctly" with Dave Emery

*If you don't know where you're going,
any road will take you there.*
—CHINESE PROVERB

During the hotly contested 2020 US Senate race in Maine, at the end of October, Colby College released its final poll of that election cycle. Among its findings were that Maine Speaker of the House Sara Gideon had 47 percent of the vote while Senator Susan Collins had 43 percent, Max Linn 2 percent, and Lisa Savage 5 percent, with 4 percent of voters undecided.

Two eager political junkies (aka "the gerbils") began chattering, "Wow, that is really something. Collins is finished if those numbers are right," said one as both rushed to see the cross tabulations to see how far ahead Gideon was with the Franco-Americans. That would tell the story. Collins had always done well among the Francos in Maine, especially in Aroostook County.

But as the little gerbils soon found out, that would be impossible. The poll had not identified and sampled *any* Franco-American voters. None. There were also none of the only other two ethnic breaks that matter in Maine: none for the Irish, none for the English/Yankees!

"Huh?" exclaimed one gerbil. "Who put this poll together?"

"Look at what they used, look at these," said the other, "this is really quite amusing."

And indeed it was. Most amusing. And most baffling. There were race/ethnicity questions all right in the poll, that was true. But instead of the essential key Maine ethnic breaks, there were—and it's still hard to believe even fifty years after the fact that the three largest Maine "tribes," the English, the Irish and the Francos had been truly identified—the following cross tabulations were listed for ethnicity:

1. White, Non-Hispanic voters
2. Black, Non-Hispanic
3. Asian
4. Other, Non-Hispanic
5. Two or more races, non-Hispanic
6. Two or more races, Hispanic
7. Refused to answer

"What is this?" asked an incredulous gerbil. "I don't get it." "I don't either, this is very weird."

Very weird, indeed.

The gerbils had a right to be confused.

Since 90 percent of the Maine population falls into the first category—always, no matter who polls and how—these ethnic breaks were and remain totally useless, telling the reader nothing about the reality of the state's current voting patterns by ethnicity. And frustrating the gerbils no end since it made no difference whether Gideon or Collins led in *all* of the last six categories or had no votes at all.

"Maybe they used a template from Texas," concluded one of the gerbils. "Or Florida" said the other.

Another embedded cross tabulation was equally puzzling as it had Collins losing up north, including in Aroostook County, her home county, by a good margin. If this were true, Collins was going to have a terrible, terrible election night. She would end up truly and finally channeling her favorite role model, Margaret Chase Smith, who lost *her* hometown of Skowhegan to Bill Hathaway in 1972.

Luckily for Collins, but of course unluckily for Gideon, she did not lose her home county by a big margin. Even more importantly, the hidden-in-the-poll Francos again delivered for her (and were undoubtedly delivering for her when the poll was taken) as she swept to victory statewide 51–42 percent (with two other candidates bringing up the rear: Savage getting 5 percent and Lynn getting 2 percent). The poll had been way off and without the Franco ethnic component, there had been no sure way to tell the authors they were making a mistake.

Polling has gotten a lot of criticism in the last few years, and as this example shows, much of it seems well deserved. Polling, and the many types of polls, are a confusing subject. So before looking at some real-life situations in Maine's recent political history, here are some Polling 101 basics and context to help understand the various roles polls can or do play in Maine politics.

Before we start, however, it is important that the reader understand that right or wrong, prescient or behind the curve, the pollster is at the very heart of most campaigns. When she or he enters the room, she or he becomes the center of attention. If they are right, big rewards. If they are wrong, everybody knows about it very soon. So it is in most campaign pollsters' best interests to be right, as right as can be.

Accurate polling depends on a number of ingredients. By far, the most important factor for any poll (or portions of a poll) is the randomness of the survey. That is to say, how were the people chosen by the polling entity? The more random the selection, the more accurate the conclusions. On one level, you can use telephone books, selecting pages and names at random from the listings until you have completed the survey.

But this method has major drawbacks. Over 25 percent or more of the population now have unlisted numbers, so this group—often the voters most likely to turn out to vote—would not even be included in the universe of calls made. And of course more and more people no longer have landlines at all; they have cellphones, and these numbers can be difficult and/or expensive to obtain.

Therefore, a much better approach is to have a computer randomly select telephone numbers from among all possible telephone numbers—listed, unlisted, and cell—in the necessary exchanges. This is more expensive for the pollster because you can't filter out businesses or other nonproductive telephone numbers just by looking at the number and name as you can with a telephone book, but it does result in superior accuracy.

Once the computer has selected the numbers, however, you have to make sure you do everything you can to stick to those numbers. You need to call back three or four times if there is no answer at a given number because it is the randomness of the selection that provides the accuracy, enabling one to make statements about the results one gets.

When the polling results are in, there is a mathematical formula that indicates how accurate they are. The degree of accuracy is qualified by a term known as the "margin of error." You often see this in the newspaper along with the polling results or it is announced by the TV personality. "Margin of error" means that if a random survey consists of four hundred respondents, then it is said to have a possible error of plus or minus 5 percent. Thus if candidate x is said to have 45 percent of the vote, he or she really could have 40 or 50 percent.

The margin of error thus shows the range within which the survey results fall. If the survey had 600 respondents, the margin of error is plus or minus

4 percent, and if 250, it is plus or minus a little more than 6 percent. And remember, these margins of error are only applicable for two choice questions, a "YES" or a "NO," or candidate x versus candidate y. If there are more candidates or choices than two, the margin of error goes up accordingly.

Also, because most reporters, editors, and TV personalities don't give the range of possibilities, people tend to think the base number is fixed, that it is really 45 percent, not the range of 40–50 percent if 400 people were called. This penchant for accepting the base numbers at face value can lead to a lot of confusion (and consternation among candidates and their supporters), especially if other polling shows different results.

Let's say that the candidate who had 45 percent in the first poll is said in a second, later poll to have only 40 percent (with the same margin of error), most people (and candidates) would interpret the data as saying candidate x was losing ground. In fact, there may have been no movement at all within the electorate, the candidate really may have had 42 percent all along, and the first survey placed him or her too high and the second too low. So much confusion about polling results could be cleared up if the media outlets presented polling data to the public as a range of possible outcomes, not as a single outcome.

But there is an even bigger caveat that should be explained and one which almost never is announced by anybody, including most pollsters. That is the extent to which the mathematical tables used to compute the margin of error are based on a .95 confidence factor. That means the margin of error is valid *but* only in ninety-five out of a hundred cases.

This is actually a very high probability, but it still means that in 5 out of 100 cases, the poll will be totally off! I have yet to see this caveat on any published poll in the state of Maine during the last five decades. But it does explain some polls that were way, way off the mark during that time.

There is also another aspect of polling head-to-head contests between candidates that is seldom understood by the news media. Over the years I have tried and tried (totally unsuccessfully) to get reporters to ask the following question of candidates or their minions: "Ok, so the poll says you have 56 percent, and your opponent has 26 percent—that's among all respondents. What are the head-to-head numbers among respondents *who know both candidates*?" Incumbents almost always have big leads over their opponents when the race begins and for most of its duration, but those leads are often inflated by what is called "the name recognition factor."

Since "recognition" is easier than "recall," most voters will pick the name they know if they are unsure about the challenger, and that in and of itself gives the incumbent or better-known candidate a seeming advantage in many polls. If reporters would only insist that the campaign pollster or even the station or newspaper's own pollster give both numbers, they and their readers or viewers would have a much better idea of how the horserace was coming.

One of the best examples of this was when Angus King ran against Joe Brennan in 1994. When that race began, Brennan had a huge lead, something on the order of 48–6 percent. At the time, many people assumed King was much better known than he actually was, having been on public television for so long. In fact, only about 13 percent of the electorate knew who he was.

But among voters who knew both King and Brennan, the horserace was actually in King's favor by a tiny margin, giving him the hope that as more and more people knew who he was, the better he would do since Brennan's huge lead was based in part on his high name recognition and King's lack of recognition.

The press corps, especially the print media, does tend to take polls seriously and their own handicapping of the candidates even more seriously. These reporters talk among themselves and get an idea fixed in their heads about who is going to win and who is not. Then they often treat those they perceive as losing as less credible; hence they give them less coverage and show less interest in whatever they are saying (however desperate they may sound at this juncture in the campaign). They often privately pronounce this or that candidate as "dead," even before the election is held.

Another problem occurs when the newspaper or TV station itself commissions the poll in question. Newspapers are notorious for doing "quick and dirty" polls to put on their front pages. As Lance Tapley has pointed out in his seminal article "Cheap News," this happens regularly. These front-page newspaper polls get readers' attention. That's what counts. Yes, it would be nice if they were spot on, but as Tapley points out, many newspapers don't really care about that, at least not much. Certainly not enough to pay for the most accurate polling possible.

They get great headlines and relevance just by putting the results in the paper. Never mind that if the elections turn out differently in the end, the papers can, and do, claim that "a lot of voters changed their minds in the interval." One newspaper poll infamously had the assisted suicide NO side down 70–30 percent with two weeks to go. Yet the NO side won 51–49 percent, defying all logic and common sense. The explanation the paper gave later was, "Many voters changed their minds over the last weekend before the election!" Never happened.

These claims are made, even though voters, rarely, very rarely, ever change their votes during the last weekend. They may appear to, but I've never seen a six-hundred-person survey that was actually conducted on the Friday before an election. Maybe a week out but not confined to the Friday before. Besides, causes and candidates always spend a ton of money to try to keep their *existing* supporter base that last weekend. True "flips" the last weekend are rarer than hen's teeth (as they used to say in Maine before all the egg farms went bust).

How to make your polls more accurate? To get the most accurate polling information, you have to make sure you are talking to people who are actually voters. You have to make sure you are really talking to someone who is going to vote on Election Day, not simply saying they are going to do so.

To do that you have to have a very "tight" filter. You need one that really acts as a lie key and ensures you get true information about who will actually be showing up. Other than a strictly academic exercise, we don't care about the opinions of those voters who don't bother to vote.

To get a true reading you have to take an additional step. After asking them if they are a registered voter and dropping anybody who is not a voter, you give the respondent three ways to sound like good, well-meaning voters. We have always preferred the following:

"What is your typical voting pattern for Maine elections?"

1. Extremely likely/never miss an election
2. Just about always vote
3. Usually vote/often vote/don't know

Respondents thus can sound like good, responsible voters no matter what type they really are (and remember, usually 40 percent of registered voters are not going to vote in most elections). If you drop respondents for #3, you can recode for your purposes, giving #1 to "Most likely voters" and #2 to "Quite likely voters." You've given the liars a choice they can feel good about, but you know what they really mean by it.

This is quite expensive to be so fussy, but it pays off in terms of accuracy. Now you throw out *all* the #3s. You don't care. They are not going to vote. Make more calls until you get to six hundred, then you have a true margin of error and not the "maybe/hopefully/not likely in this life" margin of error.

Incidentally, I can say that during my years in Maine politics, I was approached by every major newspaper in the state to do a poll at one time or another. And every time, they never would pay enough to do the job properly.

Because using the tightest of filters at the beginning, you often have to make four, five, or even six times as many calls as the poll calls for on the surface.

As Dennis Bailey recalls, the press doesn't care:

> During Tom Andrews's Democratic primary campaign for Congress in 1990, I distinctly remember a news report over Memorial Day weekend where the newscaster said, "Just weeks ahead of the Democratic primary for Congress, a new poll shows that only two candidates stand a realistic chance of winning: former Attorney General James Tierney and state Representative Libby Mitchell." Tom didn't even get a mention.
>
> I knew something was off, and when I got a copy of the full poll, my suspicions were confirmed. It wasn't a poll of likely primary voters; it was a poll of all registered voters. Big difference. The universe that was polled was essentially *all* voters, and if all voters showed up on Election Day the results were probably accurate. But that wasn't going to happen.
>
> In a primary, you're lucky to get 30 percent of eligible voters to turn out. I made my rounds to the press to explain how this cheap poll was crap, and should be ignored, but of course didn't get any takers. As far as the news media was concerned, Tom was DOA. The news media really doesn't understand polling, and only care about the top line. So, when Tom won on Election Day, no one was more surprised than the news reporters.

Some other things to consider in analyzing polls. The head-to-head matchups in candidate campaigns and x versus y in ballot measures almost always get most of the attention when polls are made public, but they are usually the least interesting, least efficacious aspects. What really matters is identifying elements that push behavior. Voters don't go from candidate A to candidate B; they usually stop at "I don't know" first, and in ballot measures, the movement is equally sequential.

Voters respond to wedge issues and influence vectors, and those are almost always the keys to winning elections. The answers to the "If you knew" influence vectors are what decide elections and what give polls their value to political campaigns. Yes, you want to know where you are when you start, but it is much more important to know what you have to do and say to get you to end up where you want to be.

This became glaringly apparent during the 2003 campaign against a big gambling casino in Sanford. Dennis Bailey recalls,

> Before we had money to do polling, we were using a message that basically said, "Watch out, Las Vegas is coming to Maine." We had flyers printed up that had these shadowy Las Vegas goons with their eyes on Maine. We just assumed that this was a message that would grab people and turn them off.

But we were wrong. After we tested it in the poll, we found out that voters seemed almost flattered that Las Vegas was interested in Maine. It was seen as a big business bringing jobs to the state. What voters didn't like, though, was seeing all the money spent at the Maine casino leaving the state to fill the coffers in Las Vegas. So, we immediately trashed all our lovely flyers and adopted a new message. We later ran a TV ad showing a map of the United States with a big money trail leaving Maine for Las Vegas, a poll-tested message that we knew would move voters. This is the real value in polling, not just the head-to-head stuff.

For political campaigns there is another approach that enables you to use relatively untrained volunteers and requires a different methodology. That is a tracking poll, a methodology Dave Emery brought to campaigning in his 1974 run for Congress in the 1st CD. It utilizes regression analysis and is also the basis for the "key precinct" projections used on election night.

For twenty years Dave has enlightened generations of Bowdoin students with his erudite lectures on polling in general and his key precinct analysis in particular. For this chapter, I asked him to tell the most interesting story about approach: how his system came into being, how it worked, and why it was the most efficacious one for forty years in both candidate and ballot measure elections.

Let Dave tell you how he devised his Maine "magic mystery machine":

The truth is, I really didn't invent anything new. I did, however, apply my knowledge of statistical analysis to my first election to Congress in 1974, and in subsequent political endeavors. Here's how it happened:

During my second term in the Maine House of Representatives (1973–1975), it became apparent to me that I had a tough decision to make. As a 1970 college graduate, I thought my electrical engineering degree was getting stale, and I couldn't live the remainder of my life on the $3,500 legislative salary. That meant I either had to leave the legislature and get a real job or find a way to move up the political ladder.

So contrary to all conventional wisdom and common sense, in January of 1974, I announced my candidacy for Congress in Maine's First Congressional District. Not only would I be running against a four-term entrenched Democratic incumbent, Congressman Peter N. Kyros of Portland, but I would be running as a Republican in the toxic political environment known as Watergate. Moreover, I lived in the wrong end of the district, far away from the southern Maine population centers. The city of Portland *alone* had twice the population of my home county of Knox; I lived in the city of Rockland, which at that time had a population of a little over eight thousand.

There is a lot more to this story, but here I will confine my tale to the development of a very special tool that I depended upon to guide my campaign, a tool that gave me encouragement and hope of victory even while the political cognoscenti wrote me off without a second thought.

Among the challenges my campaign faced was understanding where and how to campaign effectively. This was greatly complicated by the fact that I was largely unknown outside of Knox County and had little or no money in my campaign treasury. Following my January announcement and continuing into the spring, my campaign activities consisted mostly of attending Republican caucuses throughout the district where I was able to meet handfuls of party faithful, collect petition signatures, and find volunteers who might help me build some semblance of an organization.

One such contact was Peter Burr of Kennebunk. Peter's story is a sad one, but the unfortunate aspects of his life did not develop until many years later. Peter attended Yale, and at one point he was elected York County treasurer. Peter was eccentric, no doubt about it, but he was brilliant, very conservative, and he had a head for politics. Consequently, along with Kennebunk state Representative Jim McMahon, I felt I had a very good start in the very important York County.

Following the June 15 primary election in which I was unopposed, I began a six-hundred-mile walk through the First District. Congressman Bill Cohen had walked the massive Second District two years earlier and had found the walk to be a great success. Also Democratic Governor Lawton Chiles had previously campaigned this way in Florida, so I had every reason to believe it would help me as well.

I was right. My walking tour snaked through all seven First District counties, ending in Bath on Labor Day. After a summer of walking through Maine, I was probably in the best shape of my life, and I could see that people were beginning to know who I was and what I was doing. One day, while meeting with my top campaign volunteers, including Peter, I casually asked each one in turn, "How am I doing in your area?"

Of course, no one could give me a specific answer other than apocryphal stories from this person or that person with whom they had spoken. Then Peter said, "Let's take a poll!"

"How do we go about that?" I asked. "We don't have any money for a poll."

"We can do it ourselves with volunteers."

"OK, you set it up!"

We quickly realized that our calling would have to be limited to communities where we had volunteers. In those days, local calls could be made without additional charge, but calling outside the local calling area could get very expensive very fast. Consequently, we were able to generate statistically useful calls only in a few places.

These included Winthrop, Augusta, Kennebunk, Portland, Bath, Rockland, Sanford, Gorham, and a few other communities.

In early September, Peter began keeping a record of the calls as we received new data. He set up a rudimentary tracking system that allowed us to gauge progress in each calling area as time passed. Initially, the numbers were quite discouraging; I was well behind everywhere except in Rockland, with a great many "undecideds" in most places.

By the first week in October, we began to notice some movement, but it was sporadic. I began to wonder how I could relate these disparate town results to the entire district, because surely improvements in Portland or Augusta would logically suggest improvement in the district as a whole. But I didn't have the means to conduct a proper districtwide poll, and none of the Maine newspapers or TV stations had conducted surveys of their own.

Then came the epiphany!

That previous winter while I had been considering and planning the campaign, I had laboriously calculated vote percentages in every First District town for the major candidates running in the elections of 1968, 1970, and 1972. This data consisted of eight election contests: two presidential, two senatorial, one gubernatorial, and three congressional. What's more, the data included three elections that Peter Kyros had won, giving me an excellent baseline of his voter appeal for analysis. But how could I use this data?

The answer was a well-known analytical tool called "linear regression," sometimes referred to as a "least square fit." Here's what it means: if you have data that can be plotted on paper such that for every point there is a "Y" value that corresponds to a unique "X" value, you can take a ruler and draw a line through the average of the points you have plotted. That line represents a linear equation describing the data. Remember the equation "Y = mX + b" from high school algebra?

In order to set up the regression equations, I used the First District Republican percentages in each of the eight races as the "Y" axis, and for each town where we had valid calling data, I used the Republican town election percentages. The result, for each town, was a scatter plot of eight points in a pattern that was clearly linear. But how should I draw the equation line accurately? It could be done graphically by wiggling a ruler until it looks like the errors above the line exactly cancel out the errors below the line, but fortunately, there is an arithmetic process that calculates the equation of the line exactly.

Today, that calculation can be made instantly using an Excel spreadsheet or any number of other computer programs; but in 1974, that data had to be hand-calculated. Fortunately, I had recently bought a small, newfangled hand calculator, one that I still have and use to this very day!

Once these equations were set up, it was only necessary to plug in the polling results; finally, I could see what a 1st CD vote might look like within a reasonable margin of error. Separate equations for each key town were used for the projected vote; the Emery vote was calculated from the Republican percentage data, and the Kyros vote was calculated from the Democrat percentage data.

From that point on, Peter and I were able to watch the campaign progress. I was actually able to run a few TV ads during the last three weeks of the campaign, and after a week of ads, the numbers jumped! I closed to about 10 points behind going into the last week, but as the last weekend approached, both Kyros and I seemed to lose ground as the undecideds grew. My heart was in my throat! However, over that weekend, the numbers showed the race dramatically closing, and the last figures we saw put the race almost dead even, albeit with about 20 percent undecided.

I spent election night, November 5, 1974, at the radio station in Rockland to watch the returns come in. There I had access to both the UPI and AP wire service machines, plus WRKD always collected town returns from Knox, Lincoln, and Waldo Counties. The polls closed at 8 P.M., and the waiting game began. At about 8:45, I saw the Rockland voting machine totals and there was no surprise there; I had a solid lead of about 62 percent in Rockland. A few minutes later, however, I heard the mechanical clack-clack-clack of the UPI wire service machine. The first returns gave Kyros, as I recall, 77 votes to my 27. I do not have a copy of that first UPI tabulation, but I managed to save all the rest from that election night.

"Not good," I thought. "Probably some small rural town that I should have carried."

About fifteen minutes later, we heard clack-clack-clack again. This time I heard a scream from one of my volunteers who came running into the back room, wide eyed, with a yellow printout that read: House First District, 8 precincts (3 percent): Emery 592 (58 percent), Kyros 428 (42 percent).

My legs immediately turned to jelly!

At 11:10 P.M., returns from nineteen precincts came in, giving me 3,854 votes to Kyros's 3,754. These returns were immediately followed by a comment from the Kyros camp as reported by the UPI Wire Service ticker:

Top aides of incumbent First District Congressman Peter Kyros say they are not a bit worried by the fact that Republican challenger David Emery is ahead in the latest tabulations. The most recent figures show Emery ahead with 51% of the vote and Democrat Kyros trailing with 49 percent of the vote. A Kyros aide said—quote—"That's just the rural returns—If Emery can't take the rural returns, what can he take?" The Kyros aide said the incumbent congressman remains—quote—"very confident" he will be returned to the US House of Representatives.

Most ballots were hand-counted paper ballots in those days, so the count was slow. At 11:38 P.M., UPI had reported only 47 precincts of 253, but I was ahead 9,433 to 8,732.

By 12:15 A.M., the pace had picked up a bit. Eighty-seven precincts had reported, and I was leading by 720 votes, 20,923 to 20,203.

At 1:33 A.M., with 163 precincts reporting, Kyros had pulled ahead by 637 votes, 43,963 to 43,326. "This is it," I thought. "The Democratic cities are now reporting and I'm behind. Now it'll be hard to catch up."

But about that time, UPI reported the following commentary:

A big upset could be in the making in the First Congressional District. Republican challenger David Emery, the 26-year-old State representative from Rockland, is keeping ahead of four-term Democrat Peter Kyros with nearly half of the vote in. As expected, Emery picked up a number of coastal and rural communities quickly . . . the surprise coming when in the first seven precincts from normally Democratic Portland came in and Emery had edged out Kyros 1,918 to 1,915.

The next tabulations, coming at about 2:00 A.M., reported 183 precincts (72 percent) of the total of 253, and gave me a lead of 52,512 to 51,662.

As the night drew on, we swapped the lead a couple of times. At 3:26 A.M., I led Kyros by only 149 votes, 69,726 to 69,577 with 220 precincts reporting. An hour or so later with 235 precincts in, the count was Emery 78,987, Kyros 78,759.

As dawn approached, only 7 precincts out of 253 were outstanding, and I led by only 198 votes, 89,771 to 89,573.

Throughout the night I had been keeping my own vote tally. By about seven o'clock, with a tiny lead of only 121 votes according to my figures, I had accounted for all but three towns: Oakland, Newcastle, and Winthrop. At that point, I was pretty confident I had won. I had expected to lose Oakland (I did, narrowly), but I was counting on both Newcastle and Winthrop; my Lincoln County chair was from Newcastle and my campaign manager, George Smith, lived in Winthrop. As it turned out, I carried these three towns by 316, giving me a lead of 437 votes with all cities, towns, and precincts accounted for, according to my own figures.

The final unofficial UPI tally of all 253 precincts was reported at 9:36 on the morning of Wednesday, November 6. Their figures gave me a margin of 142 votes out of 186,582: David Emery 93,362 to Peter Kyros 93,220.

It should be noted that these were only unofficial results. UPI had a total, AP had another (that showed me with a lead of 679 votes), and almost every newspaper and TV station had their own figures. These discrepancies were purely inadvertent, the result of 2 A.M. typos and assorted transposition errors resulting from exhausted volunteers working long past their usual bedtimes. The pre-recount official returns as reported from all 253 First District precincts to the Secretary of State gave me a lead of 688 votes out of 187,736: Emery 94,212, Kyros 93,524.

The contest went through two recounts, one in Maine and another in Washington, DC, before the House Administration Committee. I won both. It is interesting to note that there had been a great many counting, tabulation, and reporting errors in the official town submissions to the Secretary of State's office. As I said, these were all innocent errors. Nevertheless, only 34 precincts out of all 253 in the First District reported recount results identical to the figures officially reported to the state for certification.

The final corrected count was Emery 94,744 (50.112 percent), Kyros 94,319 (49.888 percent). The total vote was 189,063, with a winning margin of 425 votes (0.224 percent). The technique we developed out of necessity during the 1974 campaign, using a system of key precincts and regression analysis, proved to be useful and accurate.

Over the following decades, I have maintained that database and have continually updated the equations, now employing more than sixty data points rather than eight, generating powerful algorithms running on a modern computer. As it turned out, many of the towns in which we had access to volunteer callers happened by coincidence to be among the best key towns; their correlations with state and district totals were then and now remain very tight, yielding trustworthy and repeatable results year to year.

But as I said, we didn't really invent a thing; we merely used mathematical analysis to take maximum advantage of the data available to us. Later I would apply this system to candidate and ballot measure campaigns. Along the way, I found some towns to be more useful to poll than others.

Below are three columns: the first represents the key precincts I remember from 1974 and a second column of the ones from 2020. See where they differ and where they overlap. I have also provided a third column for the statewide ones from 2020. Note, though, that the totals from these towns have to be run through the equations to make their projections; the raw totals are not enough.

1st CD 1974	1st CD 2020	Statewide 2020
Winthrop	Topsham	Topsham
Augusta	Winthrop	Winthrop
Portland	Bath	Farmingdale
Gorham	Harpswell	Bowoinham
Kennebunk	Bowoinham	Augusta
Bath	Westbrook	Dover-Foxcroft
Sanford	Farmingdale	Auburn
Rockland	Gorham	Gorham
Dresden	Freeport	Poland
Bridgton	Augusta	Windham

Using this system over the years under Dave's direction, Bowdoin students have successfully conducted polls with amazingly accurate results, so accurate that sometimes campaigns bought them and used them in their races. Take the example of Dennis Bailey and Bond #3, the land for conservation and public access, which included funds to preserve Maine's working waterfront, in 2012. Dennis and his campaign clients used not only the student poll on their issue, but they also purchased the thirty-second commercial that students made as a result of it.

Showing that "Team Working Waterfront" in that class deserved to be admitted to the hallowed company of professional political and media consultants, they purchased donuts and coffee for the entire class with the five hundred dollars they received for their services. The bond ended up winning 60.8 percent of the vote, so it seemed the money was well spent! Dennis learned the importance of key precincts during Angus King's campaign for governor in 1994.

> Chris called me one day toward the end of the campaign and said the tracking poll showed Joe Brennan beating Angus by six points in Westbrook. I of course thought, "Uh-oh. Bad news."
>
> Chris said, "What are you talking about? This is great news. If Brennan isn't beating Angus by double digits in a Democratic stronghold like Westbrook, he's going to have a bad night." And he did. Just goes to show there's more ways to read polls than the top line.

Quite surprising results can be foretold by these polls.

I remember in 2016 in late September, a poll by Bowdoin students supervised by Dave indicated that Donald Trump was likely to win in Maine's 2nd CD. I was dubious about those results, but a week later my grandson had a football game in Turner, Maine. As we drove to it, I was stunned at two strange sights. One, there were hardly any Hillary signs in heavily Democratic Lewiston, and two, on many lawns of trailers and small single-family homes on the road to Turner were sign after sign for Donald Trump. I quickly became a believer in the efficacy of the students' effort.

Now signs on people's lawns, put there by the owners of their homes, are really the only meaningful gauge of signs' efficacy. Most campaigns, whether candidates or ballot measures, simply hire firms to put them up on public ways. What a lot of signs prove is that the campaign had enough money to pay to have someone put them there. Not so with lawn signs. They are put up by property owners. They show commitment. I came to believe in the student poll.

At the end of the day, Trump would carry the 2nd CD in Maine by a margin of 27,996 (7.4 percent) out of 380,324 votes cast.

Polling is thus an essential tool of modern political campaigning and can produce amazing results, but unless it's done properly, it can lead to disastrous results within campaigns and to the detriment of the public's true understanding of the political process. And it is much easier for any given public poll to be more misleading that its sponsors even imagine.

*"Campaign Managers Have to Manage Campaigns, Consultants—
and Candidates" with Kay Rand and Dennis Bailey*

> *A campaign manager is a lot like a wilderness guide:
> a good one will lead you up the mountain,
> and a bad one will lead you off a cliff.*
> —COLIN HAY

Generations of Bowdoin students have read Catherine Shaw's excellent book *The Campaign Manager* in "Maine Politics," and many later reported great success from applying its teaching to their own subsequent runs for political office or working on other real-life campaigns. They often refer to it as their "bible."

Shaw calls the campaign manager "the single most important position in a campaign." One of the truest aspects of her description of what a campaign manager does (and does not do) is to call the job of campaign manager "resoundingly open-ended." I especially found that description depressingly accurate myself.

In 1972, after moving to Maine to teach at Bowdoin, I was approached by Bill Cohen to be his campaign manager in his run for Congress. My previous experience in politics had been limited to a tiny bit of working on the Gene McCarthy campaign for president in 1968 while I was teaching at Dartmouth. That experience consisted of simply getting students to go door to door after they got "clean for Gene." I did learn some fundamental things, though, like the after-action Dartmouth poll that showed that 13 percent of McCarthy's vote had actually come from good citizens who thought he was the other McCarthy, the one who was tough on communists! My fascination with polling started right there and then!

Neither Bill nor I had taken any government or politics courses at Bowdoin, and now we were jumping in free fall onto the political stage of the Pine Tree State. For any interested reader, that campaign is covered in considerable detail in my book *This Splendid Game* and more recently in *Bill Cohen's 1972 Campaign for Congress* with Jed Lyons.

Bill's congressional run was the first time I was ever a campaign manager. And the last. I found it to be a huge, huge, almost overwhelming burden and got an ulcer for my trouble. I took on all the responsibilities—for the press, for the strategy, for issue research, and for directing the field operations and meeting with the money people.

The worries, the pressures, the sleepless nights were almost insurmountable. I ended up throwing away my watch and never wore it again—of course exchanging it for a lifetime of driving others mad with my question, "What time is it?"

We won, and my relief was incalculable.

Although I never played that role in politics again, I have always had a great deal of admiration for anyone who served as campaign manager in the forty-odd elections and image-enhancement efforts I participated in later. I don't know how they keep their sanity day in and day out amid the chaos and uncertainties. My hat is perpetually off to them.

As Catherine Shaw points out, there are a wide range of "campaign managers" from the all-in, holistic role I ended up playing to what is really an office manager, carrying out the wishes of a candidate or a strategic game plan produced by others.

But whatever form they take, campaign managers are at the center of an ongoing, ever-changing, very challenging process. It is one that determines the outcome of many elections. Sometimes the candidate plays a major role in the decision making and even micromanages the process. Sometimes the candidate plays a minor role in the administration of a campaign. Sometimes she or he operates at a level in between these two extremes.

Maine has produced a lot of top-flight campaign managers and campaign directors—Bill Webster, Bob Loeb, Tony Payne, David Swardlick, Paul Hawthorne, Bill Lewis, Jesse Connelly, Marc Mutty, John Donovan, Phil Merrill, Jim Mitchell, Sharon Sudbay, Maria Fuentes, Dana Connors, Roger Mallar, Frank O'Hara, Joe Mackey, Greg Nadeau, Mary Mayhew, Jonathan Carter, Charlie Bass, Bill Cohen, Ken Hayes, Ed Kane, Peter Kelley, Barbara Holt, Neil Rolde, Carol Palesky, Abbott Greene, Bruce Reeves, Beryl Bernhard, Craig Brown, Lance Dutson, Brownie Carson, Matt McTighe, James Cote, David Farmer, Tom Daffron, Bob Tyrer, Charlie Micoleau, Ray Shadis, Steve Abbott, George Campbell, John Menario, Mary McAleney, Bobby McKernan, Leslie Merrill, Larry Benoit, George Smith, Rosemary Baldacci, Brett Littlefield, Barbara Trafton, Frank Coffin, Michael Heath, Jim Case, John Rensenbrink, Carol Allen, Sandy Maisel, Betsy Sweet, Frank Murray, Dick Pierce, Pat Eltman, Jackie Potter, Alan Caron, John Cleveland, Dave Sparks,

Sharon Miller, Edie Smith, Angela Twitchell and Connie LaPointe Brennan, to name just a few—so historically we can formulate a lot about how winning campaigns have been run in the Pine Tree State.

There are different skills required for being a campaign manager for a candidate or a cause, for a ballot measure or a bond. To have oversight over the campaign headquarters or for the field personnel, the pollster, the press operation, the paid media effort, the volunteers, the inside strategists and the outside ones, the candidate and her or his significant other(s), the friends and neighbors, supporters, and assorted hangers on takes a certain kind of person, one with a lot of inner strength and serenity.

It's a complex, multidimensional job.

The holistic campaign manager has to manage the consultants, the campaign itself, and the candidate her or himself. It takes a very special person to be able to do it all properly. Shaw describes the ideal campaign manager as "hardworking, organized, intelligent, self-confident, reliable, and loyal."

For this chapter, we turn to Kay Rand who epitomized Shaw's ideal archetype as she managed Angus King's successful runs for governor in 1994 and 1998 and his US Senate race in 2012—and is doing so again in 2024. Wonder what her longevity secret is? I have always thought she was the optimum blend of strategic thinker and superb office manager for candidate campaigns. She is someone with the perfect even-keeled temperament and force of personality to deal not only with the pressures of the campaign dynamics, but she was also able to successfully manage the very large egos of the very talented King team in 1994. In addition, she had to guide the candidate with a wide range of opinions of his own. She fits Shaw's criteria to a "T."

This is her story. Kay Rand:

It was the summer of 1993. I was working with my good friend George Campbell at the Maine Alliance as vice president for Government Relations—where I got to work with some amazing business leaders like Chuck Cianchette, people who were interested in finding a better balance between environmental regulation and jobs.

That's when I told my good friend Mike Carpenter, who was attorney general at the time, that if he ran for governor, I would heartily support him. After fifteen years as a lobbyist (Maine Municipal Association) and state employee (Department of Economic and Community Development), I was a bit disillusioned with the state of public policy—the state had just endured its first government shutdown, and the divisions between parties were getting more stark and more negative. I figured I could sit back and criticize or try to help move things in a better direction. Mike ultimately decided not to run for governor but gave my name to everyone else who was thinking of doing so.

That began a series of meetings with candidates from both parties—Tom Allen, Joe Brennan, Jack Wyman, Dick Barringer, Bob Woodbury, James Howaniec, and Donnie Carroll. I had just decided to delay a decision until after the primaries in June (The interviews were not helpful in discerning differences between the candidates; they mostly just agreed with me.) when I started getting phone messages from Angus King.

We exchanged phone calls almost a dozen times before we actually connected, and he just blurted out that he wanted me to be his campaign manager. I remember telling him he was already proving a lack of executive discernment in choosing me, since I'd never managed a political campaign. He explained he wasn't looking for a seasoned political operative but someone who knew public policy in Maine and wasn't a partisan (I was a registered Democrat but not in any way active in the party).

I knew his wife, Mary Herman. We were both lobbyists and frequently ran into each other on the third floor of the statehouse. Several of my friends later took credit for encouraging Angus to consider me (Kevin Gildart and John Marsh both stand out), but I know Mary was on board, too.

I had just learned of Angus's interest in running for governor as an Independent from Chuck Cianchette, and I remember being dismissive, harking back to Maine's only experience with an Independent governor, Jim Longley. As I was a University of Maine student, his cuts and lack of support for public education were damaging and left me with a bitter taste.

Angus convinced me to come to Brunswick to meet with him, which I did. I was expecting an interview like the ones I'd already had with gubernatorial candidates. I was wrong. Angus didn't agree with a single thing I said; he challenged everything and actually made me think anew about topics I had lobbied on for years. I left with a draft copy of the book he was writing about his interest in being governor. After reading it, I was hooked.

I was in mid-career when I decided to risk running a political campaign—for an Independent, no less, where there'd be no institutional support from a party. I had a lot to learn (and unlearn) from Dr. Christian P. Potholm, a campaign advisor to Angus. Chris offered to teach me everything I needed to know. His first lesson was to always pay his bills on time. While that was an important lesson I took to heart, he had a lot more to teach: "Being a campaign manager is an amalgam of jobs—including sweeping the floor when there's nobody else to do it." Angus was not the kind of candidate to work only through the campaign manager—when he had questions about a press release, he talked to the campaign press secretary.

When he had a question about fundraising, he'd talk to the finance director—only rarely when the "candidate" called in to the office was it for me. This was before email and texts—all communications were by phone—sometimes from his car phone, but we were always cautious about using that to discuss campaign matters—we even had a sign in his car that said, "THIS IS A RADIO!"

I learned that my job was to knit together the operation, not to be in front of it. Volunteers needed to be valued; the finance director (Diane Kew) needed names of potential donors; the field director (Jim Doyle) needed names of potential local supporters; the scheduler (Angus King III) needed next to nothing, since he knew his dad pretty well, but we did discuss priorities; the policy director (Andrew Bloom) needed help figuring out how to prioritize all the questionnaires incoming from interest groups and how possibly to answer them all (we made a commitment to do so, and I suspect Angus was the only candidate to do so).

There are egos involved in every campaign. The candidate's, for sure, but a campaign manager's ego is subjugated by so many, many others. All the paid consultants—the pollster, the media consultant, the political advisor, the fundraiser—it often felt like they were all as invested in having their advice followed as much as in the candidate's victory. Juggling all that advice, often conflicting, and keeping everyone focused while leading the candidate to believe he was really the one making the calls is not an easy thing.

Our primary pollster was Tubby Harrison from Boston, a friend of Mary Herman's brother, Tom. Like all pollsters, Tubby believed in the direction that his numbers pointed, even when the candidate believed to the depths of his soul that people just loved his stories and the way he chose to tell them. Tubby was from Massachusetts, a fact repeatedly pointed out by Joe Brennan, our Democratic opponent.

Tubby always over-polled Democrats and always had us losing; never once did he have us winning, even when we had numbers from other campaigns or public polls suggesting otherwise. Even thinking we were going to lose, I'll never forget that Tubby cared enough to show up on Election Day and hang in there until the bitter end to celebrate the victory. He was thrilled to declare his numbers wrong. This was one cool dude.

The fundraiser always believes their work deserves more of the candidate's time. In 1994, we did not hire a professional fundraiser, we had the aforementioned Diane Kew as the finance director who worked closely with a high-powered finance committee led by Jamie Broder, a friend of Angus's and a Portland attorney. In the 2012 Angus King for US Senate campaign, we had to hire a DC-based fundraiser who also believed her time with the candidate was more important than any time he might want to spend with others, including his spouse, even when she was at the same event. Altogether, it was a campaign manager's nightmare.

The media consultant *hates* it when his TV scripts are rewritten, or even worse, the candidate writes his own ads. Dan Payne was our media consultant in 1994, 1998, and again in 2012 for the Angus King for US Senate campaign. Dan was the consultant most often to disagree with the candidate, and mediating their disagreements was full of heat for me. Angus notoriously rewrote TV scripts while the storm cloud over Dan's head grew blacker.

While Angus isn't a big believer in polling research to dictate his priorities, Dan was a big believer in polling research to dictate his messaging. You get the conflict. It was pretty perpetual on our campaign. Angus thrived at getting contradictory advice from all sides. We all learned a lot from the vigorous interplay.

In 2012, one of our volunteers was a young media ingenue who had already received some acclaim—he took it upon himself to create an ad focused on an issue the candidate cared a lot about—wind energy (Angus had developed a wind project in Oxford County), but the polls suggested his role in the project was a non-issue. The candidate loved the ad. Getting that ad into the rotation for TV (something the media consultant needed to implement) was akin to WWIII. We knew it wasn't going to sway public opinion, but I argued that it made the candidate feel better. People did not see it often, but he did.

The political consultant hates it when the candidate or campaign manager panics over political non-events, such as a newspaper headline or letter to the editor that only political insiders read or care about. During the 1994 Angus King for Governor Campaign, I was repeatedly told by Chris Potholm that only my insider friends read newspapers and that I should be more worried about raising money for TV ads or direct mail to sportsmen, or whatever.

I felt vindicated a bit after listening to the tape of a focus group he conducted with "real" people. I recognized one of the voices! Chris still didn't seem to care. He didn't pay a lot of attention either when Angus reported that his friends and neighbors didn't like one of our ads or press releases. He dubbed them "Angus's Rolling Focus Group" because they always seemed to mysteriously agree with Angus on whatever topic it was.

George Smith was our direct mail advisor in 1994. George was a very good writer and was of tremendous help to us in getting the right messages out to sportsmen and liberal-Republican leaning areas of coastal Maine. I grew to love George's contrarian nature but could have easily done without all the extra advice. He had managed Dave Emery's successful campaign for Congress in 1974 and was the head of the Sportsman's Alliance of Maine, so I guess he knew some things, albeit not everything.

Then there are the friends of the candidate. All of them believe the campaign should adjust in one form or another when they run into someone who has a criticism. No one wants their friends criticized. Responding to the good intentions of all Angus's friends would have contorted the campaign into a pretzel. Making friends feel valued (and they *are* valuable) while maintaining the campaign's focus and direction was one of the toughest challenges.

The thing I knew about Angus King—if people met him, they'd like him. I always believed we would win. That, perhaps, was what made me successful as a campaign manager; I'm not sure how well I'd do without that conviction.

Here are a couple of vignettes from that first campaign, which I hope will give the readers an inside look at the dynamics of the race.

My lowest point of the campaign: As an Independent, we had to campaign like we were in a primary; we couldn't sit back until the primaries were over. Chris and Dan came up with the idea of having an imaginary "Independent Primary" so we could have image parity as soon as possible and not wait until September to show up in the polls.

We even had T-shirts made that said, "Coming Soon to a Polling Place Near You" and worked to insert Angus into all the candidate debates, and even ran TV ads like we were on the ballot in June instead of November. We had worked hard and felt good about where we were. You can imagine our dismay when, right after the primary, a Channel 6 (NBC) bullet poll had Angus trailing both Joe Brennan and Susan Collins with only 19 percent of the vote. Chris and George thought that was great since they felt Angus only had to get to 30 percent by Labor Day and be in second place to be viable in November.

Both candidates had received a bounce from winning the primary, but it was deflating for our campaign. Only George Smith and Chris Potholm thought it was great news that Susan Collins had won the primary. They thought she was out of money and out of friends, and besides, along with Dan Payne, they were sure our massive TV buy in June, with Angus winning "The Independent Primary" would make him viable while Collins languished. George and Chris were pretty sure Collins was finished. I wasn't so sure.

My highest points of the campaign: first, the July 4 parade in Bath was definitely a high point, where we felt the crowd's enthusiasm for Angus, especially compared to the reception that Joe Brennan and Susan Collins were receiving.

Second, there was another Channel 6 bullet poll in October that had Joe Brennan and Angus tied in a dead heat, confirming what we were all feeling and what our volunteer nightly tracking poll was showing. We had faith in our numbers, but I still was gratified to have some outside source confirming them.

Election night was hectic and exciting, and when it was over and Angus had won, I felt like a huge weight had been lifted from my shoulders. Well, that's understandable because it had.

Dennis Bailey adds some interesting vignettes of his own and closes this chapter with a most definite insight, namely that many worker bees and staff (to say nothing of the consultants) on campaigns don't do it just for the ideology or the party or even, in all honesty, just the candidate. They do it for moments like the one he concludes with, moments that tingle them from head to toe:

Campaigns are like a hurricane, a constant storm center setting off a different series of daily brush fires. Amid all of that, Kay was the eye of the storm—calm, cool, rational. Her reasoned, expert advice always lowered the temperature of whatever crisis was happening at the moment, and I'm sure she prevented a lot of us, the candidate included, from making big mistakes. During the 1994 governor's race, I used to drive to the campaign office in Brunswick every morning from Portland listening to talk radio (ugh!) and come into the office in a near panic. "We're getting slaughtered on the radio!" Nothing fazed Kay: Stick with the plan, keep your eye on the ball, don't get distracted.

As she explained above, the manager's job is like herding cats, but it's not just with the consultants, pollsters, and other advisers. The different personalities and quirks of the staff, even between the candidate's family, friends, and relatives, often lead to internal conflicts, jealousies, rivalries. Kay had to manage that as well. She was like the den mother over all of us.

And every time an ad went up on the air, she had to take an endless number of phone calls from our supporters who were happy to tell her it was a bad ad, the wrong message, and why isn't Angus talking about this, that, or the other thing? Note: if your own supporters don't like your ad, it's probably the right message because the ad isn't written for them. It's for people who haven't made up their mind about your candidate. See the previous chapter on "Your Friends Will Do You More Harm Than Your Enemies."

Fortunately, too, the depth of her experience in Maine politics and public policy, unusual for a campaign manager, was a huge asset to the campaign. At one point during Angus's 1994 campaign for governor against Joe Brennan, we looked at figures showing how much government had grown during Brennan's eight years in office. Someone did the math and figured out it was equivalent to hiring a new state employee for every day of his two four-year terms.

During a candidate's debate, Angus explained the figures and used the line, "It was like he got up every morning, had a glass of orange juice, took his vitamin and hired a bureaucrat." It got a huge laugh and clearly infuriated Brennan. The next day, Brennan held a news conference and released his own figures challenging Angus's data. This was a mistake because it just drew attention to Angus's claim. You never want to play on your opponent's lily pad, their argument, because you just look defensive, and like football, you can't score on defense.

The news media were all over it.

A brawl between candidates is like catnip to reporters. Kay and I were on our way to yet another candidate debate in Bangor when I kept getting paged (yes, we had pagers in those days) from a number that for some reason I didn't recognize. After two or three calls, Kay said, "Um . . . that would be the candidate."

Angus was, shall we say, "concerned" about Brennan's response and worried that maybe we had screwed up big time with the numbers. "I hope you guys are right," he said several times, making sure we both knew *he* wasn't at fault. Still driving in the car, Kay called key sources in state government who she knew to meticulously go through all the numbers again, and Brennan's.

Our numbers were solid.

We met with Angus in his hotel room just before the debate and walked him through all the numbers, explaining where Brennan got his figures and why ours were correct. Kay had written them all out on a piece of paper, and Angus wisely tucked it into his suit coat pocket as he left for the debate.

Not long into the debate, Brennan, who seemed to have a raft of notes in front of him, launched into a tirade about the orange juice line, defending his time as governor and accusing Angus of lying. Angus listened calmly, and when it was his turn to respond, he reached into his suit coat, pulled out the paper, and handed it to Brennan. "Here are the figures Joe, read 'em and weep."

It didn't matter at that point who had the right numbers. The visual contrast between the two candidates said it all. One of them calm, cool, confident. The other looking down, shuffling papers in front of him, struggling to explain a very wonky topic that probably went over the heads of most viewers anyway. It was a good day for the campaign, and it wouldn't have been possible without Kay Rand.

Campaign managers can make a big difference in a campaign. They can help—or hinder—the campaign or the cause. They are at the center of the storm and keeping everything going in the right direction is their central task.

Kay Rand was outstanding in a tough, very tough, very important race. And still is.

AXIOM #7

"Don't Expect the Press to Do Your Work for You, But Sometimes They Do" with Dennis Bailey

It's better to recall something you wish you'd said than something you wish you hadn't.
—FRANK CLARK

While Robert Redford's film *The Candidate* is an amazing and satisfying account of campaign dynamics, one of the very best depictions of the relationship between a candidate and a campaign, it is *The Ides of March* with George Clooney as the candidate, Ryan Gosling as the campaign strategist, and Marisa Tomei as the reporter that best captures the complex relationship between a campaign and the press. And for what it is worth, it is my pick for the best campaign movie of all time. This one is the real deal.

In the film, the reporter, Ida, uses the campaign manager, and the campaign manager, Steve, uses the reporter. But in the twists and turns during the campaign, the reporter burns the campaign manager badly when he most needs her. So when, against the odds, the strategist's candidate wins, the reporter seeks him out and asks the Gosling character, "Aren't we still friends?" He replies ironically, "Ida, you're my best friend" and then bans her from any further access to the president elect.

Would that in real life campaign strategists could wield that much power over the press! Most reporters and their editors consider it their God-given right to have access, whether the subject wants it or not.

In reality, reporters, editors, and publishers in Maine play a variety of roles as campaigns play out with regularity and varying interactions between the press and those campaigns.

For example, here in Maine, although they profess otherwise, the major newspapers in Maine, the *Portland Press Herald (PPH)* and their satellite papers, the *Kennebec Journal* and the *Waterville Sentinel*, the *Bangor Daily News (BDN)* and the *Lewiston Sun* have owners and editors with political points of view and don't always confine those views to the editorial pages.

Nor are all reporters immune from biases and favorites. For years everybody in politics knew that the principal political reporter for the *BDN*, John Day, while capable of occasionally savaging Republican candidates, usually favored them, while Steve Campbell for the *PPH* loved skewering Republicans and best-lighting Democrats.

For this chapter, let Dennis Bailey, who has served as press secretary and campaign strategist for more campaigns than anyone else in recent Maine history, explain how the press operation of a campaign works and how the world of reporters (with their editors and publishers) really operates. "Dennis is the one operative you want on your side in any campaign, ballot measure or candidate; he's invaluable," I've been told in more than one campaign.

Dennis Bailey:

The first rule for any candidate to remember is: news reporters are not your friend. It doesn't matter how chummy and charming they may seem, they will never hesitate to burn you if they have the goods, and sometimes even when they don't. So give them access, return their calls, let them in on certain things, but never think this will guarantee favorable coverage.

It won't.

In fact, it's well known that some reporters often do an initial profile that is very favorable of a candidate just to gain better access, feel part of the "team," and get juicy information on the candidate or his/her opponent. Reporters are never part of your team.

Similarly, news reporters will almost never do your work for you. OK, I say almost never because, well, sometimes they do. One episode I recall from the 1990 Democratic congressional primary was both a home run (for the candidate I was working for, Tom Andrews), but also it was a mistake.

It started innocently enough at a candidates' forum in Portland when the front-runner, Attorney General James Tierney, handed out a glossy new brochure. On the back page was a list of his accomplishments, and one of them struck me as rather odd. It claimed Tierney was "instrumental" in bringing Exxon to justice after the disastrous 1989 Valdez oil spill in Alaska.

Huh? I had never heard of this.

I followed the news pretty closely, and it seemed like this was something Tierney would have crowed about years before the primary. If it were true. The next day I called a reporter who I knew well and who was closely following the race, Lee Burnett of the small afternoon newspaper the *Biddeford Journal-Tribune*. I faxed him a copy of the brochure and suggested he might want to check it out.

He immediately called the attorney general in Alaska who literally chuckled when Burnett read him the claim on the brochure. He explained to Burnett that all Tierney had done was sign a letter with nearly every other attorney general in the United States suggesting that Exxon be held accountable for its crimes. In other words, "instrumental" was a bit of a stretch.

During his years in public life, Tierney had been downright solicitous of the press—casual, friendly, accessible. I know because before I was in politics, I was a reporter and frequently took Tierney's calls. But like I said, none of that was money in the bank. None of it protected him from what was to come.

Even though it's hardly unusual for candidates to puff up their résumés and accomplishments, this one was too glaring an example to ignore. Burnett's story touched off a wave of coverage, especially when it was picked up by the always important local TV news stations. I recall an anchor at the leading Portland station asking the reporter who covered the story on air, "Did Jim Tierney lie?" It really didn't matter what the answer was, it's not the kind of conversation you want people to have in the weeks before an election.

The coverage was compounded by Tierney's refusal to defend the brochure or even say anything about it, which brings up another rule: never say "No comment."

Reporters love it when someone declines to comment. It gives them a license to write a one-sided, he-said-she-said (or doesn't say) story. Reporters like black and white. What they don't like is gray. They don't like complications or confusing details.

Tierney could have said anything—blame a staffer, call it an oversight, promise to change it in future printings, whatever. He could have made it gray instead of black and white. It might not have made the story go away, but it certainly would have lessened its impact. And news anchors wouldn't be questioning on air if he was a liar.

But in the end, even though the story benefited my candidate (without my fingerprints on it), I still consider it a mistake for one reason: I really didn't know if Tierney had been instrumental in the Valdez episode. For all I knew, Burnett could have called up the Alaska AG and been told that, "Yes, Exxon would have never been brought to justice without Jim's help."

That would have backfired and given Tierney's campaign a big boost. Just like a lawyer who never asks a witness a question he doesn't know the answer to, I never should have gambled by giving Burnett the story when I didn't really know what he'd find out. In the future, I learned to wrap these kinds of stories in an airtight bow before handing over the gift to a reporter. They like it better that way anyway.

Another incident from the Andrews campaign illustrates how campaigns sometimes use the press. We got a call one afternoon from a local TV reporter who was doing a roundup of the race and wanted to come in to the campaign office that afternoon and interview Tom. We went into Red Alert. Tom was the underdog in the race, and no one was expecting him to win. So we decided to do a little staging to show we had a busy, active campaign.

We called in a few volunteers to sit at a table and stuff envelopes (even though most of our mailing was already done), and we had staff members in other rooms keep dialing the campaign office numbers while the cameras rolled. What viewers saw that night was a beehive of activity. While Tom was talking, phones were ringing, people in the background were scurrying back and forth, volunteers were hard at work. It's a small thing, but visual images count for a lot. Not every campaign thinks about them. I've seen some candidates give similar interviews in a suit and tie from what looks like a law office. Yeah, that's a winning message. Voters love lawyers.

Although social media has made significant inroads, TV still rules as the dominant medium for news and information. It used to drive me nuts when I worked for Governor Angus King, and he would become irate about some item in the eighteenth paragraph of a *Press Herald* story when the same story the night before on the six o'clock news—where most people saw it—was overwhelmingly positive.

Every politician complains about the press, but yes, it does help when the press is on your side. During the campaign against the big Sanford casino, every paper in the state was against casino gambling, and they would often liberally quote our news releases in columns and editorials. In most cases, press releases don't have the impact they used to. Reporters want exclusives, and if every reporter has the same news release, they don't consider it news. You often get more mileage if you convince a reporter that no one else has this "scoop," or that you're giving it to this one reporter ahead of its release. I've used this method to turn a story of what would have been buried somewhere inside into a front-page headline.

If I were an editor for a newspaper or TV station, I'd give my political reporter a sabbatical to go work on a campaign for a year. When they came back, they would be able to provide more depth and insight in their future reporting. Because the truth is most reporters don't understand the real nuts and bolts of a campaign, all that goes into it and why.

They know the TV ads and the FEC expenditure reports, but that's about it. They have preconceived ideas about campaigns and issues (although they'll deny it with their dying breath), but they often miss the bigger picture.

When I served as communications director for Governor King, there was one statehouse reporter in particular who had a habit of coming into my office late on a Friday and ask to speak to the governor about a story he was writing for the following Sunday's paper. In other words, the story was written. He just needed a quote from the governor, something like, "Governor King denied blah blah blah. . . ." The issue was invariably complicated, and we offered the reporter an opportunity to sit down with the governor on Monday for a full discussion.

Nope, he only needed ten minutes, he said; the story was running Sunday. We knew what was up, and so did the reporter. A discussion about the issue with Angus would edge the story into the gray zone, make it less black and white, less impactful but more factual. Like I said, reporters aren't always interested in that.

Likewise, there was another statehouse reporter, a conservative, who regularly wrote a weekly column savaging Angus. The guy never came to Angus's daily press briefings, never even met the governor. I finally suggested he sit down with Angus, spend some time with him. "I'm not going to do that," he said. "I might like him."

Dave Emery likewise provides some valuable insight into the world of editors and editorial boards:

All candidates and officeholders have had testy encounters with the press from time to time, but in most cases, this stems from the fact that the relationship between the press and politicians is necessarily adversarial. The candidate's job is to present himself in the best possible light; the press's job is to check facts and challenge assertions as well as to report the news. Reporters and editorial writers don't always get it right, but neither do candidates and officeholders.

I can think of a few times when I was aggravated by news stories and articles, but there was only one time during my career that I was really *pissed*. You see, I'm a fanatical Red Sox fan, and I've attended dozens upon dozens of baseball games over the years at Fenway, at Yankee Stadium, in Baltimore, and at several other parks around the country. Back in 1978 when I was nearing the end of my third congressional campaign, the Sox found themselves facing the Yankees at Fenway for a one-game playoff to determine the American League East winner. *And* I had a ticket! Game day, October 2, was a Monday, and I was in Portland for my campaign editorial board interview with the *Portland Press Herald*, scheduled for that afternoon.

"Reschedule the editorial board," I said to my chief of staff. "I'm going to the ballgame instead!"

"But you can't. You're running for reelection. That won't look good in the papers."

"I don't care! I've got a ticket, and I'm going to the game."

"Absolutely not! They'll crucify you!" came the adamant response.

So finally, I gave in to the withering pressure from my campaign manager and congressional staff, and at the appointed time on playoff day, I presented myself at the offices of the *Portland Press Herald* on Congress Street, where I was greeted by Columnist Bill Caldwell. He escorted me to the conference room, but only one other person was there. I had expected the room to be full of columnists and editorial writers, and particularly Jim Brunelle and editor-in-chief Don Hansen, as was the usual practice.

"Where is everybody?" I asked."

"Oh," said Caldwell. "They've all gone to the game."

I could feel my neck getting redder and redder as I took my seat, suffering through the small talk and assorted banal minutiae before getting into discussions concerning the campaign and the issues of the day. I don't remember much else about the editorial board, but I remember watching Carl Yastrzemski hit a foul popup to third for the last out; the Sox lost 5–4. I watched the last three or four innings of the game at the Portland Jetport restaurant and lounge before boarding my flight back to DC. No Fenway Franks for me that day, but at least I had had a cold beer.

Another incident involved John Day, at that time in Washington for the *Bangor Daily News*. In 1978, the Maine delegation was in the throes of developing a strategy to resolve the Maine Indian Land Claim, a complicated and controversial matter brought by the Penobscot and Passamaquoddy people against the state of Maine. They asserted that most of northern Maine (12 million acres, in fact) had been taken from them illegally, and they demanded compensation.

The Maine congressional delegation at the time consisted of Senators Ed Muskie and Bill Hathaway, with Bill Cohen and me, the delegation chairman that year, in the House; Jim Longley was governor. To make matters worse, Cohen was running against Hathaway for the US Senate seat, and Maine Attorney General Joe Brennan was running to succeed Longley as governor.

Delegation meetings were usually held in Ed Muskie's private hideaway office in the capitol. He acquired this privilege through seniority, and it was quite convenient to meet there whenever the House and Senate were in session and particularly for meetings away from prying eyes and ears.

Delegation meetings concerning the Land Claim could become testy, but whenever they included Longley and Brennan, they were often tempestuous! One such meeting was punctuated by a loud and feisty exchange between Muskie and Longley over Longley's objection to the establishment of *a nation within a nation*, as he put it.

Unbeknownst to the delegation, John Day had camped outside the Muskie hideaway, hoping to get comments from each of us as we left the meeting. He could hear that there was raucous argument going on inside, but he couldn't quite make out the words. He tried everything he could think of to get one of us to spill the beans to the embarrassment of the combatants, but as chairman, I had suggested that we draft a common statement and that no one stray from it. Fortunately for our ability to work effectively in a strained political environment, the delegation held together, and John Day never got quite the juicy story that lurked just out of earshot.

Here is an interesting sidebar about the press in politics. For a long time, newspaper editorials were widely read and widely believed and thought to have a major impact with their content late in the election cycle. And before TV and twenty-four-hour news cycles, they did.

But in recent times, readership has fallen off substantially, and today only about 12–13 percent of readers say they pay attention to the editorials, and because of the huge importance of television, late editorials are basically useless. To be valuable, endorsements have to be made early enough so the editorials can be cited in subsequent TV advertising. At least ten days out is a necessity to maximize impact. Today, things are more likely to be "electronic drives print," at least when there are editorials involved.

Phil Merrill recounts another way of dealing with the press and editors: "When I was running for governor in 1978 and campaigning in Biddeford against Joe Brennan, Barry Hobbins and I got the idea to go door to door on a few streets, including the street where the editor of the *Biddeford Journal*, Brian Thayer, lived. We did some houses and then marched up to his place, acting as if we didn't know it was his street. He came to the door and chatted, and we later got the endorsement of the paper. He was very impressed we were going door to door all over the city. Great fun."

Phil remains one of Maine's longest-serving political activists and consultants, from running Ed Muskie's senatorial bid in 1976 to Joe Brennan's gubernatorial effort in 1994, to his wife Barbara Merrill's Independent run for governor in 2006.

Sometimes (even often during some election cycles) the curtain of "objectivity" at newspapers gets a little frayed, and keen observers can see behind it. A most amusing example of this occurred in the 1994 gubernatorial campaign for governor. The *Portland Press Herald* was solidly for Joe Brennan and the *Bangor Daily News* was solidly for Susan Collins. They had no interest in having the Independent candidate Angus King becoming governor, and both their reporting and more blatantly, their editorial pages, reflected that bias.

Both papers were quite vociferous in advocating for their favorite candidate and most unwilling to credit Angus King's rise, first to second place (by Labor Day) and then as he steadily rose in October. Both papers constantly supported their respective candidates, even as the situation on the ground changed dramatically.

There was simply no daylight in their editorial suites for Angus King.

Therefore, the following account of what happened at the end of the campaign seems even more amusing. Some background is in order to understand the dynamics. In the Republican gubernatorial primary that year, Susan Collins staggered through, winning with only 21 percent with Sumner Lipman getting 17 percent and six other candidates (Jasper Wyman, Judy Foss, Paul Young, Mary Adams, Charlie Webster and Pam Cahill) splitting the rest.

At the time, most in the King campaign were disappointed, thinking Collins was the Republican's strongest standard bearer. Paul Carrier of the *Portland Press Herald* even wrote rather gratuitously, and without any polling evidence, that Collins's win "bodes ill for King." Not surprisingly Steve Abbot, Collins's campaign manager, thought her victory "strikes a blow at Angus King."

At the time, George Smith and I saw things differently and were delighted with her as the Republican's choice. Collins had a top campaign manager, Steve Abbott, and one of the very top Republican strategists and staff guys in Tom Daffron (who along with Larry Benoit and Kay Rand combine special talents in both roles). But we were confident the McKernan wing of the party (which had supported Foss) and the conservatives (such as Mary Adams and Charlie Webster and Sumner Lipman) would not lift a finger to help her. She was out of money and nearly out of friends.

By contrast, King used June and then the summer to go on TV after "winning the Independent Primary" where he was, happily, unopposed. Week by week, backed by 1000+ gross rating points (GRPs) and hard work, King rose in the polls. By Labor Day he was in second place in even the newspaper polls, albeit much farther back in them than in Peter Burr's nightly tracking ones. In fact, Collins closed her Portland headquarters and tried to keep fighting from the 2nd CD. The King campaign took good advice and ignored her, focusing entirely on Brennan.

Focus groups, though, had shown that while undecided voters liked King, they felt more comfortable with Brennan as a known commodity and without some contrast ads, they were inclined to stick with him. In reality, King had a pretty Democratic profile so the contrasts would have to be about style and approach and past performance of Brennan, not on his issue positions. There were plenty of the former and Dan Payne, King's media guy, had them ready to go. He also gets credit for rebaptizing the "negative" ads as "contrast" ads.

But Jim Brunelle of the *PPH* seemingly singlehandedly held up the King campaign's use of them. Brunelle had been with King on his PBS *Maine Watch* show and was firmly against "negative" ads. Please dear reader, do not think we are talking about the negative ads of today's Crazy Town, which are lies, distortions, and bizarre, often other-worldly total fabrications. We are talking about saying things like, "While in office Joe Brennan would get up, brush his teeth, and add a bureaucrat."

As Dennis Bailey put it, "Angus just didn't want to go forward with anything negative. He fought it all the way. It was very frustrating."

Finally, when the polling numbers stalled, Dan Payne and the rest of the campaign staff, including the very influential campaign manager, Kay Rand, urged him to take action.

I remember with some fondness a meeting during which, tired of hearing how "Jim" wouldn't like this or that, I jumped up and went to the easel in the front of the room and drew a diagram of the Blaine House and a stick figure in front of it. Then I ran a big arrow through the figure saying, "The road to the Blaine House runs through Jim Brunelle, not around him."

Although unmoved by my plea, later King finally did consent to some mild contrast ads—but only after the Brennan campaign foolishly went negative first, accusing King of lying and asking if voters thought a candidate should have to take a lie detector test.

These, of course, were all it took for Brunelle to decry "negative advertising" yet again, but the *PPH* then published its own poll on October 29 that showed Brennan with 33 percent, King with 28 percent, and Collins out of it at 15 percent. The next day the *PPH* vigorously endorsed Brennan again, saying he was "the right person at the right time to get Maine going again, and he deserves the voters' support." King got but half a sentence of thin, thin gruel for "his unusual perspective."

But now comes the fun part. The Brennan campaign then released the findings of their "poll," one which claimed to show King fading and Collins coming on strong in the 2nd CD. Later Democratic strategists would call it a "leak job" of dubious origin and dubious methodology. "Trust me, this was not a Tom Keily poll" (the respected Democratic national pollster) said a Democratic operative.

The *Bangor Daily News* gladly and eagerly went for the Brennan campaign ploy—or at least the editor and publisher did. For as Phil Merrill, campaign manager for Brennan, recalled humorously years later, "The whole poll was legitimate, but we only peddled a small part of it, the part that showed Collins gaining in northern Maine. The reporter at the *BDN* we gave it to said, "I know this is phony as hell, but my editors say I have to run with it."

As Chris Lehane (a top national Democratic operative, press secretary for the presidential effort of Al Gore, and author of the excellent campaign film *Knife Fight* starring Rob Lowe), who was on the inside of the Brennan campaign, put it: "The *BDN* was desperate for a fragment."

Understandably, but ill-advisedly, the *BDN* took the fragment of a fragment and ran with it, using it to editorialize again on her behalf.

On November 5, 1994, the paper declared of Collins: "She can win." Well no, actually she couldn't, but what's a little hyperbole when you have a newspaper you can use for a shout-out. But the *BDN* went even further, casting doubt on both other candidates: "This campaign has turned sour . . . the two men, King and Brennan, have clawed at each other through last week, even as they slipped in the polls."

These assumptions, of course, left aside the reality that neither man was slipping in the real polls, and that Collins was truly dead in the water. Brennan was holding his own and King was finishing strong.

Now comes perhaps the most deliciously ironic element of all. Collins really did pick up some votes in northern Maine after the *BDN* editorial. But on Election Day, the exit polling showed that Collins's gains had actually come at Brennan's expense in Penobscot, Aroostook, Washington, and Hancock counties! Thus in a limited, but still satisfying way, the *BDN* actually helped elect King, which one can only imagine was the reverse of their intent.

King would finish with 35.4 percent, Brennan at 33.8 percent, and Collins far back at 23.1 percent. Green candidate Jonathan Carter received 6.4 percent and Mark Finks 1.3 percent.

But think of what the results might have been if the *PPH* and *BDN* had handled the 1994 governor's race with true objectivity. King probably would have won by more, perhaps even by a lot more. We'll never know, thanks to the paw prints of various editors.

So, although you can never count on the press doing your work for you, sometimes they do so.

Even if inadvertently.

In addition to the numerous political reporters listed in the opening memorial, the contributors would also like to acknowledge other notable political beat reporters/editors during the period under review: Lance Tapley, Bill "B. J." Johnson, Bill Frederick, Peter Jackson, Willis Johnson, Nancy Perry, A.J. Higgins, Todd Benoit, Lee Burnett, Pat Callahan, Steve Campbell, Paul Carrier, John Day, Don Carrigan, Liz Chapman, Al Diamon, Jerry Harkavy, John Lovell, Jeanne Meserve, Bill Nemitz, Francis Quinn, Naomi Schalit, Susan Sharon, Keith Shortall, Jeff Toorish, Joshua Weinstein, and last, and by no means least, Dennis Bailey, who trained with your mob. Thanks to friend and foe alike. "It was nothing personal, just the nature of the business."

AXIOM #8

"Ballot Measures Are Different Than Candidate Elections"

*Men fight and lose the battle and the thing they fought for comes
about in spite of their defeat, and when it comes, turns out not to be what they
meant and other men have to fight for what they meant under another name.*
—WILLIAM MORRIS

Ballot Measure campaigns—referenda and bonds—are very different from candidate campaigns. Although most of the political axioms in this book, such as "All the big mistakes are made early," apply equally to both candidate and ballot measure campaigns, ballot measures themselves display many important differences.

Often candidates, the general public, and even political operatives fail to see how significant those differences are because ballot measure campaigns are unique. Parallels drawn from normal candidate electoral experiences are sometimes inappropriate, and the requirements for successful ballot measure campaigns must be present for consistent success in this area.

Let's look at some key elements of ballot measure campaigns:

THE PLAYING FIELD IS MUCH WIDER

For one thing, with ballot measures, the initial playing field is much wider; that is, usually there are more voters "in play" in ballot measures, often *many more* than in partisan elections. That is especially true today since the playing field for Republicans, Democrats, and Independents in candidate campaigns has shrunk considerably over the last twenty years with excessive partisanship. I would estimate, for example, that in the 2020 senatorial race between Susan Collins and Sarah Gideon, that no more than 10–15 percent of eligible voters were truly "in play" at any given time and susceptible to being persuaded to switching candidates.

By contrast, in ballot measures, it is not unusual to have two or even three times that number of persuadable voters in play. Of course, if an issue is on the ballot for multiple times—such as casinos or Gay Marriage—that initial percentage declines. For example, the persuadable universe in play between the proposed small casino on Passamaquoddy land in Washington County in 2002 (45 percent) differed markedly in size from the much smaller Oxford Casino persuadable universe in 2010 (10 percent).

But in general, one of the biggest differences between candidate campaigns and ballot measures is that with initiatives, there are no partisan underpinnings. Very broadly, in a candidate campaign—at least 40 percent vote for the Democrat and 40 percent for Republican almost automatically are in play, and so at best you can persuade 20 percent of likely voters. In a ballot measure, there are no such partisan connections (unless it is a social issue and even there more "play" in the universe is discernible), and that's why we see wide swings in ballot measures as voters get more information.

In a ballot measure, a much bigger percentage of the electorate can be persuaded one way or the other. That's one reason why a measure can start off with over 70 percent support and still lose. Or a NO side can be behind by forty points and still win. For example, in 2000, some polls showed the Physician-Assisted Suicide referendum in Maine with nearly 70 percent support with just five weeks to go *but it still lost.*

THERE IS MUCH MORE OPPORTUNITY FOR COMMAND AND CONTROL

A second, even more consequential difference is the amount of command and control a campaign can have. Where candidate campaigns are subject to interference from party state committees, national party committees, and outside interest groups, and by law cannot coordinate with independent expenditures, ballot measure campaigns have much more freedom to run their own campaigns their own ways. Ballot measures also, in the opinion of Lance Dutson, bring "the pure joy of not having a candidate to manage." Amen to that, say many consultants dealing with referenda.

In this regard it is essential that ballot measure campaigns pretest internals before submitting them to the signature gathering process or the legislature. In 1996, the failure of the Natural Resources Council of Maine to pretest the ingredients in their complicated "Compact" proposal resulted in a target-rich environment during the subsequent election. The Forest Ecology Network, for example, discovered that the Compact more than doubled the size of the clearcutting already allowed and made a lot of political hay telling everybody in the environmental community.

This occurred when a highly popular competing measure drastically reducing clearcutting was already on the ballot. Environmentally concerned voters across the state were thus confronted by dueling authority figures having radically different talking points taken from the same authority universe.

Also unlike candidate campaigns where outside groups may spend more than the candidates, in most ballot measures it is possible to control most, even 100 percent, of the TV commercials. In this regard, there is a much greater likelihood that the campaign will be driven by professionals and not subject to the input of the friends, neighbors, spouses, and partners of candidates the way candidate campaigns can be.

BALLOT MEASURES ARE MORE FOCUSED THAN CANDIDATE ELECTIONS

A third major difference is the huge discrepancy between and among issues. Candidates have to have opinions on hundreds of subjects and are sometimes at the mercy of subject oddments as are found in party platforms such as, "But the Republican Party platform is Pro Life and you are Pro Choice," so where do you really stand?

But in ballot measures, it is often possible to reduce the issue spread down to only two! Take the campaigns to shut down the Maine Yankee nuclear power plant, for example—it came down to only a relatively simple choice between "health and safety" issues and "economic" ones. Therefore, in that type of environment, campaigns can concentrate on nuances, consistent imagery, and influence vectors. This additional focus is very important and makes running campaigns much, much simpler.

Along these same lines, in candidate campaigns with the multiplicity of issues, candidates are usually all over the lot with overlapping positions. Ballot measures provide greater opportunities to frame the debate by staking out and keeping voter attention on the best argument or the most important influence vector.

In ballot measures we call these "lily pads," and they allow you to jump on one and make it your own as when we discussed the dueling lily pads of "health and safety" versus "economics." Competing binary choices like that are a campaign manager's dream. As we shall see, however, in the clearcutting/forest compact environment, it was a nightmare for the YES side. The NO side benefited enormously from the confusing nature of the referendum, the conflicting authority figures from the same universe and a poor choice for the name. As Megan MacLennan warns, "A lily pad has a maximum occupancy of one."

In the case of the Maine Yankee shutdown referendum, The NO side was helped considerably by the inability of the other side to stay off the NO's best lily pad, the economic costs of shutting down the plant. The more they climbed up on it, the worse they did. Likewise, the NO side let their best "health and safety" lily pad drift away from the centrality of the debate. With good riddance, since it could have cost the NO side the election. Had the YES side stayed exclusively on the health and safety issue, they might well have won.

Therefore, if you ever find that the other side has a commanding and winning lily pad, don't ever try to climb up on it; you simply lose voters, sometimes even those you already have.

Or in the words of an astute Bowdoin student, Peter Carter, "If you are riding a horse, and it dies, get off it." The influential Maine Republican consultant and blogger, Lance Dutson, puts it best in consultant Zen-speak when warning clients not to get involved in the other side's best arguments. He says simply, "Remember, it takes two hands to clap." Subtext: we don't want voters clapping on their issue!

LAWYERS AND CAR DEALERS ARE IMPORTANT: FOR THE SAME REASON

In ballot measures, it is more important to have assurances that the client will be represented by experienced, aggressive, tenacious legal counsel. This is especially true at the beginning of the election cycle. You want very good legal counsel as the proposed legislation and ballot wording is being put together. Candidates run, and lawyers help them with the paperwork of filing and of keeping campaign records, but they don't have a vital role in putting them on the ballot; they just run.

In ballot measures, you want very good legal beagles putting together the language that describes and implements the measure, but *not* until all the elements possibly to be included have been evaluated by polling. You do not want your legal team drafting *their* language of what you are trying to accomplish. You want them to draft a bill that implements what *you* want to accomplish and only what *you know* can be won at the polls. You assess the elements *first* and then have them draft the ballot measure. Control over the wording of the ballot measure is a critical part of the process and without it, the adage "All the big mistakes are made early" comes into play. Research at the beginning of the cycle is critical to subsequent success.

Later in the process, you will need them to argue cogently with the secretary of state who has to approve the ballot language as this will almost always in the face of opposition come from the other side. In the end the secretary of state has the final say on the wording that will go on the subsequent referendum.

As Dennis Bailey indicates, this is a very important step:

In another casino referendum in 2011, proponents posed the question, "Do you want to allow a slot machine facility at a harness racing track in Biddeford?" Casinos *NO!* protested the wording because the actual bill didn't stipulate Biddeford as the location of the slots parlor but allowed it to be built anywhere within twenty-five miles of the harness racing track in Scarborough.

The secretary of state agreed and changed the ballot language to read, "Do you want to allow a slot machine facility at a harness racing track in Biddeford *or another community within 25 miles of Scarborough Downs*?

This was important because changing the language suddenly put voters in Portland and South Portland in play who might not have cared about a slots parlor in Biddeford but wouldn't want one in their hometown.

Voters rejected the Biddeford slots parlor 55–45 percent.

Tough, astute, and dogged legal counsel is also vital in decorticating the opponent's proposal. In the 2000 forestry referendum, the YES proponents, concerned about the eleven thousand Small Woodlot Owners Association of Maine (SWOAM) members' reactions to various restrictions within their proposal, argued that some of the provisions wouldn't apply. A strongly worded opinion from Pierce Atwood pointed out trenchantly that they *would* apply, thereby undercutting the YES side's position.

Another area where you need dedicated and tenacious counsel is in dealing with the television stations. I have never been on a campaign where we went to the stations to protest an ad that was misleading enough to try to get it off the air. But on various occasions, opponents have gone to the stations to object to ours—especially those they deemed effective. Sometimes the management of a TV station has a personal viewpoint that can creep into the oversight process. Then you need effective legal engagement.

Sometimes, though, legal pressure is not enough, and you really need to bring in heavy hitters in terms of the advertising clientele—that is, entities such as car dealerships and law firms, that advertise year in and year out. You need them to put a word in with the station manager as to the desirability of making sure freedom of speech is not compromised.

This factor has not been extensively studied, but I am aware of several instances in which large car dealerships have threatened to withdraw future advertising dollars from certain TV stations that refused to run ads considered controversial from the station's point of view.

AS LONG AS LEGAL: SOURCES OF FUNDING DO NOT MATTER

Unlike candidate elections, where sometimes the issue of who is donating to your cause comes up and your opponent can make some headway by pointing this out, in ballot measures, dollars are more symbolically cost-free. Often, however, in candidate campaigns, learning about a funding source is more likely to reinforce the voter's existing position than change that voter's choice, but sometimes it can rebound negatively on that candidate.

In ballot measures, the sources of your funding do not matter. What matters is your ability to put 1000 GRPs of television on the air weekly. If the voters' attention is to be kept on your side's most efficacious influence vectors and their attention away from the other side's best ones, you need a constant barrage of imagery to keep and to persuade voters. This battle of the lily pads can only work with a well-funded television campaign.

BALLOT MEASURES TAKE PLACE IN A MUCH MORE BIPARTISAN BATTLE SPACE: TODAY'S ENEMY IS TOMORROW'S FRIEND

In ballot measures, unlike partisan politics, there are no "inveterate animosities." This cycle's ally becomes next cycle's opponent. Ebb and flow of comradeship. Take Jonathan Carter. Carter helped Angus King defeat Joe Brennan by taking a good percentage of the vote in Brennan's old state Senate district in 1994. But later in 1996, Carter helped defeat the King-supported "Compact." And despite long antagonism between Carter and the paper industry, he found common cause with SWOAM to defeat the Compact the second time around (1997). On that occasion, many paper companies were not unhappy to see that process play out the way it did.

On the other hand, the Maine Audubon Society, which had supported the Compact put together by the forest products industry and the NRCM in 1996 and 1997, turned against the Carter-modified clearcutting application proposal when it reappeared in 2000.

Note: Carter was a major player on the Maine political scene for quite a long time. As head of the Green Party, he ran for political office a number of times and also managed the Green Party candidacy of Pat LaMarche. For background on the Maine Green Party, its founding by John Rensenbrink and its political activities, see Rensenbrink's very incisive *Against all Odds*.

THE CLEARCUTTING/FOREST COMPACT SAGA

The period from 1995 to 2000 shows a pattern of three separate referenda on clearcutting, the paper industry's practice of leveling large swaths of forest, leaving an ugly gash in the forest. There was one in 1996, another in 1997 and a final one in 2000. Taken together, these three referenda are also a marvelous indicator of many important aspects of ballot measure politics.

First, they illustrate how *not* to make forest practices policy and underscore the pattern of the legislature often abrogating its responsibility until forced to accept it.

Second, they underscore how complexity is the enemy of passage when it comes to ballot measures.

Third, they define the element of confusion in action.

Fourth, they exhibit most of the axioms presented in this work, each in action in one series of interlocking and overlapping ballot measures.

Part of the reason is that ballot measures, unlike candidate campaigns, do not like complexity and ambiguity. In ballot measures, complexity hinders, simplicity helps (whereas in candidate campaigns, "fudging issues" is a major ingredient of any campaign).

FEAR DRIVES OUT FAVOR

Remember that in ballot measure campaigns, the NO side almost always automatically gets 5 percent at the end of a cycle because people who can't decide or who are confused just say "No." In fact, a good rule of thumb is that the YES side needs to start with 60 percent in order to win, depending of course on the quality of the campaigns involved.

See chapter 9 for an examination of the important adage, "Fear Drives Out Favor" in the context of changing very popular referenda proposals into defeats.

BALLOT MEASURES LIKE SIMPLICITY

Ballot measures like simplicity and manageable lily pads that have been pre-tested. Ballot measures do not like complexity and various free-floating lily pads that can be turned against the proponents of their measure.

To set the stage, in 1995 Jonathan Carter and his Forest Ecology Network collected fifty-eight thousand signatures to put a clearcutting ban on the ballot. Saying "It's a David versus Goliath struggle," he certainly spoke for many Maine people about the unsightly and destructive nature of clearcutting. At that time perhaps 60–70 percent of Maine people opposed clearcutting, at least in its existing form. Some environmental organizations such as the Sierra Club and the Wilderness Society supported the ban as well.

Because they opposed both Carter and his proposal in part because of the importance of clearcutting in dealing with the spruce budworm infestation, the Natural Resources Council of Maine (NRCM) and two large paper companies went to Governor King and proposed a new, complicated competing measure, one with quite different provisions.

Other environmental groups such as the Audubon Society and the Nature Conservancy then joined with Governor King and elements of the forest industry, including the large paper companies, to put forth an alternative measure. They called it a "Forest Compact." *Portland Press Herald* editor George Neavoll urged King to join NRCM and push for the Compact.

The Forest Ecology Network probably was not totally incorrect when it claimed the new proposal was created with the "express purpose of defeating the Citizen's Referendum to Ban Clearcutting."

Even today with a healthy distance of forty years, it is still not clear why "Compact" was chosen as the name of the twenty-seven-page document. Was this a hangover from Pilgrim times? Inquiring minds might still like to know why it wasn't simply called a "Compromise" since it so clearly was cobbled together to try to please both the paper companies and the environmental groups. Instead, the alternative was named "The Compact for Maine Forests to Become Law to Promote Sustainable Forest Management Practices Throughout the State."

This choice of words was quite astonishing because in virtually any polling or focus group efforts, six out of ten Maine voters statewide supported the idea of a "Compromise" around forestry issues. Insiders believe the culprits for the name were several paper companies whose home offices did not like the sound of "compromise."

Perhaps even a more palatable name would not have changed the internal provisions that proved so baffling to voters (and difficult to explain!). But it certainly might have picked up 3 percent difference since the measure lost twice, once in a three-way contest and then more surprisingly in a two-way one. Also, a "compromise" might not have been so susceptible to both parody and caricature by the Forest Ecology Network (FEN), which viewed it as a cynical sellout.

For example, the Compact called for allowing 75-acre clearcuts. The FEN pointed out that this doubled the size of existing clearcuts. Naturally some emoted, "Say what? Now they can only cut 35 acres per year, how is this an improvement?" Proponents then offered a strange defense, namely that companies and people would never cut that many acres! An odd defense surely, asking voters to take on faith the very companies that had promoted the disliked practice in the first place!

Talk about mistakes made early—and in haste—and not polled on enough. You can be assured that all the internal elements of the Compact had never been tested with Maine voters. For example, it ended up calling for making state audits of compliance *voluntary* and contained provisions for allowing up to over a million acres of forest to be clearcut over a ten-year period. Carter's Forest Ecology Network savaged the Compact from one end of the state to the other using its very provisions.

On October 31, 1996, Carey Goldberg, a reporter for the *New York Times,* wrote a headline—"Logging Debate in Maine Makes a Referendum Impenetrable." An accurate description. And the confusion and cross currents of forest practices policy did not end there; the battle would go on for four more years. When in doubt, vote No.

Massive TV advertising on all sides (Carter's group spent almost $900,000, and the Compact supporters spent $1.2 million) succeeded in confusing many. On Election Day 1996, Maine voters said "A pox on both of your houses,"

Ban Clearcutting	29.2
The Compact	47.4
Against Both	23

Because neither proposal received 50 percent, another vote took place the following year on the Compact alone. This turned out to be an opportunity to *really* confuse voters.

One reason that the Compact went down to defeat was the strong opposition from Jonathan Carter and his Forest Ecology Network when combined with forestry proponents usually on the other side of his issues. Another is, as Bob Deis, one of the most effective ballot measure operators in the entire country, puts it, "Competing measures have sometimes been successfully used as a strategy to defeat a measure, by creating more confusion and uncertainty about an issue."

Although the Compact had had the support of Governor King and some of the large landowners along with the NRCM, which took over and ran the campaign in 1997 along with the Audubon Society, it had been opposed by

SWOAM and other environmental groups such as the Sierra Club as well as Republican property rights conservatives as well.

On Election Day in 1997, after having been attacked from a variety of sides and entities, the Compact for Maine's Forests, worded on the ballot as "Do you want the Compact for Maine's Forests to become law to promote sustainable forest management practices throughout the state?" was defeated 52.5–47.5 percent. Ironically, that total was virtually the same percentage (47.6 percent) that the Compact had gotten the year before in the earlier three-way competition.

This example indicates that when it comes to authority figures in ballot measures, political authority figures are not usually persuasive, especially if the proposal is complex and multi-dimensional. Governor McKernan was unable to persuade voters in 1992 to support widening of the Maine Turnpike and according to opponents of the widening, became a target instead. In this case Governor King was not persuasive enough on the issue of the Compact to overcome all its flaws by himself. Voters may like their elected officials but still not find them persuasive on particular issues.

Why? First, they are injecting partisanship into the debate. A Democrat messenger will turn off a high percentage of Republicans. A Republican messenger turns off a high percentage of Democrats. And voters don't usually trust politicians or give them high credibility on specific issues. Voters may like their governor or any elected official but won't necessarily be persuaded by them on a particular measure. "She's doing a great job as governor, but I disagree with her on this issue."

In fairness to Governor King, he was successful changing minds in other ballot measure fights in Maine including the 2003 Casinos *NO!* effort where he starred in a television ad and played a very visible role. And in the Gay Rights referendum of 1995, he was very persuasive to women who worked at home, suburbanites, and Independents, albeit not persuasive to Franco men or males along the Maine coast. In general, it's a mistake to use political figures on bigger platforms with the general public, although they can successfully be narrow-cast.

Three years later in 2000, ANOTHER referendum pushed by Carter was held on requiring clearcutting permits. Called "An Act Regarding Forest Practices," it gave voters a clearer, binary choice. Initially the environmental groups were split. The Sierra Club, for example, supported the Carter proposal, but other environmental groups such as the Audubon Society were neutral (but later turned against it).

The anti-Carter effort enjoyed the strong support of SWOAM members and the paper companies. The NO side benefited from an extremely strong campaign team with Abby Holman as campaign manager, Jeff Romano, Jeff Toorish, and George Smith playing key roles, and Joe Cowie handling grass-roots and GOTV efforts. Cowie's efforts were instrumental in jacking up the anti-votes in the mill towns of Jay, Rumford, and Bucksport, areas that had underperformed in the 1996 and 1997 votes. Cowie is one field operative who always earned his money and then some. Jimmy Robbins and Steve Clarkin also played important roles in that campaign.

Finally, in 2000, when it became a case of dueling authority figures, SWOAM members would prove to be very efficacious for the NO side, more so than the other authority figures on the YES side. Extremely effective commercials by Erik Potholm included SWOAM members telling how much they loved the Maine land and wanted to preserve it and pass it on to future generations. "It's a lovely piece of ground, I want us to keep it that way."

Initially, polling in 2000 had shown that while the proposed measure started with a margin of 57–27 percent, when initially presented to voters and even after first being exposed to the anti-ideas, almost 2–1 (48–23 percent) still supported it, although the large number of undecided voters offered hope for an opportunity to change minds.

Most telling to me was that the early polling showed that 51 percent of Francos supported the Carter proposal, and 26 percent were undecided. But when the votes were eventually counted, the Francos would lead the way, opposing the Carter proposal (28.7 percent YES to 71.3 percent NO statewide). Indeed, Franco opposition would finally register a 2–1 margin NO vote in every Franco geographic breakout, including an astounding 5–1 drubbing in Aroostook's St. John Valley.

Knowing that landowners would be forced to cut timber every year or lose their harvesting rights was 7–1 negative, while knowing that a thousand miles of new woods roads would have to be built was 4–1 negative. Losing thirteen thousand forestry jobs statewide because of the proposal was 3–1 negative and "could cause increased sprawl" was 5–1 negative.

Authority figures abounded as Maine guides were 11–1 positive, SWOAM was 5–1 (with thirteen thousand members), the Director of the Maine Forest Service was 6–1 and the Dean of the University of Maine School of Forestry was 10–1.

The basic NO strategy was contained in its lead tag line, "Carter's Bad Idea: It's Even Worse Than You Thought. Vote No on 2."

As the campaign wore on, it began to start hitting on all cylinders. The TV was changing minds nightly, SWOAM members were doing great outreach, and the field preparations were all having effect. In late September, the

Maine Audubon Society announced its opposition to the Carter proposal saying, "Maine Audubon cannot support the referendum as drafted." There was significant SWOAM and Audubon membership overlap.

At the same time, the NO side headquarters rocked with mirth in late September when the NRCM endorsed the Carter referendum. The NRCM had torpedoed Carter's clearcutting ban ship in 1986, and Carter had returned the favor by torpedoing the NRCM's Compact ship in 1987. Now, after Carter's new 2000 vessel was taking on water from a nice three-torpedo spread from his opponents, and was listing badly to port, there was Brownie and company swimming toward it. Good theater.

As they paddled toward the soon-to-be shipwreck, Brownie Carson and the NRCM tried to assure SWOAM members that really, the measure they feared would not actually apply to them. Tough sell that, especially when their own forestry organization was now adamantly against the clearcutting proposal.

Equally important, though, was the Maine Audubon Society/Sportsman's Alliance spectrum of the Wild Wild East that kicked in again, pulling their respective constituencies together with six out of ten voters coming together to vote NO. It was going to be fun.

Our October 18 tracking poll showed the NO side was firmly ahead 57–27 percent, and I was elated. In keeping with the military metaphors flying around headquarters at the time, I wrote to the command-and-control group with considerable enthusiasm, beginning, "I love the smell of napalm in the morning." It was one of the joyous moments in those rare campaigns when you know you are going to win no matter what the other side can do or will do.

Unlike on election nights when you are normally so tired and relieved it is all coming to an end and your responsibility is over, in a situation like this with an insurmountable lead and plenty of firepower of your own still coming, you have a couple of weeks to enjoy the endgame. Those are the golden days. That is a sweet spot that doesn't come often, but when it does, you enjoy it immensely.

On Election Day, the Carter proposal was defeated 71.6–28.3 percent, so at least some of the earlier hyperbole and rash talk about sinking ships had been warranted.

Note: there is considerable irony in the cluster of these three ballot measures. As Karin Tilberg, head of the Forest Society of Maine, points out, the 1989 Maine Forest Practices Act was gradually implemented by the Maine Forest Service over several decades and "pretty successfully ended clearcutting in Maine" despite the defeat of the proposed bans.

IN BALLOT MEASURES, FEWER PRESS CONFERENCES ARE USUALLY A BETTER STRATEGY

As we saw in chapter 1, unlike in candidate campaigns where candidates try to get their hands on a public microphone at all costs, in ballot measures, one wants to avoid them because if one has a press conference the attending reporters will always check with opponents to get their side of the announcement. The result is usually mush or a tie at best, and in the public's mind nothing is gained. These "he said, she said" events are not worth the effort and are often counterproductive. Far better to use your good authority figures and influence vectors in your thirty-second ads.

A most amusing example of this occurred in the second Widening of the Maine Turnpike referendum in 1997. Several sympathetic reporters tipped off the YES side that Brownie Carson, then head of the NRCM, and one of the leaders of the NO side, had scheduled a press conference out by a toll booth on the Maine Turnpike. The YES side, led by Joe Cowie and Jim Betts, quickly assembled a team of counter-protesters who held up signs that read "Honk and Wave if You Support the Widening" and "Safety is a Quality of Life Issue," as Brownie gave his talk.

As cars whizzed by, many honked and waved, and the news story that night was not about whatever point Brownie had been trying to make but about the visuals of so many drivers honking and waving in favor of the widening of the highway. Reporters love drama, and there it was right in front of them, courtesy of Joe Cowie and Jim Betts.

Not surprisingly, Brownie looked angry and frustrated and hostile—not often a good look for the nightly news—in delivering whatever his message was.

So, final advice: whenever you get an urge to hold a press conference during a ballot measure campaign, especially one in the open air, go to the gym, work out, or take an ice-cold shower instead.

ASTROTURF BEATS REAL GRASSROOTS IN MOST BALLOT MEASURE CAMPAIGNS

Another shibboleth of ballot measures is the proposition that "Astroturf beats grassroots" in which you hire people to (1) get your issue on the ballot, (2) put up your lawn signs (if any), and (3) spend the bulk of your money on TV, relying on motivating voters that way.

In ballot measures you can often purchase all the trappings of a grassroots effort without the cost and problems of true grassroots campaigning—without all the usual concomitant tasks of the care and feeding of grassroots supporters and the difficult task of supervising them on a statewide basis. Lance Tapley called that kind of grassroots effort "Astroturf."

In Save Maine Yankee I, at Chuck Winner's direction, using the Maine driver's license list, the campaign mailed out cards urging people to sign up to keep Maine Yankee. Of course a lot of Mickey Mice and Donald Ducks dutifully returned their cards signed. In the end, Save Maine Yankee ended up with a campaign band of thirty thousand—then and I think still—the largest campaign group in Maine history. All for only $70,000 or so. Astroturf may be more expensive, but it does get the job done.

Also, while organizing candidate campaigns you can rely on worker bees from previous partisan efforts. In ballot measures there are usually no similar standing armies waiting to be mobilized.

A further differentiation between candidate campaigns and ballot measures is the differing targeting possibilities. In a candidate campaign you have the basic Republican/Democrat/Independent split. Imaginative candidate campaigns can add ethnic groups or religious groups or others as well.

In ballot measure efforts, targeting moves between R/D/I to psychographics groups (lifestyles and mindsets), giving a much wider range of possibilities for TV targeting. Such groups as "The Cruel Yuppies," "The Gold Coast Joggers," "Rich Republicans with Sailboats," and the "Nests of Back-to-Landers" can all be brought into play. Advertising firms love moving in these directions and often do their best work with them as they are freed up from the ideological constraints of partisan politics.

CONTROL POSSIBILITIES ARE MUCH GREATER

Perhaps the biggest difference between candidate and ballot measure campaigns is the degree of control the campaign can—and must—have. There is control over the extensive research opportunities at the front end of the cycle to let the research guide and then tightly control the messages, the authority figures, and the combinations of psychographic targeting.

You control the "out front," "public" face of the campaign and are not subject to the whims of a candidate. You also can control the makeup of the umbrella "steering" committee, the public face of the campaign. Of course the steering committee is not allowed to do *any* steering, and its members should be chosen for docility in that regard. One breaks this caveat at one's peril. You can control virtually *all* aspects of the media effort—TV, radio, print, direct mail—with no input from the partners, spouses, or friends of the candidate. It's marvelous.

That is why, from a consultant's point of view, all the above reasons add up to a marvelous package of possibilities that usually make ballot measures much, much more fun than candidate campaign ones. They give the consultant more authority and control, a situation that is always desirable from the consultant's point of view.

We close here with another interesting point about the differences between candidate and ballot measure campaigns and their degree of difficulty. This comes courtesy of Matt McTighe, who has been the astute campaign strategist and manager for both types. He served as director of the gay marriage referendum of 2012 and many other ballot measures, as well as the gubernatorial campaign of Mike Michaud in 2014.

He points out, "The real difference between the two is that with a candidate campaign, you are, at best, selling potential. You are asking voters to put their faith in what this person will possibly do. With ballot measures you are selling impacts and outcomes. If you vote *this* way, *that* will happen. Ballot measures are much simpler."

In the next chapters, we will be looking at the choices ballot measure operatives have in terms of choosing both authority figures (to deliver their messages) and influence vectors (to persuade the persuadable voters) as well as the role played by the fear factor.

AXIOM #9

"Fear Drives Out Favor" with Edie Smith

Hell, I never vote for anybody, I always vote against.
—W. C. FIELDS

In terms of ballot measure realities, the most powerful reality is the axiom "fear drives out favor." To have the NO side in any race is to have an advantage of +5 percent because if a voter is confused, she or he will vote NO at the end of the campaign. To have a successful ballot measure wanting a YES vote, usually you need to start at 60 percent.

One notable exception to this was the bond issue for public television in 1999. Most at the Maine Public Broadcasting station, WCBB, couldn't believe that any campaign had to run in favor of such a public good, but the initial polling showed only 40 percent of most likely voters willing to vote YES to digitalize public television. Assumptions that "everybody" supports public television, especially children's programming, proved suspect when Maine voters were polled on the need to spend tax dollars to keep it going.

Luckily, Rob Gardiner, then president of Maine Public Broadcasting Corporation at Channel 10, took matters into his own hands and decided to run an effective campaign to ensure that the bond passed. At this point, Gardiner had had a long and distinguished career, previously serving as the executive director of the Natural Resources Council of Maine (1978–1983), director of the Maine Bureau of Public Lands (1983–1987) and then president of the Maine Public Broadcasting Corporation. He showed the same quality of leadership in assembling a topflight campaign team led by George Campbell and Edie Smith and utilizing the media skills of Bob Cott of Creative Design and Marketing.

The decision was made to inject a considerable amount of fear into what had been viewed simply a "feel good" ballot measure by making it about "saving Big Bird." The concomitant television spot "Keeping Maine's PBS Alive," which suggested that without this bond Big Bird would go the way of the auk, was very persuasive. The ballot measure won with over 60 percent of the vote (64.3–35.6 percent). A significant turnaround.

"The campaign had turned public perception of the referendum question from a highbrow rescue plan for a station that already received lots of public donations to a campaign to save the hearts and minds of little children by saving Big Bird," said Edie Smith. "The fear of hurting our children overcame the favor of throwing money at a snooty TV station." Without Rob Gardiner providing the leadership he did, the bond might well have gone overconfidently down to defeat.

Saving Big Bird another time took the skill set of Pat Eltman, who when appearing before the Legislature's Appropriations Committee after it proposed cutting the funding for public television, opened a very big box and pulled out feather after feather—large yellow feathers. She then announced, "You just plucked Big Bird. Big Bird is no more." Appropriately shamed and laughing, the Appropriations Committee reinstated the money for public television.

Pat, one of the top Democratic GOTV specialists in the country, began her national work in 1983 working for the presidential campaign of Walter Mondale (and every Democratic one since then), and she is still at it doing significant political work at the local, state, and national levels. She has handled Maine gubernatorial, Senate, congressional, and state representative races and local contests with equal skill and dispatch, always setting the standard for "field" and "doors" and effective strategies at all levels. For almost fifty years she has been the "go-to" person to get things done in the political realm. Pat is one of the great Maine operatives known to one and all. Her spirit name, "She Who Must Be Obeyed," tells you everything you need to know about her.

The fear driving out favor principle was very successfully used by the "Stop the Widening of the Maine Turnpike" referendum of 1991. It called for the "deauthorization of the widening of the Maine Turnpike." Despite many traffic studies showing the need for widening the two lanes to three south of Portland and many public figures endorsing the project—from Governor McKernan to police and safety officials as well as business leaders—the much-needed project was defeated by a very effective campaign run by opponents.

Alan Caron was the campaign manager, while Brownie Carson and Tom LaPointe were skillful leaders both in terms of the media, free media, and grassroots efforts. Dave Vail, Rick Freeman, and Lloyd Irland also authored an important report supporting congestion pricing (variable tolls) to shift traffic away from peaks.

Carson has been a major player in Maine politics over three decades, particularly on environmental matters. Not only did he oppose the widening of the Maine Turnpike, but he also opposed the construction of the Dickey Lincoln and Big A dams and as executive director of the NRCM, he would be instrumental in a host of environmental initiatives and always focused on making Maine's water, air, and land better than it had been. Although he channeled Savonarola a bit too many times for many insiders, he was always a force to be reckoned with.

The anti-widening side offered all sorts of appealing alternatives to more cars and more pollution—boats, carpooling, et cetera—and cast great doubt on the need for the project throughout the rest of the state. Some of it, of course, was pure pixie dust. Can you imagine the family from Boston stopping in Kennebunk, leaving their car, and boarding a boat for a leisurely sail up to their destination in Bar Harbor in order to reduce traffic on the Maine Turnpike?

But it was great messaging on TV that turned the debate around by playing to the adage "fear drives out favor." To this day I can still close my eyes and see a white-clad Karin Tilberg looking like a Druid priestess, standing out by a marsh, calling on one and all to save the "sacred wetlands" as we called them. On the news, she stood beside them, talked of their virtues and how they must be saved. Tilberg, a member of Maine Audubon, was a very believable authority figure on the news and in the free media. In these early stages the anti-widening forces were supported by a coalition of thirty environmental groups.

Even all the media wizardry of Chuck Winner and company, called back to Maine from California after his highly successful Save Maine Yankee campaign, could not get Maine people to vote for the widening. Barbara Trafton, a leading Maine environmentalist, served as a very resolute and effective campaign chair, and Roger Mallar and Tony Buxton provided first-rate leadership as well.

Bob Deis, who was the on-the-ground presence for Winner Wagner during the widening referendum, said this unfortunately was an example of a client not taking good advice. "We tried to keep McKernan from speaking out on the turnpike, but he insisted on being in some of the ads, and he ended up poisoning the well and the opponents did a good job of taking advantage of it."

Alan Caron's polling showed that the environmental opposition ran its course early on, and the deauthorization effort needed to broaden its base of support. He shifted focus to the needed road, bridge, and other projects statewide and framed the debate as an opportunity to send a message about waste and inefficiency in government.

It was the very powerful and effective closer commercial ad written by Caron and produced by the Washington firm Joe Slade White, which won the day. As Caron says,

I remember that ad because it led to record voter enrollment across the state in the last week, and because I wrote it. We had a Washington firm doing the production, but on our script. When they sent it back somewhat softened, I wouldn't run it until they got it right. That ad, in my mind, moved the numbers by at least fifteen points in the last week.

It also generated a massive inflow of campaign funds so that in the final days of the campaign, it averaged eighteen to twenty views per viewer per day.

The ad was devastating.

Telling viewers the project was "gold plated" and would cost $100 million, the ad said it could be stopped if people would only vote NO and "send a message" to politicians like Governor McKernan who had promoted the widening in an earlier ad. The commercial occurred during an election cycle when voters were highly distrustful of government. It became a defining message to just say NO to them for any and all sins.

The masterful anti-widening commercial turned the election around and the widening project went down to a frustrating 59–41 percent defeat—along with our tip of the cap to the professionals on the other side who utilized their advantages so effectively and framed the debate so cogently in their favor.

In an interesting follow-up to this effort, Karin Tilberg would go on to prove that she could save dry land as well as wet, sacred, or otherwise. Subsequently as the head of the Forest Society of Maine, she would be part of a major effort to stabilize the Great North Woods by getting, and overseeing, one million acres under conservation easements.

A few years later in 1997 when I did some exploratory polling work for Dana Connors and the Maine State Chamber of Commerce, Maria Fuentes and the Maine Better Transportation Association, and others still interested in the widening, I found out which wetlands had been utilized so effectively by Karin Tilberg.

I was driven out to see them firsthand. Imagine my surprise when I discovered that "the sacred wetlands" were actually the six-foot-wide drainage ditches alongside the existing highways. I was floored. Drainage ditches masquerading as sacred wetlands. Genius. It doesn't get any better than that in our business. I was very impressed with that frame. The second time around would require maximum effort to be successful in the face of such wizardry.

We showed the new polling about the widening to Governor King and his staff and asked to have a new referendum on the subject that the legislature put out to the voters. As Maria Fuentes, the very talented campaign manager for the YES side remembers, "There were many groups such as the Chamber and some agency people who worked hard to make sure the legislature sent it out to the people. But the campaign was a new ballgame."

Dana Connors was the overall head of the effort as chairman, and he and Maria deployed a very skillful press and ground-game team, including Joe Cooper, Chris Esposito, Jeff Romano, Joe Cowie, and Anna Lidman. A very vital campaign staffer was Jim Betts, who had worked to defeat the widening in 1991 and was known to friend and foe as "King of the Street."

"We had a great team and the best media company in the country," Maria says, "so we covered all our bases, but we didn't know what the opposition was going to do this time around. We went for a full-court press."

The YES side knew we had to come on strong and wipe out the residual opposition from the previous vote. Erik Potholm came up with an outstanding media strategy, and in a series of very effective commercials using EMTs, firemen, and ambulances getting stuck in actual traffic jams at 5 P.M. outside Biddeford on the Turnpike, upping the fear quotient for one and all. Even today the commercials remain powerful and emotionally charged.

In effect, the YES side would be using more fear to drive out all the other side's previous fears! Heart attacks versus sacred wetlands—priceless!

The resulting commercials were amazingly effective as Erik Potholm and his team tapped a deep emotional chord, hitting a fear that trumped the other fear of tax revenues spent on a road.

As one of the EMT guys in the ambulance so powerfully put it, "There is nothing worse than trying to get somebody to the hospital to save their life and then get stuck in traffic."

Virtually every night these commercials played, and they changed minds. So effective were they that I still remember the soft data one of our callers tabulated. An elderly gentleman from Bar Harbor said he had voted against the turnpike widening last time around but this time was voting for it. When pressed, he told the caller, "Look, I've got a bad ticker, and if I have to be rushed to the hospital with a heart attack, I sure don't want to get stuck in traffic."

Leaving aside—or actually celebrating—the fact that if he was in Bar Harbor, he would be trucked to Ellsworth or Bangor hospitals and never would he be on the highway off Biddeford, you have to say, "Well, I guess that was an effective message if it frightened him enough to vote YES."

This time the widening side got 60.6 percent. Fear drives out favor. And personal fear even drives out other fears like the loss of even "sacred wetlands."

The 1987 campaign for Land for Maine's Future used a similar approach after focus groups showed real concern on the part of Maine voters that they were losing their land and its heritage to sprawl and changing land use patterns. The initial idea for this implementation of the effort to save Maine land for future generations came from Angus King and is probably his greatest contribution to the state. He enlisted the help of Pat McGowan and Dick Barringer and took the concept to Governor McKernan and his right-hand man Bob Moore. Carol Baudler of the national Nature Conservancy and Kent Womack and Mason Morfit of the Maine chapter decided to go all in and run a campaign worthy of the goals involved. Others instrumental in its passage were Bill Townsend and George Smith of SAM.

Roger Williams of Roger Williams Advertising then produced an excellent series of ads built around that fear of losing public access after a productive focus group in Lewiston showed real Maine people really feared the loss of access to their favorite spots in nature. Williams came up with three dynamite ads for Citizens to Save Maine's Heritage, one "Signs," a second "People," and a third "Bud Leavitt."

Each ad concluded with a big iron gate crashing down and cutting off the public from a scenic waterway. Jane Williams and Betty Angell did a masterful job in ad placement where swing and undecided voters would see the ads the most. Nightly tracking polls showed their impact in real time and measured progress among the various demographic and psychographic groups.

In a parallel effort, George Smith led the Sportsman's Alliance of Maine (SAM) in strong support of the bond as well, reaching out to hunting and fishing groups all across the state.

Bud Leavitt, outdoor writer for the *Bangor Daily News* and sometime fishing companion of Ted Williams—it is said in parts of Maine that "Ted Williams fished with Bud Leavitt, not Bud Leavitt fished with Ted Williams"—turned out to be a most effective authority figure. Writing an outdoor column for forty-six years, and a widely read and beloved book, *Twelve Months in Maine*, as well as hosting a popular TV show, *The Bud Leavitt Show*, his appeal crossed many demographic groups and bridged the gap in this election between the hunting and fishing community and the environmental groups.

Over and over, with much gravitas, he intoned the somber message, "If we don't make more Maine land public, someone else will make it private.

Vote YES." In the ads, Maine people across the state pointed to real Maine places where access had been denied and what needed to be saved.

Bud hit a walk-off grand-slam home run for the home team with that message.

The bond campaign with its $35 million price tag won convincingly by the margin of 64.9–35.1 percent and set up a pattern of successful land acquisition bonds in the future and establishing the Land for Maine's Future Board. The Nature Conservancy and Audubon were the lead groups supporting and raising money for that first bond and established a precedent of winning public access that still offers hope for Maine's future. Without Carol Baudler from the national Nature Conservancy putting the team together and keeping it that way, the project would not have been a success.

Fear was also the central driver of the much closer assisted suicide vote in 2000, but only after a series of positive messages had set the stage for their use. At one point, public polling had assisted suicide ahead 70–20 percent, so it was very important to show voters the extent to which there were alternatives. Nurses, doctors, and other health care workers talked convincingly about palliative care and Maine Hospice, led by Kandyce Powell, explained that help was already present for those dying.

Also instrumental in that campaign: the Roman Catholic Diocese, Marc Mutty, and especially Juliana L'Heureux, who represented both the Diocese and the nurses. Edie Smith was the outstanding campaign director for George Campbell and his Governmental Services, while Erik Potholm handled the media with skill and dispatch.

But even after all the positive influence vectors had been used on TV, the measure allowing for assisted suicide was still headed for victory. Then very powerful ads, highlighting the possible future roles of HMOs in the dying process, abuses in the similar law already in place in Oregon, and especially the closer ad that underscored that under the proposed law, suicide pills could be sent through the mail, were powerful vectors. The closer featured a teenage girl going to the mailbox and taking out such a shipment, and that turned the tide. The little girl reaching for the suicide pills in the mailbox proved to be a powerful and enduring image, one that changed numerous minds at the end.

Undecided voters thought about all these perils and turned the tide during the final week. The assisted suicide referendum saw the NO side eking out a 51–49 percent squeaker.

The Bear Hunting Ban referendum of 2004 was another ballot measure in which fear drove out favor quite effectively, but it turned out not the fear you might suppose. Edie Smith also ran that one.

Before we deal with the "fear factor" in this election, it is important to lay out that the emphasis on this dimension, while key to the close outcome, could only have come into play with the NO side down by 2–1 if there had not been a very coherent and professional overall effort to get within striking distance.

Edie Smith, then head of the Eaton Peabody Consulting Group, faced an almost impossible challenge and a well-financed ($1 million) Humane Society of the United States (HSUS) effort to eliminate bear baiting, hounding, and trapping. She put together a truly extraordinary effort under the umbrella committee, "Maine's Fish and Wildlife Conservation Council," which had tested very well. Edie's field director, Will Gardiner, did a masterful job of bringing together the disparate parts to make a coherent whole out of the 14,500 members of Maine's Fish and Wildlife Conservation Council, the Maine Professional Guides Association, the Maine Trappers Association, the Sportsman's Alliance of Maine, and Eve Rice and the 975 women of SWIM (Sporting Women in Maine).

Edie and her brother, the executive director of SAM, George Smith, also put on a fundraising clinic, going from nowhere to over $3 million from people all over Maine and the United States who saw the referendum as a direct threat to their hunting heritage. Every time the National Humane Society upped the ante, they matched it. Every time the national Humane Society floated in new TV buys under the radar, they caught them in the act.

George Smith tapped into his national contacts to make sure they realized what was at stake in Maine. Rob Sexton and the US Sportsmen's Alliance, Sandy and Joe Hosmer of the Safari Club International and many others such as Skip Trask and Ed and Cate Pineau responded to the call as well.

Governor Baldacci, too, deserves a great deal of credit. When the bear biologists and other members of the Maine Department of Inland Fisheries and Wildlife were threatened with a gag order, and even some of his own staff wanted him to stay out of the fray, the governor stood tall and supported his notion of "science, not emotion or politics" should determine game management in the state of Maine.

He insisted that the people who know the bears the best needed to be heard. Dick Davies and Paul Jacques were also invaluable in the entire effort, as was the Department of Inland Fisheries and Wildlife whose members stood up to those who would make game management a perpetual political food fight in the legislature.

As media consultant Erik Potholm rightly anticipated that the proponents would use the most graphic and heart-wrenching scenes of bears trapped and snared and persecuted, he countered with a very effective series of ads featuring wildlife professionals.

The media stars of the NO side included the state's bear biologist, Jennifer Vashon, who taught the cruel yuppies of the south a valuable scientific lesson while Jack Knight, Gloria Curtis, Craig McLaughlin, and Tenley Meara, Bowdoin's own registered Maine Guide, projected credibility and authority.

For his part, Dave Emery did a truly magnificent job in his tracking polls, picking up even small movements along the voter net. He remains one of the few pollsters who are consistently able to project outcomes when the voting patterns are turnout driven. Seldom has anyone so carefully calculated and calibrated an election outcome with such a high voter turnout. In this case, the higher the turnout the better for the NO forces, and on Election Day, as Maine voters hit the 70 percent level, the tide turned decisively. Emery was once again right on target.

In terms of the print media, Maine's premier outdoor writers such as Paul Reynolds and Tom Hennessey were effective in combating the propaganda and emotional attacks of non-hunters. Except for the *Portland Press Herald,* all the major dailies urged a NO vote. The Portland paper weighed in heavily in support of the YES side in editorials, columns, and reporting. Fair enough, but then they had the gall to refuse to have their editorial board even *meet* with opponents, including the state's bear biologist! That was a sad day for balanced journalism indeed.

It was a tough, hard, bruising campaign with many dimensions, rather like playing chess on five or six boards at once.

Through it all, Edie Smith masterfully controlled the action, directed the allocation of resources, and kept her side on the winning strategy. Edie deserves a place in the Maine political hall of fame. She's done it all—fundraising, signature gathering, GOTV, and campaign managing not just candidates but ballot measures in Maine and elsewhere (I also sent her to Florida and Virginia for the Nature Conservancy, and she won both of those). Most importantly, she managed three of the toughest fought and closest campaigns yet—Casinos *NO!*, assisted suicide, and bear hunting. That is why she is known to political insiders as "The Queen of the South—and the North."

She remembers the bear-hunting referendum as her most difficult and satisfying campaign:

Our opponents included Cecile Gray, John Glowa, Darryl DeJoy, and Robert Fisk and named their coalition "Maine Friends of Animals" and "Citizens for Fair Bear Hunting." They also used the word CRUEL over and over and over and over. It was their mantra. Baiting, hounding, and trapping are CRUEL. We raised over $3 million. Back in 2000, that was a gasp-worthy amount. Paul Jacques was deputy commissioner of DIF&W; Dick Davies was a senior advisor to Governor Baldacci. Both were very helpful.

When the national organization, Humane Society of the United States (HSUS) entered Maine in 2004, they came loaded for bear (pun intended). They were intent on stopping bear hunting in our state, starting with three of the most popular (and effective) methods: baiting, hounds, and traps.

HSUS was not your local animal shelter—in fact, they had nothing to do with any shelters in Maine. They were a national fundraising and lobbying machine with an agenda to stop hunting and to make money. They saw Maine as a relatively inexpensive state to sponsor a referendum campaign due to our small voting population and our (relatively speaking) inexpensive media market.

While they found Mainers to act as spokespeople (Cecile Gray, John Glowa, Darryl DeJoy, Robert Fisk), they made the mistake of hiring a campaign manager from Massachusetts—Katie Hansberry, an attorney who practiced litigation in Massachusetts and graduated from Bowdoin College. Not a hunter. Not even close.

HSUS and Hansberry spent a year portraying bear guides and bear hunters as slovenly, lazy hunters who were killing the precious bears. HSUS and Hansberry called Maine bear hunters murderers. It was a smear campaign. So how do you fight a smear campaign based on emotion? You wage a truth campaign ultimately based on fear. Fear drives out favor.

Polling showed us we had to concentrate our message on baiting. People misunderstood what baiting really was—they thought it was throwing a bunch of donuts in the middle of the woods, then sit and wait for the bear to come. We had to educate Mainers, especially those in southern Maine, that bear baiting was a regulated form of hunting, with rules and regulations. Bear hunters in Maine were conservationists and just all-around great guys and gals.

Polling also showed us that we would lose if we talked about hounds and traps. Very few black bears were taken by those methods, so they weren't instrumental in managing the huge number of bears in Maine (around thirty thousand). They also conjured up much more emotion around the issue of cruelty to bears. So—we never said "hounds" or "traps."

We had the facts behind us, namely that bear baiting was highly regulated and also the best way to get a clean shot at a bear, making sure that you were shooting an adult bear and not a cub.

We had an amazing team behind our NO effort—groups such as the Sportsman's Alliance of Maine, Maine Professional Guides Association, Fish and Wildlife Clubs from every corner of Maine, with the management team, including George Smith, Skip Trask, Don Kleiner, Chris Potholm, and James Cote. James cut his young teeth on this campaign and then went on to be hired as the campaign manager in 2014 when a similar question, again sponsored by HSUS, appeared in Maine.

James did a masterful job in 2014 defeating the question and sending HSUS on their way with their tail between their legs. James is now one of the best lobbying and political advocates in Maine, especially when it comes to issues of Maine's outdoors. Media was handled by the second-to-none firm of SRCP Media, led by the brilliant Erik Potholm.

The bear-hunting ban side focused almost entirely on the fear side—of what the bear hunt did to bears. They were chased by dogs, caught in traps, lured by donuts, and then killed, all unnecessarily in their view. In fact, some respondents in focus groups were convinced they were chased by dogs into traps and then shot.

These assertions, quite naturally, turned voters against the practice and given the fact that this was the late twentieth century, it seemed to make a good deal of sense that the whole idea of hunting bears—by any means—was more than a tad anachronistic. It was unnecessary, it was cruel, and it was horrible. Proponents of the bear-hunting ban played the fear card and played it very well.

That is why, perhaps, the proponents of keeping the bear hunt made only little headway with some of their arguments. Maine's bear biologists, especially Vashon, made her scientific assertion that Maine's black bear population was simply too large for the carrying capacity of its range. She stated that it required a yearly hunt that, in turn, needed the methods employed because black bears were not readily encountered the way deer or moose were. Her assertion made some progress.

In this context, effective ads such as "Bear Reel" and "Biologists" by Erik Potholm showing a very concerned animal control officer asking for help in the face of mounting bear-human interactions again had some effect on the numbers but still, the YES side maintained a meaningful lead.

More fear was needed. A black bear had been sighted in a school yard in South Portland, and the resulting "Bear Fear" ad drew accusations from the YES side that the NO side had recently trapped a bear in northern Maine and trucked it south to film it in the schoolyard, mercifully after school hours. The NO side pleaded "Not guilty" but had a good laugh about it.

But the one ad that really stuck in my mind and in others—and those generations of Bowdoin students were forced to listen to it over and over, even though the vote had long passed—was called, cleverly, we thought, "Bear Eats Baby."

Edie Smith describes how it came about:

Erik and I were standing in a conference room at Eaton Peabody in Augusta, holding a videotape a woman from Aroostook County had sent us.

It was a video she and her husband had taken of a bear attacking a baby moose and hauling it off into the woods in its mouth. Talk about the perfect killer ad . . . but the video was shaky, and the bear and unlucky baby moose were off in the distance and often a bit blurry.

Darn—what to do? Erik said to me, "Close your eyes." And then he played the shaky video with us just hearing the audio. "Ohmygosh, look at that bear—ohmigosh, the bear is headed for the baby, ohmigosh, the bear has the baby, the bear took the baby, the bear took the baby!!!!" said an anguished woman.

That final thirty-second ad was just a black screen. Then you heard the woman screaming.

"Oh look. Look. It's a bear. A big bear. Oh. Look at it. Look, it's going after the baby. No, oh no, no, not the baby, Oh no."

At this point an equally disturbed but firm radio announcer (known as "the Voice of God") intoned, "This time it was a baby moose. Next time it could be a real baby."

What fun!

But as Election Day approached, bear fear had been used up, exhausted. It had done its job, but more fear and fear of a different kind had to be employed because of the huge vote deficits being run up in the Portland DMA where city folk saw no real black bear threats, even to their birdfeeders.

Gloria Curtis was the grandmother who came on the TV begging voters not to stop the bear hunt. She was the sole provider for her two grandchildren. Her business was catering to hunters, especially bear hunters. "Without the bear hunt, I'll be out of business, and we'll have to go on welfare. Please don't do that."

This ad entitled "Bear Grandmother and Granddaughter" was significantly persuasive in southern Maine, so although the NO side would still lose in Cumberland and York counties and tie in Sagadahoc, it would be by a much smaller margin than before the TV ad ran.

The NO side would carry the day in all other counties on the way to a victory of 54–46 percent, losing only Cumberland and York counties and tying in Sagadahoc. All the other counties voted NO with Aroostook leading the way with 65 percent of the vote.

For Edie Smith, this election night November 2004 was her proudest moment:

In Brewer, we had a huge room full of Maine bear hunters, who had been maligned in the press for over a year and were scared to death of losing not only their livelihoods, but their dignity. They couldn't understand why the people of Maine would believe all the lies told about them and their methods of keeping Maine's bear population in check.

We had warned the crowd that we wouldn't know the final numbers until the wee hours of the morning, since the larger towns and cities reported first, and they would lean YES on the question. The rural areas and our base of support would report later in the evening. I kept calming the crowd throughout the evening whenever a town's numbers came in that were a "NO."

The NO votes and YES votes were neck and neck throughout the evening. But around 1:30 A.M., the NOs started taking hold. And at 2:30 A.M., as I was surrounded by big, burly bear hunters desperate to have their lives restored, the TV stations started calling the race, and announced the NO votes won 53 to 47 percent.

As the final votes were announced, I started feeling all these arms around me as the guys and gals started hugging me—like a massive group hug. Tears streaming down their faces, thanking me and my team for believing in them and believing in their heritage. They had been vindicated by the voters of Maine.

That was my proudest moment. It was when I realized that I had truly helped these wonderful people. Me and my team. Feeling the gratitude and love in that room at 2:30 in the morning will be a feeling I will never forget.

Dave Emery remembers that night very vividly as well:

I remember the very somber and funereal gathering in Brewer that evening as the early returns came in. The assembled group of bear hunters and Maine Guides were convinced they were losing badly. They didn't believe me when I assured them they were actually winning.

The early returns from southern Maine were indeed grim, but as soon as the central and northern Maine vote began to come in, the NO side pulled ahead for good. I knew from the votes coming in from the 2nd CD, and particularly those from Androscoggin, Penobscot, and Aroostook counties, that we were winning.

Small towns and Franco-American voters from northern Maine strongly supported bear hunting. The hunters and guides who had not left the party early in disgust were incredulous, and very grateful, when the returns finally flipped to NO.

Note: several years later my wife Sandy and I while driving in northern Maine stopped in Patten. There in the general store there was still a poster of the Vote NO campaign. "Our son Erik did that," we said proudly. The proprietor answered quickly and with feeling, "Your son saved Patten, Maine."

It doesn't get better than that on the campaign trail.

Of course that gave the axiom a new dimension: "If one kind of fear doesn't get the job done, add another kind." I'm quite sure the YES side banked on "fear driving out favor" and used it effectively to blunt the upside potential of the NO vote but in the end, a different kind of fear prevailed.

Perhaps the best example of fear(s) driving out favor was the Palesky Tax Cap referendum of 2004, an effort designed to put a curb on rising property taxes across the state.

Who wouldn't want to lower or cap property taxes?

Out of the box it was extremely popular. The provisions were simple and straightforward and very appealing.

Thus, 2004 saw a very popular concept—the reduction of property taxes—thrust upon the Maine political stage. Carol Palesky and her Maine Taxpayers Action Network gathered over fifty thousand signatures to cap property taxes at $10 per $1,000 of property. The Maine legislature punted on the proposal and sent the very popular measure (70 percent approval) out to the voters. Governor Baldacci was under considerable pressure to put the measure out for a vote in June of that year, a moment when it was most likely to win, and facing reelection in two years, he was urged to stay out of what looked like a most popular issue with voters.

Instead, he courageously insisted that the vote be held in November and then put together a campaign team of note, choosing his former chief of staff, Larry Benoit, as campaign manager. Benoit, one of the top staffers in recent Maine history, was also an unusual political operative for being highly successful at both candidate and ballot measure elections (such as the TABOR and People's Veto of the tax reform law). Most campaign managers are either good at one or the other. Larry also ran independent expenditures.

He worked for Peter Kyros, Ed Muskie, and then managed George Mitchell's highly successful 1982 and 1988 senatorial campaigns. He was also Sergeant at Arms of the US Senate and chief of staff for John Baldacci. I have always felt that Larry did not get the credit he deserved for steering the 1982 campaign which began with Senator Mitchell facing a 35 percent deficit in the public polls and 20 percent in his own.

In the Palesky referendum, he hired Dennis Bailey to do the press and media relations. Benoit also kept the fractious coalition of the Maine Municipal Association, the Maine Education Association, the AFL-CIO and AARP together—no easy task.

The Maine Chamber of Commerce led by Dana Connors also assisted and Martha Freeman, head of the State Planning Office as well as Jonathan Rubin and Todd Gabe compiled the devastating "kitty casino" kill switch that if the Palesky proposal passed, the sales tax would have to increase by 80 percent and the income tax by 64 percent just to keep the current levels of municipal services across the state.

Talk about fear driving out favor: images of police and fire cuts and educational shortfalls drove many sectors of the Maine electorate into opposition as the Anti-Tax Cap coalition showed more and more commercials highlighting the disastrous consequences of its passage. Even conservative Republicans such as George Smith, who wrote a powerful column indicating why those who wanted tax relief should vote against the tax cap, became energized. As Dennis Bailey relates:

> On the tax cap, I remember that it began turning around when we pointed out that out-of-state owners of camps and beachfront condos would also be getting a big tax break, and Maine taxpayers would have to make up the difference to repair the roads, fund the schools, and so on. It turned what looked like a measure for the hard-pressed middle class into a gift for the wealthy.

Phil Harriman, who favored the measure as a protest when the legislature failed to act, remembers the mood switch in voter sentiment:

> The turning point was when I received a call from a client who wanted me to hear it from him first that he was donating a significant sum of money to defeat the question. You know when money pours in and the Chamber of Commerce and pro-government associations are on the same team you are going to lose.

This campaign resulted in an overwhelming victory for Governor Baldacci and could not have been achieved without his leadership. By a margin of 64–36 percent Maine people voted down a proposition that earlier had a 70 percent approval rating. Fear of unintended consequences firmly drove out the favor for property tax relief.

Incidentally, this "fear of losing existing services and benefits" strategy was also used in the various referenda previously, most notably in the 1971 effort to repeal the state income tax. It failed by a margin of 75–25 percent when this tactic was utilized.

One final "fear" ad—this one with no Potholm paw prints on it. In 1986, New England Telephone wanted to pass a referendum to promote "measured service." Jack Havey and his team of John Christie and Beryl Ann Johnson did the advertising in favor of measured service.

But Ralph Nader cut a simple, but extremely effective, commercial based on the fear of "having a pay phone in every home." If I remember correctly, it was the only TV ad the NO side ran, but it was more than devastating and the NO side won by a considerable margin.

So Maine political history is shot full of successful ballot measure campaigns that used the powerful influence vectors which produced fear in the voters and led to the adage "fear drives out favor."

But finally, we should note that as Bob Deis observes there are real limits to fear, especially false fear:

> Some zealots on an issue think tricks and deception are acceptable to achieve their goals and that voters can easily be fooled with scare tactics.
>
> In 1987, for example, in that nuclear shut-down effort, the antinuclear zealots tried to make voters think Maine would be the site of a federal high-level nuclear waste dump if Maine Yankee continued to operate. They ran slickly produced ads purportedly showing a supposed radioactive waste container falling off a truck on the way to that future dump. They also sent mail to people in various towns telling them—falsely—that their community had been selected as the site for a nuclear waste dump.
>
> In fact, the claim that the continued operation of Maine Yankee had anything to do with the federal decisions on dump siting was totally and demonstrably false. I remember saying that to their lead political consultant, who considered himself to be a clever hotshot. He responded by saying, "Perception is reality, Bob."
>
> In today's post-Trump era, that may seem prescient. But when it comes to ballot measure proposals, as opposed to candidates, it's an oversimplification. Most voters start out being wary of controversial measures they have to try to figure out and vote on. And, most still have reasonably good bullshit detectors when promoters—or opponents—of a measure are making extreme and alarming claims.

Deis does have a valid point as widespread efforts to raise the specter of "Furries," people thinking they were animals or pretending to be such creatures, taking over restrooms as well as BIW and other defense contractors turned out very much to be a non-starter "fear" in the New Hampshire senatorial and the Maine 1st CD congressional races in 2022. Indeed, the claims of "Furries" ascending brought down quite a measure of ridicule on the heads of those raising the "threat."

"If It's Not on TV, It's Not Real:
The Centrality of Media" with Erik Potholm

Let everyone, then, have the right to tell their story in their own way.
—IGNAZIO SILONE

O f all the elements of ballot measures, the one that gets the most attention usually—and rightly so—is the media. It is always a vital element in ballot measures, and in contested ones it is the most important one. As Jonathan Crowley rightly points out, the thirty-second spot is the bread and butter of campaigns generally and of ballot measures particularly. TV spots are also the most glamorous and almost always the most expensive portion of a campaign budget.

I have been very fortunate to work with a number of high-quality media firms all across the country, ad creators such as Stuart Stevens (New York), Will Robinson (Washington), Luckie and Company (Atlanta), Kohnke and Koeneke (Minneapolis), Brown Inc. (Santa Fe), Michael White and Associates (Portland Oregon), Mullen and McCaffrey (South Hampton), and Sanome Partners (San Francisco), among others. Watching them turn polling findings into images on film has been very rewarding and illuminating. In the process, I learned just how good our Maine and Maine-inspired firms can be when it comes to creating powerful ads that convert viewers.

To initially interest the reader, we list here some of the best commercials in Maine produced in order to win or defeat a referendum. There are many others, of course, and the interested reader and certainly most of the consultants listed in this work would have equally persuasive commercials to tout.

When it comes to commercials, we are all experts, each of the consultants mentioned in this book and not just those of us in politics but just about everybody else. We know what we like. We know what we think are effective, often based on how we react to them.

But this list is different in that it is based on weekly or nightly tracking, which actually recorded their impact on the Maine electorate. When these were on the air you could see the numbers changing, literally before your eyes. Other political observers and consultants may have additional commercials equally well tracked (and hopefully future editions of the book can reflect them), but these are the ones I'm confident were measured enough so their standing is firm. The list is chronological rather than being in a rank order:

"Professor Hughes on Maine Yankee" (Chuck Winner, 1980) Save Maine Yankee
"Chuck" (Jack Havey, 1983) Moose Hunt
"A Pay Phone in Every House" (Ralph Nader, 1986) New England Telephone Measured Service
"Bud Leavitt: Signs are Everywhere" (Roger Williams, 1987) Land for Maine's Future Bond
"The Issue is Choice" (Bob Cott, 1990) Sunday Sales
"Gold Plated Highway" (Alan Caron/Dave Dickson, 1991) Stop the Turnpike Widening
"It's Just Not Maine" (Will Robinson, 1995) Special Rights
"EMT Stuck in Traffic" (Erik Potholm, 1997) Widen the Maine Turnpike
"Little Girl and Suicide Pills" (Erik Potholm, 2000) Physician-Assisted Suicide
"Bear Hunting Grandmother" (Erik Potholm, 2004) Bear Hunting
"Harlan Gardner: Four Generations Machias" (David Loughran, 2012) Gay Marriage

Looking at all of them together, there are some commonalities. First, these ads all have high concentrations of emotion, emotion that impacted the voters and moved them from one position to another.

Second, with a couple of exceptions, they all have what are called "high production values." They are clear, the voices are authoritative, and they are "clean" with few distractions. They tell with feeling and strength and clarity what the viewer is supposed to do—and all these ads proved that they could.

I have learned a great deal working with some terrific media people who have done work in Maine—people like Chris Duval, Will Robinson, Greg Stevens, Mike Harkins, Jack Havey, Al Caron, Mark Harroff, Roger Williams, Bob Cott, Dan Payne, Chuck Winner, Bob Deis, Paul Mandabach, and Dan Osgood. Top guns.

But none, as the unsolicited testimonials in this work will attest, have been more effective than my son Erik over a variety of campaigns. It has been one of the great pleasures of my life to work with him on a lot of successful ballot measures in Maine—Widening the Maine Turnpike, Physician-Assisted Suicide, Bear Hunt Ban I, the Research and Development Bond and Casinos *No!*, along with many others.

Here is Erik's take on the keys to political advertising, how he broke into the business, and the importance of having great mentors in life:

Some of the best advice I got in politics came from the legendary Doug Bailey. Doug was one of the first Republican political ad makers in the business. His firm, Bailey Deardorff and Associates, was a powerhouse consulting firm in the 1970s and 1980s. Doug was a true visionary and went on to become founder of the political Hotline—a bipartisan, daily briefing on American politics. Today, there are all kinds of daily political email briefings, but the Hotline was the original and you could only receive it by fax.

I took a class Doug taught at George Washington University on political advertising. His class bolstered my initial interest in advertising. When I asked him for his advice on how to break into the industry, he said, "Find a mentor, that's the key." He was right. That was the key.

I've been very lucky to have a lot of great mentors. Right out of college, I worked for Bob Deis of Winner Mandabach campaigns. He's a great political strategist, excellent writer, and truly one of the best in the business when it comes to sharpening the message in ballot measures. He taught me many keys to winning referenda and I've always carried those lessons with me.

Then there was Greg Stevens, a Maine native, and one of the true icons in the political advertising business—he created the famous Dukakis tank ad in the 1988 presidential race. Greg took me under his wing and gave me a front-row seat to high-profile US Senate and gubernatorial races around the country. Another example of how small the political world is with its Maine connections is that my dad had hired Greg Stevens to be Bill Cohen's Maine field director in his 1978 Senate race.

Greg taught me the keys to developing effective advertising and I saw how he ran a successful advertising agency which would help me years later. The most important lesson he taught me was that quality matters in advertising. He believed in high-production values because you are competing not just with political ads, but also corporate ads in the marketplace. And people will receive impressions about your candidate based on the quality of the ad—how it looks and feels to them. It's not a good first impression if the candidate's ad looks cheap and poorly produced. Like a used-car commercial.

The audience will see that and make a certain judgment. To that end, Greg believed in hiring the most talented and creative people (directors of photography, editors, producers, music composers, etc.) in the business to ensure that the final product had the highest production values. And his best advice was to invest in people and retain them—don't let them go in the off-season. Your firm's work will benefit by having talented and experienced people who know what they are doing. To this day, we often quote Greg's key lessons when we are facing an important decision at our firm.

Of course, the most important mentor in my life has been my dad. He strongly "encouraged" me to volunteer on campaigns when I was in middle school (even though I wanted to be out on Casco Bay lobstering—I eventually did both!). He taught me many important lessons about life and how to win campaigns—always reminding me what matters most, what to ignore and what not to get distracted by in the daily political grind (which is often hard to do). One of his greatest strengths was devising the overarching framing and narrative and staying disciplined in sticking to it.

Most importantly, he always was there any time I needed counsel, or to gut check my ideas or instincts. His polling conclusions and reading of complex data were always spot on, and when he spoke, campaigns and candidates listened and did exactly what he told them to do. Well, maybe not always, but most of the time or they wouldn't be his clients very long. Campaigns can often stumble because of internal paralysis or candidate second-guessing on important strategic decisions. But successful campaigns usually have a very strong and decisive internal voice who cuts through that, makes decisions, and executes the game plan. He was always that strong, unwavering voice.

My Dad always took charge of campaigns no matter what collateral damage to the egos around the table. So, for a long time, when I was starting out, I'd meet someone for the first time, and they would ask me if I was Chris Potholm's son. I'd answer, "Yes, I am. But don't worry. I have his brain, but my mom's personality." If they knew my dad well or had heard about him, they would laugh and were probably relieved.

If you are interested in getting into politics, or frankly any profession you are passionate about, find a good mentor. It makes a big difference. At Greg Stevens's firm, I started out as a low-level production assistant and learned every detail of production. To this day, young staffers roll their eyes when I remind them of how we would finish a spot at 5 A.M., and I'd take the ads to the airport and send them counter to counter on a Delta or USAIR flight to the client who would then take them to the stations. Now it's all digital transmission. They simply make sure the right ad is uploaded correctly.

I've been writing, directing, and producing commercials all over the country for the last twenty years at the highest levels. I've produced advertising for presidential campaigns, national committees, Fortune 500 companies, and for great leaders like Governor Greg Abbott of Texas and Governor Mike DeWine of Ohio. I've also created advertising campaigns for over thirty successful ballot measure campaigns, many of them in Maine. I've also been lucky to work with many talented political operatives, on both sides of the aisle, around the country.

What makes a good ad and what goes into ad making? My dad listed some of his all-time Maine favorite TV ads earlier. As he said, we all have an opinion when it comes to what makes a good ad. The candidate's closest friends and supporters often have the most vocal opinions. It makes me smile when a close supporter of the candidate tells them they don't like a particular ad, usually about a certain issue or policy. Of course, the supporter usually needs to be reminded that they are not the target demo. We are trying to convince the "undecideds" or "persuadables." If we have to convince the candidate's friends, we're in tough shape.

But what are the key elements in advertising that actually move public opinion? In my view, the best advertising comes from stories. Stories are memorable. They bring the viewer in and grab your attention. The best ones are emotional. And when the person on-camera delivers their story with raw emotion, it's pure gold. They pull at your heartstrings. People remember stories. That's why I am a big advocate of testimonial ads (someone or multiple people on-camera).

The best stories often need sixty seconds to truly develop their narrative. When we have tracked ad effectiveness through tracking polls, the sixty-second stories always stand out. They are the most memorable to the electorate and most effective.

One of the most powerful TV spots I directed and produced involved Ohio's emergency room nurses who were battling COVID at the height of the pandemic. We asked them questions (using an Interratron to interview them and keep a safe distance for us and crew). They spoke in their own words, describing the conditions of patients they were seeing every day.

Some patients were on ventilators and sometimes the nurses had to hold a patient's cellphone so they could say goodbye to loved ones. It was an incredibly poignant testimony. Everyone on set had tears coming down their faces during these interviews. The spots were extremely powerful. They were designed to grab people's attention, especially those who didn't think COVID was a deadly threat.

It's not easy for the "average" person to go on-camera in front of a large crew of people they've never met and be themselves. That's why it's important to spend considerable time in pre-production. A key part of pre-production is conducting pre-interviews and research to identify in advance who would be best on-camera. We never want to show up on set not having pre-interviewed someone, and we always want to know, to a high degree, how they may perform. Even then, people can get nervous and tighten up once the camera rolls. That's why it's always important to film more people than you intend to actually use.

Shoots are also huge financial investments. A small two-person, documentary-style crew can be less than $10,000 for the day. But shoots with multiple cameras, significant light packages, jib arms, drones, actors, props, and set designs, can easily run $30,000 to $50,000 per day, depending on where you are filming.

Given those expenses, it's critical to maximize the day and film as much as possible. After all these years, one of my colleagues still hates shoots because they can be incredibly stressful. If you need to film outdoors, you worry about the weather. No matter where you are, you're concerned about sound and noise and controlling the location.

That's one of the most important words on a shoot: control. You want to do everything you can to control the setting and be free of costly interruptions. You don't want a great "take" ruined because of noise or someone inadvertently walking into the scene. Some of those things you can control for. That's why scouting weeks in advance and securing the right locations with the proper permits is essential. But other things you can't control. Like when the teleprompter equipment breaks down.

The alternative is that the candidate, or talent, then needs to memorize the script or film it in short bites. One time we had a last-minute shoot to film a closer ad at the end of the campaign. We were filming in the middle of the woods on a Saturday. The camera broke. Fortunately, we were able to get a new one couriered to the location from about two hours away in Boston. Daylight was running out quickly, but we still got the spot filmed. That's another rule of filming—you need to be willing to adapt and willing to adjust if circumstances change. Or as I like to say, "plan B is to make plan A work." You film the ad; you just do it differently.

The first rule of advertising is to get noticed. It's also the most forgotten rule. Especially in politics. Voters complain all the time that all political ads look alike and sound alike. And they're right. Especially in October. If you live in key media markets like Columbus, Manchester, Portland, or Las Vegas you know what I mean. Nonstop, voiceover ads featuring dark images and graphics slamming down on the screen.

Ads need to be memorable, interesting, and cut through all the other ads they're competing with. Be creative. Stand out. It's important to have a creative "hook" in the ad that gets attention. That "hook" might be an interesting setting or location that reinforces the message.

In 2006, my colleagues filmed Mayor Bob Corker, who was running for the US Senate for Tennessee, at the United States and Mexico border to talk about immigration. Because of its location, it got immediate attention and traction with voters. Corker went on to win the primary and general election. In the 2022 cycle, there were countless candidates filmed at the border as immigration continues to be a key issue, especially among Republican primary voters.

Credibility still matters in advertising—especially in this age of misinformation. This is particularly true in ballot measure campaigns because you are often educating voters on a new proposal or issue they know nothing about. Voters and consumers are bombarded by information constantly in their daily lives. They don't know what to believe. As a result, it's extremely important that your message be delivered with credibility and non-partisan messengers in ballot measure campaigns. If you use partisan messengers, you will turn off a section of the electorate.

In both 2004 and 2014, national animal rights groups tried to change Maine law and ban key bear-hunting methods (baiting, trapping and use of dogs) to kill bears. Supporters used very powerful imagery of bears that had been caught in traps to try to make the case that these were inhumane hunting practices. The footage was powerful, emotional, and persuasive. But the referendum was defeated because our side had more credibility. Maine's bear biologists strongly opposed the ballot measure. They had enormous credibility with voters, and voters listened to and trusted these Maine experts who spent their days studying bears and the bear population.

Here's another example. In 1991, Maine voters rejected a proposal to widen the Maine Turnpike. It was my first campaign as a full-time staffer. We had all the money and our opponents had very little. For weeks we controlled the air waves, framed the issue, delivered our messages, and had the lead. So, this is how you run a successful campaign, I thought. But about ten days out from the election, I remember coming home after work and seeing a devastating ad by our opponents on the 11pm news. "$100 million dollars just to gold-plate a small stretch of highway?" My heart sunk. I knew it was powerful.

Given voters' frustration with politicians in Augusta, it did a perfect job of tapping in to the political environment of the time with a "send them a message" call to action. It was a knockout ad produced by Joe Slade White's agency (one of the all-time great ad makers in politics). It showed me the power of television. Frankly, it further inspired me to go into advertising because I saw how it changed the race so dramatically.

It also demonstrated an often overlooked dynamic in campaigns. The political environment you are operating in matters. A lot. If you can connect your messaging to the environment of the time, and what voters are really feeling, it makes your ads even more effective. The opposition did that. And sometimes no matter what you do, the environment is too powerful against you. Ask any consultant who has been on the wrong side of a "wave" election.

Fast forward to 1997. My firm had been hired to produce the advertising to pass the Turnpike widening. Times had changed. There was no anti-Augusta environment at the time. Based on extensive research, we developed a series of powerful ads that featured Maine's fire chiefs and EMTs who respond to accidents on the Maine Turnpike. They urged voters to widen the highway for safety reasons. We won convincingly. The *Portland Press Herald* called the ads "authenticity that is effective." We even won counties that were far away from where the project was located. That's the power of TV. But it was the credibility of the fire chiefs and the EMTs that was the difference.

One of the great advantages today for ad makers is the available online inventory and social media platforms on which to run and post longer format pieces. Ad makers can shoot and produce longer spots for social media (and much shorter ones like 6 and 15 seconds to build frequency to a specific target). If it's a compelling video and gets traction (especially in a nationally targeted race), it can go viral nationally and attract huge online contributions.

Mark Putnam, one of the best and most creative Democratic ad makers in the business, has produced a number of longer format pieces that have helped his clients gain national media attention and raise millions of dollars. That's another advantage of politics today: access to viewers and dollars nationally. Not just in a particular state or district. In the old days, you'd send a press release about an ad and maybe get some print, blog, or local TV news coverage if you were lucky. Or maybe CNN or Fox might air it. Today an ad can explode with viewers through social media sharing and online news outlets. Of course, the story must be powerful to achieve that kind of success. And many candidates today mistakenly think their video will automatically go "viral." It won't—unless the story is compelling, unique, and well-presented.

So, what *doesn't* make a good ad? One of the most common mistakes political ads make is saying too much in the ad. There always needs to be clear thematic and supporting points. But not too many points. There is often a tendency by campaigns to jam in too many attack points. They try to throw the kitchen sink at the opponent and end up putting in too much information.

They simply don't understand advertising. The truth is when you try to say too much, you say nothing. The average viewer simply cannot absorb all that information and remember all those points. The best and most effective advertising is simplistic in its messaging. It's clear and concise. Bob Deis of Winner Mandabach was the first to tell me to turn off the volume and watch a TV ad. Do you still get the message without the audio? You should if it has a clear message.

The other big mistake in political advertising is that many ads often lack an overarching theme (or tagline) or they change taglines every week, as if searching for that magical connection to change the dynamics of the race. This is a sharp contrast to most corporate advertising campaigns which have consistent taglines and are disciplined to stick to it. Develop a theme and stick to it. That's essential to building the narrative you want. It's an advertising "campaign"—there should be an ongoing narrative to it. Ads should not be bouncing from one thing to another without a common thread. Why? Because it won't stick with voters.

Edie Smith, who has worked on dozens of Maine campaigns, including managing some of the toughest ballot measures, shares her experiences with Erik on the campaign trail:

In the Physician-Assisted Suicide campaign of 2000, Erik and I were standing by a mailbox at a house in Augusta, getting ready to film a little girl going to that mailbox and taking out a clearly labeled package of "death pills."

One of the fatal flaws of the ballot question and the legislation behind it was that the act of assisted suicide had to be carried out by the patient alone, taking about thirty to forty pills. And those pills could be sent in the mail.

The video shots showing the girl walking toward the mailbox, opening it and taking out the package weren't emitting the emotion Erik wanted. Darn—what to do? Erik said to me, "Let's take the back of the mailbox off and shoot into the mailbox from the back, so the shot shows the girl's small, delicate hand open the mailbox, reach in, and take out the package, then a wider shot of her walking away slowly." It was a Stephen King moment. Scary. Jolting. We had our killer ad.

I believe hundreds of people helped us win, but it was the power of those commercials that put us finally over the top. Erik is like the Francis Ford Coppola of Maine—30 or 60 seconds—every little detail matters to him and his commercials show it.

But what about the new, digital media? Here are a few views of this new world, about which I know so very little. I bet you'd like to know more too. For example, do they upend the world of influence vectors and authority figures?

Lance Dutson, for example, believes that "the real truths of political advertising and political messaging on digital platforms are just as true as ever. You need to capture emotion and feeling to carry the day just as earlier."

He suggests that today perhaps 20–25 percent of most media budgets need to go to the newer forms, and this number climbs to 30–35 percent if digital is to drive fundraising as well as reinforcement and conversion.

Dutson believes that today's social group dynamics, "with their hard-core silos of believers," require specific digital platforms, for sometimes they are the only way to penetrate these targets. He also adds that, as with lawn signs and banners, it is important to make sure that candidates or cause leaders see your message traffic on the media platforms they watch. "That reduces stress all around."

Will Robinson, the award-winning producer and highly successful ballot measure guru of the aptly named New Media Firm, disagrees. For him, "The new digital media requires very different skill sets, targeting aspects, new approaches and especially new ways of thinking."

As Angus King points out, the new Internet-driven media and the emergence of AI has already changed and will continue to change politics into the indefinite future. "Deep fakes," for example, give new meaning to the whole concept of negative advertising.

Regardless, whether new or old or a powerful mix, media will continue to determine the outcome of many ballot measures as well as candidate campaigns.

AXIOM #11

"Influence Vectors and Authority Figures Decide Elections: If You Can Find Them"

It's about the right message to the right people at the right time.
—ELAINE FRANKLIN

Edie Smith writes,

> On my political journey, I learned three key lessons on how to win a campaign: (1) listen to your pollster, (2) listen to your pollster, and (3) listen to your pollster. You can't win without good polling data. Pure and simple. If your campaign is a ship, then the polling data are your sails, your rudder, your engine, and anything else that steers you in the right direction and keeps you on course. No data means no direction means getting lost and drifting away.
>
> Polling is an art *and* a science. The science comes in the form of hard data—how did people answer the questions you asked? The art comes into play in several areas—how to phrase the questions, how to interpret the data and how to turn that interpretation into winning campaign strategies. Interpreting the data means doing a deep dive into the crosstabs. Without proper crosstabs, based on usable units, you will never win consistently. Crosstabs, which present the overall findings by various subgroups, open a whole new way of looking at the world. They are the perfect joining of art and science.

In this chapter, we look at the vital influence vectors and authority figures that are essential to winning ballot measures. They are the operational parts of the crosstabs or "internals." They are what give polls their ability to change the future. They are the demographic and psychographic breaks that segment the voting universe into manageable units and enable a campaign to focus on individual portions of it for the purpose of changing minds.

As in candidate elections you try to get on issue "lily pads"—ones your opponent can't get on with you. In ballot measures, you test for messages that will move the electorate toward your cause or away from your opponent's, irrespective of what your opponent is saying.

In effect, while they interact, both sides are using dueling influence vectors. Choosing the wrong message or the wrong authority figure, let alone both, can doom virtually any ballot measure effort.

What moves the electorate? What causes them to go, first to "don't know" (because voters normally don't go straight from "YES" to "NO" or vice versa, they usually stop at "don't know"), and then to the opposite of where they were initially? What pushes voters along a spectrum of not voting on an issue to becoming "somewhat likely to vote" on that issue to "guaranteed to vote" on that issue?

Also, whereas candidates have to have opinions about hundreds of subjects, they usually have a few campaign staples to repeat ad nauseum, but in ballot measures, you can, indeed must, focus on a very few influence vectors. These are the statements or aspects that respondents say that if they knew, would make them "much more likely to vote for that" or "much less likely to vote" for or against something if they knew it were true. Thus "staying on message" becomes critical in ballot measures.

Polling at the front end of the cycle is critical to finding both the right messages and the right authority figures. But good campaign management is critical to get those messages out in the media. This must happen regardless of whether supporters like or dislike the messages (see chapter 2). Of vital importance, then, is tracking the impact of the media to see if they are really working.

In the beginning, you might test a dozen messages to see which work best, but at the end you will be concentrating on only one or two. This whole process echoes the words of Winston Churchill, "Out of intense complexity, intense simplicities emerge." Or as Pat Eltman, puts it, "Every campaign comes down to Education, Environment, Employment." Let's look at some of the influence vectors operative in some specific campaigns in Maine politics over the last decades.

In the assisted suicide referendum of 2002, for example, the best influence vectors pushing voters *away* from approval of Physician-Assisted Suicide ranged from "was opposed by many Maine doctors and nurses" (3–1 negative), "has no safeguards to ensure that the person seeking suicide assistance is making a voluntary choice" (6–1 negative), and "suicide pills can come in the mail" (8–1 negative), to the "HMOs could encourage patients to commit suicide in order to save money" (10–1 negative).

Not surprisingly, one very influential ad would indeed feature some poor old man looking glum when the HMO apparently did just that! Another, which really ended up moving the needle because of its striking visual impact, had a young girl getting off a school bus and going to the mailbox and finding a box of suicide pills when she opened it. The audience was left wondering if—or when—she would use them, whether by mistake or by design.

Winning by only 51.3–48.7 percent in 2000, the NO vote suggests how great was the need for really powerful influence vectors in combination with the right authority figures (which we look at below).

As we saw in chapter 1, the Sanford casino had a very negative set of dimensions, dimensions that had been totally lacking in the previously contemplated Passamaquoddy gaming facility. Even with the passage of several decades, it is hard to see how the Sanford casino could have given the NO side a better set of influence vectors to attack as long as opponents put them on TV and educated the voters about them.

For example, knowing that although the state of Maine got 25 percent of the profits from slot machines, it got nothing from roulette, and other games were 10–1 negative. Knowing that the reporting of the profits would be confidential so the state of Maine would have no way of checking receipts was over 20–1.

Knowing that the agreement was "permanent and could not be renegotiated in the future" was 30–1, and of course the kill switch was the provision allowing teenagers as young as twelve to work and gamble in so-called games of chance, which was 80–1 negative.

When it came to the highly controversial bear hunting referendum of 2004, one that would have banned the taking of bears by means of trapping, chasing with dogs, or baiting, there were also some very powerful influence vectors discovered in the pre-campaign testing.

Because initial sentiment looked something like 2–1 in favor of the proposed ban on bear hunting with traps, dogs, and baiting techniques, the measure had a good chance of passage. One of the most powerful vectors in the package that drove support was the trapping element that was held in very low regard by the general election voters. Even voters who were unsure about baiting bears or using dogs to hunt them were against catching them in big steel traps.

The trapping element was such a negative that the pro–bear-hunting side gave some consideration in the runup to the election to have the legislature ban the trapping component of Maine's bear-hunting portfolio in order to help defeat the eventual ballot measure. But in the end, the Sportsman's Alliance and others chose to stand firm and decided to win or lose together, telling the interested legislators not to proceed with that approach.

Fortunately for the supporters of bear hunting in Maine, there were powerful influence vectors that sharply reduced the support for the overall measure and eventually saved the trappers as well.

For example, if one learned that bear-human encounters have increased substantially, suggesting the need to eliminate those bears, voters said they were less inclined (10–1) to support the ban. Likewise, learning that a bear had shown up in a South Portland school playground and had to be shot diminished support to a ratio of 8–1. Also, finding out that the proposed law would make it a felony for a farmer to shoot crop-destroying bears made Mainers less likely to support the ban by a margin of 11–1.

So, the NO side had some powerful arguments, and when coupled with very credible authority figures, gave opponents of the proposed law the hope that they could be successful *if* these various powerful vectors could be brought to the public's attention by equally believable authority figures.

But having great authority figures and influence vectors on paper does not, of course, guarantee success in real-life campaigns, so the advice to the coalition at the time was simple: "Don't be discouraged. This is a tough fight. And it is important to always remember that the NO side will be behind right until the very end."

It would, indeed, turn out to be a very close, hard-fought contest right through election night. When you think that in the twenty-first century people were still arguing that taking bears by traps, dogs, and bait was a viable public policy, you can see why it might be an uphill battle. Luckily, it was being played out in the Wild, Wild East of Maine, and the NO side would win 53.9–46.9 percent!

In similar fashion, Jonathan Carter's anti-clearcutting referendum in 2000 started out with a substantial 2–1 lead in the early polling, and you could certainly argue that the Wild Wild East mindscape would definitely support his vision for a future return to less clearcutting. But while initial support was widespread, it was also thin.

And because of its many flaws, the proposal contained within it the seeds of its own destruction. Influence vectors pushing voters against the referendum were strong. For example, knowing that landowners would have to cut trees every year or lose the right to harvest them over time was 8-1 negative. Knowing that a thousand miles of logging road would have to be cut in order to carry out the proposal was 6–1 negative. Learning that the proposal would "devastate" the existing Maine Tree Growth program was 6–1 negative and tied in nicely with the authority figures found as well.

An interesting variation on the use of authority figures occurred in 1988. Alpha One, a disability and elderly advocacy agency headed by Steve Tremblay wanted research done to promote a $5 million proposed bond for adaptive equipment for the "handicapped." I put handicapped in quotes because the polling showed clearly that a substantial majority of Maine people and those in that category preferred the term "people with disabilities." This bit of information had considerable effect, not just on the verbiage of the referendum but more broadly afterward by advocates.

This low-budget effort to pass the bond was headed by "Maine Citizens for Independence" because by a margin of nearly 9–1, voters would be more inclined to vote YES if they knew it would help people with disabilities become more independent. Moreover, a margin of nearly 9–1 favored the bond if they knew people with disabilities *wanted* to work. Remember the work ethic at play in the original Passamaquoddy Nation Casino where a similar pattern emerged? Maine people like to see Maine people working.

For authority figures, a person in a wheelchair who wanted to work—or in the case of Steve Tremblay, the head of Alpha One, who was already in a wheelchair *and* working—was an 8–1 believable figure. Considering all these elements and featuring Tremblay in an ad done by Chris Duval and backed by a very modest 750 GRP TV buy produced a victory of 65.5–34.5 percent. I've subsequently wished we'd had a bigger TV budget. I would dearly have loved to bludgeon that 34.5 percent down further.

A variation on this theme of Maine people wanting to help Maine people occurred in 1995 and featured the $15 million Education and Medical Bond, which was designed to help Maine people stay competitive in a variety of fields. The name "Citizens to Keep Maine Competitive" tested very well (10–1 believable), as did the vectors of bringing more businesses to Maine (8–1), as did providing rural Maine seniors with access to telemedicine (8–1).

John Cleveland was the campaign manager, and Chris Duval and Connie McCabe of McCabe and Duval again did the media. Tom Davidson, Evan Richert, Peter Wylie, Ray Poulin, Denny Gallaudet, and Greg Scott were also of assistance, and the bond eventually passed 59.8–40.2 percent.

Another campaign that shows the intertwined role of authority figures and influence vectors in action was the 2009 attempt to repeal the school consolidation law that had been passed in 2007 under Governor John Baldacci. Baldacci worked very hard to affect taxpayer savings by the consolidation of school districts. At the time, I remember being surprised to learn that Maine had the highest ratio of teachers to students *and* superintendents per teachers of any state in the Union.

I had a hard time believing that Maine students needed more supervision than any other students in the country and/or that Maine teachers were so unruly that they needed more superintendents per teachers than any other teachers in the nation. I still do.

Another factoid that has stuck in my brain all these many years was that, whereas Boise, Idaho, had one school district, the similar population of Portland and its environs had fourteen.

Of course, local control is the bedrock of Maine life, and schools are the bedrocks of local control and serve many community purposes other than just instructing students. But Maine citizens could not have property tax relief and business as usual at the same time, or so they were led to believe when the legislature passed the measure.

Kevin Raye, state senator from Washington County, led the fight for the repeal of the consolidation law and in 2009 got it on the ballot. To defeat it, Governor Baldacci put together a very strong team. Larry Benoit was put in charge of the overall effort, while Newell Augur was the campaign manager. Dana Connors, Warren Cook, and Oakley Jones headed up the opposition, and Erik Potholm did the media. The umbrella group was called "Maine People for Improved Education."

The polling showed that opposition to the measure was strongest around the cost of reversing consolidation, which came in at $72 million for the next two years (8–1). Surprisingly, perhaps, the best authority figure was "a school superintendent who favored consolidation"—that is, someone on the front lines who had seen it in action (4–1).

Here the group found an excellent one, William Shuttleworth, superintendent of RSU-1 Bath. Erik Potholm tested him on camera and created very powerful and persuasive ads in which Shuttleworth delivered the best influence vectors with considerable gravitas. The tag line, "It costs too much and hurts our schools," was clear, direct, and decisive.

The repeal was defeated 59–41 percent. Best of all, as Shuttleworth wrote afterward, "Nearly every town where school district consolidation was taking place, the NO vote carried and usually by a majority of victory greater than the 59 percent to 41 percent margin showed."

To further understand the principles of authority figures, this example may help:

Some time ago, a major bank in Maine asked me to test authority figures and influence vectors to see how to get more people to use their banking services. They were stimulated, they said, by some ads for a competitor featuring Gold Medal marathoner Joan Benoit Samuelson. I had known Joan when she was at Bowdoin. I even had her in class. Even more impressive perhaps, one day when I was jogging around Bowdoin's Pickard Field track, she was jogging in the other direction (and for quite a bit longer, I imagine), so when she subsequently won her Olympic medal, I was able to let one and all know I had "trained with Joannie."

So I was doubly happy to do the poll. The results confirmed that people were impressed that she banked with her existing bank. But they didn't believe that they would necessarily get the same treatment as she did if they banked there. It was not that they didn't believe Joanie when she said in the ad she got excellent service. It was that they didn't believe they would get similar service simply because she did. The soft data was also pretty consistent, "Of course she got treated well. Joanie Benoit would be treated well anywhere." Many respondents said she would be a good authority figure for running shoes or a sports drink like Gatorade "because she would know what was good and what was bad in that realm." I guess they figured the running shoes wouldn't treat their feet different than hers.

I've always remembered this set of conclusions because they capture the essence of matching authority figures to products. Some people and organizations are very believable on some subjects but on others not so much. In doing ballot measures, finding the "right," that is, most efficacious authority figure lies at the heart of winning those elections.

Next, we will examine some Maine ballot measures and see which vectors and authority figures worked best and which ones would not have worked if they had been employed or didn't work very well when they were used. Remember the dueling lobstermen in chapter 3?

Most people realize that some arguments work better than others. Most people will accept this notion, even if you call them by their polling name "influence vectors" as we have done in the preceding chapter.

But many people do not realize the role that certain "authority figures" can play in multiplying the impact of your side's argument. Some figures are more believable than others overall, and some figures are more believable to some groups of people. When polling in ballot measures, to be effective you have to match those influence vectors with the proper authority figure for that issue and in that particular election cycle.

You have to use the proper authority figure to get the target population(s) to change their minds from "I don't know" to the harder "I'm on the other side."

There is a wide disparity from one person to another and even from the same person on different issues. For example, in the Save Maine Yankee referendum, the highest-scoring authority figure was "a foreign-born scientist," while an American scientist was regarded as less persuasive. Remember, Save Maine Yankee had to settle for an American scientist, Professor Will Hughes of the Bowdoin physics department, because he looked and sounded "foreign"—and also very, very authoritative.

Parenthetically, sometimes the polling shows that a seemingly natural ally on an issue should not be used by the campaign as an authority figure. An excellent example occurred during the assisted suicide referendum of 2000. Initial polling in 1999 showed the pro-suicide forces well in the lead, something like 45–30 percent, with 25 percent undecided. Many of these undecideds were least likely voters, so the practical, operational situation was 2–1 against a NO vote.

Strong and very believable authority figures were needed on the NO side.

Interestingly, the strongest authority figures did not come from the most committed opponents. Of all the authority figures tested, the Maine Christian Civic League members and the evangelical and fundamentalist communities already had the strongest aggregate numbers against the proposal—above eight or nine out of ten of them were already against the bill. Naturally, they wanted to play a big role in the campaign.

They were firm, committed, and passionate about the issue. They wanted to be involved in the campaign. They wanted to be spokespeople and be in the TV ads. Their pastors were very believable authority figures to them.

But there were problems with this strategy. Big ones.

First, despite what you might guess, many Catholics were initially undecided on the issue of assisted suicide, and the evangelical or fundamentalist Christians were not very useful on that front because, although there is commonality with Catholics on some specific issues (such as abortion), on a wide range of issues Catholics don't necessarily find evangelical and fundamentalist Christians believable.

Besides, the campaign already had a strong ground (and pulpit) game prepared for that undecided Catholic cohort using the Roman Catholic Diocese of Portland, in particular their very able team of Mark Mutty and Teresa McCann-Tumidajski, the Diocesan Respect Life Manager. They worked extremely hard and were very effective in not only staying on message, but also were consistent when energizing committed Catholics from one end of the state to the other.

Interestingly, the early polling showed four out of ten Franco-Americans undecided on the issue, so we declared, "Francos can keep the NO side in the hunt, but they cannot win it alone." Catholics alone could not win the issue either. But Teresa McCann-Tumidajski and Mark Mutty of the Portland Diocese made a major outreach effort to all Catholics in the state and eventually converted most of them to the NO side. Considering both accomplishments after the vote, McCann-Tumidajski said, with verve and feeling in her after-action report, "Long live the Francos."

No, the biggest problem to defeating the assisted suicide coalition was the group that was most favorable *to* the proposal. These were members of the upscale Protestant churches such as the Episcopalians and Congregationalists and the WASP tribe more generally. Something like 65 percent of this cohort were voting YES at the beginning. It was clear that most of them would reject any messages coming from the Christian Civic League or fundamentalist Protestant leaders, and yet they were the group from which we needed to draw in order to win.

The data was very persuasive with upscale Yuppies as well, especially non-evangelical WASP Protestants (where the "Death with Dignity" proposal was positive 61–25 percent, with only 14 percent undecided), so putting the Christian Civic League front and center would be detrimental electorally.

Much better for the purposes of conversion (and reinforcing the NO side's own supporters) were the American Medical Association (12–1 believable), a spokesperson for Hospice (9–1 believable), and the Maine Medical Association (6–1 believable). They were the best message senders, so they went into the commercials, not the leaders of the Maine Christian Civic League.

Kandyce Powell, head of Maine Hospice, and Julie L'Heureux, head of CHANS Home Health, as well as Gordon Smith of the Maine Medical Association ended up being very effective "out front" faces for the anti side.

Also, the initial polling showed that the original name for the anti-assisted suicide umbrella group, "Citizens Against Assisted Suicide," did not test as well as "Maine Citizens Against the Dangers of Physician Assisted Suicide," so that became the name for the entity fighting the referendum, especially after it tested best against the other side's group name, "Mainers for Death with Dignity."

Another ballot measure where dueling authority figures came into play was the complicated set of public and private maneuverings about forest practices. Overall, this is probably the best civics lesson on why ballot measures and referenda are not the best arena for accomplishing complicated public policy.

The overlapping clearcutting/forestry compact campaigns could also be studied as a perfect indication of "your friends will do you more harm than your enemies" as dueling environmentalists such as Jonathan Carter and his Forest Ecology Network clashed with the Nature Conservancy and the Natural Resources Council of Maine, confusing voters no end in two successive referenda.

After the defeat of the compact, Carter and the Forest Ecology Network proposed another referendum that would not ban clearcuts outright but would require landowners to get permits. In 2000, in order to get the proper authority figures for this proposal, we did considerable research. Governor King and Dennis Bailey, in particular, were anxious that something be done when the results showed Carter's proposal was ahead 59–23 percent, so we sought the best authority figures.

On clearcutting, Maine guides were 11–1 believable, the dean at the University of Maine School of Forestry checked in at 10–1, and the Small Woodlot Owners Association of Maine (SWOAM) came in at 5–1 but also carried with it a veritable army of 11,000 members; adding family members and friends, you got a potential army of 50,000 or so. SWOAM brought an instant ground game. Not Astroturf this time. Real grassroots.

Erik Potholm would turn these earnest folks who oversee our forests at the ground level into media stars. I still remember one very passionate woodlot owner persuasively saying in an ad, "It's very pretty ground. And we want to keep it that way." The statewide audience believed him.

Also opposing Carter was a good chunk of the environmental community in Maine: the Nature Conservancy, Audubon, and likeminded groups. The Natural Resources Council of Maine (NRCM) opposed it initially and then late in the game, endorsed it. The Sierra Club stood fast with Carter and provided the effort with several hundred thousand dollars in support.

With Abby Holman as campaign manager and Jeff Toorish as spokesperson, Jim Robbins as co-chair and Steve Clarkin from International Paper, the team was solid. Also invaluable to the effort were George Smith and SAM, with the whole campaign tightly controlled using the numerous themes outlined above. The NO side would win in 2000, but here we will confine our analysis to see how one set of efficacious authority figures, in this case SWOAM, were able to prevail against a host of other authority figures (many of which were in conflict on the various elements of woodcraft).

Generally nationwide and usually in Maine, political figures are *not* good authority figures in ballot measures. But there are exceptions. Angus King was good with some segments on Gay Rights and Casinos *NO!*. John Baldacci, Attorney General Janet Mills, and Joe Brennan were also good on Casinos *NO!* and bear hunting, and all played a positive role in those referenda. As we've seen, Baldacci was also quite strong in the Carol Palesky Tax Cap referendum of 2004.

The bear-hunting referendum of 2004 also provides an interesting internal look at dueling authority figures. The organization behind the proposed ban—the national Humane Society—was believable to 57 percent of Maine voters, while not believable to 33 percent (or roughly 2–1) *on this issue*. But when voters learned it was the Humane Society's stated position that they would ban all hunting, the believability of that organization in Maine flipped to only 35 percent believable, with 56 percent now finding it not believable.

Edie Smith declares,

Authority figures came from crosstabs, and you must select and embrace two to three authority figures for your spokespeople. Polling will tell you who should be the public faces of a campaign. Obviously, in a candidate campaign, the candidate is front and center. But who else should speak out on behalf of the candidate to convince the voters this is their guy or gal.

The selection of campaign spokespersons was especially important in the 2004 anti-bear-hunting referendum. We couldn't just have a bunch of hunters coming out of the woods saying they wanted to keep killing bears. The polling told us people needed to hear from trustworthy wildlife experts, using data and facts, and saying that harvesting bears was based on sound science, and that we had to harvest bear for their own good. We had over twenty-three thousand bears in Maine in 2004, which was too many. So who polled the highest? Who could change minds of Maine voters who thought hunting bears was cruel? Polling #1 was wildlife biologists. Even better . . . female wildlife biologists.

There we hit the jackpot in that category—Maine's leading biologist on black bears was a woman, Jen Vashon, who was an experienced wildlife biologist at Maine's Department of Inland Fisheries and Wildlife. And she knew more about black bears than anyone on the planet.

We put a female hunter in our first ad as well: Tenley Maura (now Scofield), a Maine native, bear hunter, registered Maine guide, articulate, friendly, relatable, trustworthy. She talked science, not sport. She got the campaign off on just the right foot.

The Wild, Wild East continued to live with power and majesty as the NO side had a number of *very* believable authority figures within a wide cohort of typologies. Maine guides, for example, came in at 3–1 believable, game wardens at 6–1 believable, while bear biologists scored best at 11–1. Given the huge lead of the stop bear-hunting effort, the NO side would need all the credible authorities it could get.

Fortunately, the newly created umbrella group opposing the ban chose as its public umbrella group, "Maine's Fish and Wildlife Conservation Council," which had tested at 10–1 as did the Sportsman's Alliance of Maine (SAM) at 6–1.

Note: in all referenda and ballot measures, the names of umbrella groups should be tested beforehand for their believability quotient. It is one dimension the campaign always has control over—but only if it carefully tests names at the front end of the cycle. You would be surprised at how many individuals and groups plunge into campaigns without testing their authority figures and simply come up with names for the group as if pulling them out of a hat.

These very positive figures on bear hunting were enhanced by the ratio of voters agreeing (72–11 percent) that "science, not politics or emotion, should guide our wildlife decisions."

While political authority figures are not always very believable on specific issues, sometimes they make critical decisions and provide leadership to ensure defeat (if a NO vote is wanted) or assist in winning (if a YES vote is required).

The following case study illuminates this—the Tax Cap referendum of 2004—and puts the mix of influence vectors and authority figures in perspective. In 2004, a very popular concept—the reduction of property taxes—was thrust upon the Maine political stage. Carol Palesky and her Maine Taxpayers Action Network gathered over fifty thousand signatures to cap property taxes at $10 per $1,000 of property. The Maine legislature punted on the proposal and sent the very popular measure (70 percent approval at the time) out to the voters.

The Tax Cap Yes! side strongly favored having the vote in June. Governor Baldacci was urged by many Democrats to put the issue on the ballot that June so it would not be giving Republicans an advantage in turnout come November. But the polling was clear: the 58 percent the YES side had in June (among "most likely voters") went to 46 percent in November (again with "most likely'" and "somewhat likely voters"). He could easily have acquiesced at a time when the Palesky initiative had the support of 58 percent of the voters of Maine, and many in his own party were afraid of their possible defeat in the fall if it were on the ballot.

Instead, Baldacci insisted on having the referendum in November in order to give the NO side enough time to prepare and to ensure that the maximum number of people would be voting on this momentous issue. Baldacci put his reputation on the line because he thought that a 3–1 popular issue was bad for Maine, and because he believed that in a democracy the system worked best when the most people voted.

No doubt channeling Claude Rains playing Inspector Louis Renault in *Casablanca*, Baldacci rounded up the usual suspects by turning to his former chief of staff, Larry Benoit, giving the NO side a formidable head. Benoit did a very effective job. One of the very few consultants with senatorial (Mitchell), congressional (Baldacci), and gubernatorial staff experience (Baldacci), and having served in both candidate (ten, including five primaries) and ballot measures (three, two of which are covered in this book) as campaign manager, as well as one for independent expenditure campaigns, Benoit is one of Maine's premier political operatives.

This time, he ran a nearly pitch-perfect campaign, guiding it through a maze of possible errors and keeping warring factions at bay. Believe me, as a strategist on ballot measures, a well-run campaign is such a relief in the middle of all that turmoil. Larry Benoit certainly ran one in 2004.

Moreover, his experience and expertise showed in the allocation of campaign resources: 70 percent TV, 17 percent consulting, and 8 percent direct mail, email, phone banks, and GOTV (utilizing a very effective door knocker, the one thing scholarly articles stress works in real-time action).

Benoit also chose Wes Bonney to be chairman of the effort, and along with Kay Rand and Stephanie Clifford (field director), he kept a fractious coalition of the Maine Municipal Association (MMA), the Maine Education Association (MEA), the AFL-CIO, and AARP in line. Mark Grey, executive director of the MEA, helped fend off nationally generated bad advice, while Martha Freeman, head of the State Planning Office, Jonathan Rubin, and Todd Gabe provided the policy ramifications of the "meat ax" approach of the Palesky initiative (which would have caused an 80 percent jump in sales taxes and a 64 percent increase in income taxes to pay for the $750 million state revenue shortfall).

George Smith, a leading Maine conservative, and Dana Connors, head of the Maine State Chamber of Commerce, joined forces to argue against the Palesky referendum and thus legitimized Republican opposition. Dennis Bailey was instrumental in convincing the Maine press corps that the passage of the tax cap was not inevitable.

Erik Potholm, hired by Benoit over the objections of some partisan Democrats, produced a series of dramatic and powerful thirty-second ads, using no politicians or interest group spokespeople, but simply real Maine people whose lives would be impacted by the passage of the referendum. He then followed up with strong closer commercials featuring firemen and EMT workers.

There were excellent NO authority figures: a fireman, an EMT worker, and a public school teacher all scored very highly, coming in at 15–1 believability. And there were also a host of powerful influence vectors. For example, knowing there would be massive layoffs of firefighters, police, and EMTs would influence voters to vote against by a margin of 76–3 percent, and raising the income tax and the state sales tax was also very determinant at 20–1. Again as we saw in the Casinos *NO!* campaign, the real problem was not a killer vector, it was convincing supporters and friends *not* to use these themes too early in the campaign.

If we were able to get out all our messages combined with our best authority figures, as in the polling, the voting public would flip on this referendum from 58–18 percent for it to 27–47 percent against it.

Targets abounded with Francos 2–1 in favor of the measure—and other groups like women who worked at home and were highly persuadable. I wrote, "If we take 60 percent of the Franco vote and 60 percent of the women in the home vote, we will win no matter what the other side does."

Support for the Palesky referendum came from a variety of sources, including Eric Cianchette, Phil Harriman, David Delorme, and others on the Tax Cap Yes! campaign.

The NO's very effective campaign effort resulted in an overwhelming victory. By a margin of 64–36 percent Maine people voted down a proposition that earlier had a 70 percent approval rating. Fear of unintended consequences firmly drove out the favor for property tax relief.

The result was not only a smashing victory for the NO campaign, but it also underscored the strong leadership of Governor Baldacci. He had proven to be unafraid to risk defeat for a principle, unconcerned about newspaper popularity rating and unwilling to be deterred by the odds against him.

Another example of authority figures making a difference occurred in the 2009 campaign to repeal the school consolidation and enables us to look at another of the Pine Tree State's targets of opportunity and substance in ballot measure campaigns.

Regarding targeting voters, I have never subscribed to the current fixation on winning elections by getting out only your own voters (that overworked "base"). That's important, surely, but I've always found conversion of your opponent's voters to be vital and efficacious. Think of math—if you get one of your opponent's supporters, it's like getting 2 for 1—you take away one from them and add one to yours.

Getting out only your own vote exclusively leads almost invariably to thinking about suppressing your opponents' base vote, which is not healthy for democracy at all. To play the wider field, though, you have to have better messages, better TV, and especially better targeting. But it is worth the effort.

This is where "women who work at home" come into play. They have been our "hidden advantage" targets in so many ballot measures that we have lost track. In fact, next to the Francos, they have proven to be the most dependable targeting/outcome group in ballot measures precisely because they are persuadable with the right messages and cheap TV.

Early on, we discovered that while men and women who work outside the home often track on major issues, women who work inside the home most often do not. Moreover, the cohort of women who work at home is almost always filled with more undecided voters on most issues than the other two groups.

So the most efficacious cross tabulation for sex/occupation in ballot measure campaigns is this:

Men
Women who work at home
Women who work outside the home

You might ask, "What about the differences between 'men who work outside the home' and 'men who work inside the home?'" In forty years our research has indicated there are no significant statistical differences between these two groups.

The more you aggregate the targets, of course, the more accurate your poll. So to get at that cohort, you need to isolate them statistically. But isolating the "women working inside the home" is not fashionable—even by other pollsters—to say nothing of feminists, purists, academicians, many Bowdoin students, and politically correct observers. So sometimes you have to ask an additional question by doing "males working outside the home," "males working inside," "females working outside the home," and "females working inside," and then combine the first three, leaving you with targeting gold.

Whatever you have to do to isolate this group, you must do it.

It's referendum-winning gold.

Why? For a lot of reasons actually: (1) the "women in the home" cohort almost always has a higher undecided percentage than either of the other two; (2) being at home all day, this group watches much more TV than the other two groups; (3) that TV is cheaper to buy, often much cheaper; (4) if you target the "women in the home," you automatically reel in a lot of senior citizens of both sexes, and they are the demographic most likely to vote and the demographic most likely to watch the most TV; (5) "women who work at home" are often doing other things while the TV is on, so you have to have a lot of impressions; and (6) they are often slower to decide on issues, but once they do, they are also less likely to change their minds.

And very valuable targets they are—and have been.

In the first Land for Maine's Future bond, for example, in the initial polling, 47 percent were undecided compared with 23 percent of "women who worked outside the home."

In the forest compact ballot measure, there were three times the number of undecided "women working at home" (40 percent) than either "men or women working outside the home."

In the Sanford casino effort, there were three times as many undecideds in the home as men or women outside the home.

In the bear hunt effort, it was almost 3–1 as well, and in the Widening of the Maine Turnpike II, three times as many "women working at home" were undecided as "women outside the home." Also, in terms of support, 57 percent of "women outside the home" initially favored the widening compared with 37 percent of "women in the home"— no doubt because many of them drove to work.

In assisted suicide, "women in the home" were 35 percent undecided, the highest of any of the sex/occupation groups.

So in ballot measures, putting in influence vectors, authority figures, and cohort targeting, winning an election is, at base, a fairly simple proposition. Find out where different groups are on issues, find out what will change their minds, and find out who are the best messengers to deliver those influence vectors. If you can find reliable targeting groups and can stick with them, you will do especially well, even very well in ballot measure elections. If you can, you need to keep your own client or cause from doing it their way and losing.

Always pay close attention to what messages brought by what authority figures move Franco-Americans and women who work at home. They will reward your attention to detail on election night.

AXIOM #12

"Avoid Hummingbird Tongues and Other Impedimenta"
with Dave Emery

There is no greater harm than that of time wasted.
—MICHELANGELO

At the end of the critical second day of the Battle of Gettysburg, after Maine's very own Joshua Chamberlain and the rest of the Union line had done their splendid work, General Jeb Stuart showed up at General Robert E. Lee's headquarters. Having ridden around the entire Union army and captured thirty or forty wagons of supplies and ammunition, Stuart fully expected to be praised. But since Lee's army had been blind without Stuart's cavalry for several days and was in danger of losing the battle, Lee was not impressed. Instead, he said peevishly something to the effect of, "These are but impedimenta."

This chapter will try to show how when you move from candidate campaigns to referenda and bond ballot measures you can—happily, securely, and without fear of penalty—jettison a great deal of impedimenta yourself.

But before we leave this understudied subject of bumper strips, posters, lawn signs, and campaign literature, we have to deal with another type of impedimenta that can consume a great deal of time: the "union bug."

Do hummingbirds have tongues?

I suppose so, but I don't really know.

Whether they do or not doesn't really matter to me. Such a thing seems both outside my experiential plane and irrelevant to it, although there are undoubtedly people who care about such things.

In my forty years in politics, I've come up with few equivalents of hummingbird tongues in political campaigns that can match the union bug.

When you look at the many, many Maine campaign bumper strips over the years, you should marvel at them because they are often the product of a huge amount of debate, time, effort, and money, and think of how useless, except for the impact on the candidate's psyche and that of her/his supporters, they all have been in terms of getting votes.

The union bug turned out to be the most famous of hummingbird tongues I encountered in politics. Back in the 1970s and 1980s (and even before), unions were a big deal, and whether a candidate, particularly a Republican candidate, used a union printer was always a matter of great debate. Never mind that the handout or flyer said, no matter what the pretend newspaper said, they all *had* to have a tiny symbol on the bumper strip or poster that the printing had been done by a union shop, hence the union bug.

I always thought that was nonsense in terms of political outcomes, but in my early campaigns, it was an act of faith on the part of most Republicans. Supposedly you would be "punished" at the ballot box if you hadn't put a bug on your literature. So we started off doing that as a matter of course. We were usually punished more by the complaints of many small, independent printers who resented the heavy-handed demands of the union shops and therefore didn't contribute to our campaigns.

But as time went on and we saw that organized labor—labor unions—especially their leaders, would not go for a Republican under almost any circumstance, the union bug didn't get us very far. Also, Republican candidates or officeholders often tried to avoid at all costs going to the AFL-CIO conventions. Once, I told the candidate he didn't have to go. For this perspicacious insight, I got sent instead. It was quite an experience, a fine young college professor like me striding out onto the stage and being booed lustily, even before I opened my mouth, when my affiliation was announced. George Mitchell, who was on the stage with me, was highly amused. He always enjoyed a good laugh on the campaign trail.

I rather enjoyed being booed on the stage of the convention as a matter of principle since I knew that nothing we could do or say would get their endorsement anyway. I also had fun mocking the COPE rating scales, which invariably flunked any and all Republican candidates out of the box.

But I also learned at these conventions that regardless of what the official position of the labor leadership in the state, rank and file union members would decide how to vote for themselves, and often they would come up and tell me afterward what they really cared about and what aspects to highlight to differentiate our positions from those of the Democratic candidates of that era.

In any case, I soon decreed that the bumper strips could be printed by anyone friendly to our cause, union shop or not. Guess what? Nothing ever changed. I believe the vote totals were the same without the bug as they would have been with it.

As I did more and more polling, I even discovered that if you divided the respondents into non-union households, union members, and union households, the best gauge of how union members were actually going to vote was the difference between what union members said and what their households said. The household members were more likely to be honest or at least less cautious in their responses. And they most often reflected the true views of the union members themselves.

The union households tended to reflect the eventual vote better since sometimes the union members said what they thought they should say while the households generally reflected the actual preferences of the individual members and their families.

So the union bug joined the tongues of hummingbirds in the irrelevant box for me and for practical purposes when doing Republican candidates or ballot measures.

But that does not mean the bug doesn't continue to be required for many Democratic or Independent candidates. For them it remains something of a necessary merit badge.

That's why if you check the campaign literature and posters and bumper strips of candidate campaigns—say the previous materials for Tom Allen, John Baldacci, Jean Hay Bright, John Nutting, George Mitchell, and now those of Chellie Pingree and Janet Mills and virtually all Democrats—you will find them. So, too, will Independent candidates such as Angus King materials carry them. When we look at the Republican bumper strips and materials, you are unlikely to see the union bug with such candidates as Susan Collins, Paul LePage, or Bruce Poliquin. So don't bother looking; they don't matter anymore than the occasional *weevils* did in Jeb Stuart's food and supply wagons. If you're a Democrat, you put the union bug on automatically, so no wasted motion.

Another piece of even more troubling impedimenta are the annoying vinyl strips on the bumpers of cars. We used to call them "bumper stickers," but I am informed they are now called bumper strips. They have been associated with modern politics in America since the dawn of the age of the auto. Just about every politician who runs for anything has one, often more than one (doubly useless, but more of that later).

Most bumper strips are plain and unmemorable. Usually, they contain some bright colors and the name of the candidate, usually both or their last name, but sometimes only their first (see below for these oddments).

Most bumper strips are imminently forgettable, especially the ones for ballot measures such as "No on One" or "Yes on Three." In fact, thinking back over forty years of Maine campaigns, I can remember only a few truly distinctive message bumper stickers.

The first of these was during an antinuclear campaign in 1980 when many people wanted to shut down the Maine Yankee nuclear plant, and although they had a half dozen slogans, the best one was "No Nuke of the North." Maybe it was because I had watched *Sergeant Preston of the Yukon* growing up, but it hit a cord with me and was clever enough to stand out.

The second and to my mind still the most distinctive and catchy was during the Equal Rights Amendment battle when the YES side came up with "God Is Coming and Is She Pissed." Maine people with Maine oomph. Of course, the ERA referendum lost, but you can't blame that on the very pithy and distinctive strip. One of my all-time favorites actually. Try it out, next time you are arguing with someone about religion. Any religion.

The third from my very own hometown of Harpswell appeared when a huge liquefied natural gas facility was proposed for it. It said simply, "Keep Your Pipe Out of My Bottom." The vote against the facility was mammoth! Why wouldn't it be with that super powerful seacoast town imagery? *Post hoc ergo propter hoc*? Those lobstermen do know a lot about a lot of things.

Finally, who knows who or why or what import, but one of the most amusing bumper strip mysteries for me remains the one that said, "Get Religion: Lick a Witch." I never found out what its creators meant, but it's stuck with me all these years. Whatever its true purpose, it does make you think in a way "Angus 1994" or "No on 2" doesn't. Try it sometime in another religious discussion.

When I first started out in politics, I wasted a lot of time thinking about what bumper strips should look like and what they should say. I was sure they really mattered.

For Bill Cohen's first campaign in 1972, I thought "Cohen Can" had a nice ring to it as it promised hope for the future of the state's and nation's problems. I liked it, that is, until one of Bill's law partners pointed out that some crafty Democrat or Republican primary opponent could take Cohen's own bumper strip and cut it in half, rearranging it so it said, "Can Cohen."

Being new to the game, I thought that *could* happen, and I didn't want to take the blame when it did, so we settled on the more innocuous "Bill Cohen for Congress." Prosaic perhaps, but it was simple and conveyed the message. I say "settle" because it took about two weeks and fifty hours of argument with staff, family, friends, and your odd passersby to come up with the words and colors.

Oh God, what about the colors? Red on white? White on red? Red, white, and blue? Red and purple? Red and green? Green and yellow? On and on into the night. And many gin and tonics. In the process, all sorts of arguments came into play: "Would someone who was color blind be able to read it if the colors were red and green?" And so on.

And the "cuter" candidates and campaigns get, the greater the likelihood of mistakes.

As Dave Emery writes,

> Of course, bumper strip mistakes can be made, and the consequences can be hilarious! One of Angus King's early strips flashed some artsy fartsy panache. The message was simple, just two words, two lines, one word per line, "Angus" with "governor" below it, a single "g" serving both words. The problem was that the "g" was printed in a somewhat darker color, and consequently, when reading the bumper strip from a modest distance, it clearly read "Anus." Hence, an acquired nickname whispered in Republican circles around the statehouse.

Now in subsequent campaigns, I figured out that bumper strips were utterly unimportant as far as getting anybody to vote for the candidate or the cause, and all the scholarly literature agreed, saying they have no impact.

You can track small but sometimes discernible impacts in races for "literature drops," get out the vote efforts (GOTV), and "door knockers" (small pieces of literature left on doorknobs by volunteers). But I know of no truly empirical studies to show that bumper strips win votes or influence outcomes in elections—none at all.

So the next time I had control over a campaign, this time for governor, I simply decreed, "No bumper strips." Naively, I thought that would be the end of things—no more hassle over them.

But the aggravation was only the beginning. My God, this supporter and that relative and a host of friends and that friend of a friend kept telling the candidate's wife or husband, "We have to have bumper strips." "We need strips; we're falling behind." "I saw six of his opponents and none of his or hers; we have to fix that." "Where are our bumper strips? We're going to lose this race if we don't get some soon."

Everything, including poor fundraising, was blamed on our lack of bumper strips. Thus cometh (at considerable psychic cost) "Potholm's First Law of Bumper Strips": "They are worthless, but you have to have them!"

I finally figured out a way to use this law to my own advantage. Whenever I was asked to take on (or over) a campaign, or formulate the strategy for enabling it to win, I would insist on controlling the polling and the electronic media (i.e., television and radio) but let the candidate and the field people (and all their friends and neighbors and casual know-it-alls) or the cause people in a ballot measure, have complete charge of the bumper strips and road signs. That concession always made me seem reasonable and yet left real power over what mattered in my hands. And it relieved me of endless hours of argumentation because, for a color-blind person like myself, it was not only boring, it was also quite challenging.

Occasionally, quite rarely actually, a very well-known candidate or one with considerable hubris, will have a sticker with their first name only. "Olympia" for Senator Olympia Snowe, or "Hillary" for Senator Clinton or "Angus" for governor and then Senator Angus King.

Or, as Dave Emery writes,

> But opportunity awaits those who are clever enough to seize the moment. Nelson Rockefeller, then the governor of New York, ran for president in 1968, losing at the Republican National Convention to Richard Nixon. He had printed tens of thousands of bumper strips that simply read "Rocky!," many of which were on their way to the dumpster following his loss.
>
> But that year there was a Democratic candidate for governor of Indiana named Robert Rock. Some very clever person on his campaign team acquired them and trimmed off the "y!," thereby converting impedimenta waste to windfall. But like Rocky before him, Rock lost as well. Bad karma.

Normally I am of the "Roy Blount" school of thought on these matters. Blount once said with considerable insight that the only people who should wear Greek fisherman's hats were those who were (a) Greek and (b) fishermen. With first-name bumper strips, they are best left for mega-star musicians such as Madonna or Cher or Sting or mega-star international soccer players such as Pele or Ronaldo.

But when they work, as in the case of "Olympia" and "Angus," here in Maine, they do take on a certain distinctiveness.

Luckily, you never need bumper strips for ballot measures, not really.

Campaign buttons are also impedimenta of the first order—a time-consuming and monumental distraction in the best of situations!

Dave Emery provides some valuable context:

> Since the 1970s or so, they have morphed from painted metal discs with sharp pins designed to draw blood or pull threads from fine fabric, into simple paper stickers that can be worn on your jacket, stuck to a washroom mirror, or just forgotten until they bung up the lint filter in your clothes dryer. Very few of the old-style buttons are

in use today, which is too bad because paper stickers are not collectible; they simply don't last.

But go to any flea market and you'll almost certainly find a collection of old campaign buttons for sale. I've even found some of my own on occasion! Keep an eye out for a yellow button that says, *"Emery for Congrefs."* printed in brown. You see, back in 1974, I used some artsy fartsy panache as well. The *"f"* was meant to replicate the old colonial spelling style, as in *"Congrefs of the United States"* from the original Bill of Rights. I thought it was supremely clever of me, but most people didn't get it; others thought it was some kind of a misprint. Anyway, as I recall, we ordered only five hundred, so they're pretty rare today. I bought one for twenty-five cents at an antique mall a few years ago, but please don't feel obligated if you ever find one; I know most folks wouldn't give a plugged nickel for a politician's memorabilia these days. Impedimenta! Case in point!

Lawn signs are perhaps worth a bit more, if only to build name identification for candidates and causes that are not well known. Lawn signs used to also be a reflection of a candidate's grassroots support, but increasingly they are simply put up by candidates or causes who hire firms to do this work for them. But from beginning to end, lawn signs are a trial and a tribulation, albeit a source of ongoing amusement. For example, Mary McAleney and Pat Eltman recount the magical appeal of signs and the urgent calls during the fall of 2022 from a Democratic candidate for the legislature. "Where are all my signs? I need more. I need them *now*." The incumbent representative was unopposed.

As Dave Emery says,

I am always amazed at candidates who insist on printing a thesis on their lawn signs. Don't they know you can't read more than a couple of words while whizzing by at 45 miles per hour? The best lawn signs I ever saw were used in Belfast by State Representative Walter Ash Jr. The name "Ash" filled up the entire sign, and you could read it a mile away. I don't remember if he added "for Representative" at the bottom, but it didn't matter; all you needed to see was "Ash." And since it's not that easy for a prankster to convert such a large "h" to an "s," he was good to go!

Dave continues,

My most memorable experience with signs occurred during my 2016 state Senate campaign. My good friend Mike Thibodeau, then the state Senate president, arranged for a billboard-sized sign that was hauled around on a flatbed truck. It was massive . . . not unlike the famous Green Monster at Fenway Park!

Mike arranged to have the sign, flatbed, and all, hauled in the Rockland Lobster Festival parade. It was certainly noticed! So much so that the festival organizers subsequently banned all candidates from future festival parades, citing my sign as the reason. I never much liked marching in parades, and I'm certain that no lobster-eating tourist from New York ever voted for me anyway.

Some sort of campaign literature is necessary, if for no reason other than it provides some frame of reference as a candidate introduces himself to his prospective constituents; it is essentially a business card for politicians. Such literature can be a simple card, a folded brochure or even a tabloid-sized newspaper.

I must confess that I was once in love with the tabloid approach because they are cheap to produce and can accommodate any number of photos. But mostly, I liked the idea because they provide room for lots of text, giving me plenty of space to expound on all issues, great and small. Of course, no one reads these things except opponents and reporters looking for misstatements, factual errors, inconsistencies, and controversy. And tabloids are too heavy and bulky to carry around conveniently. Impedimenta! Consequently, I have concluded that a well-designed card with interesting photos, a brief bio and a few succinct issue bullet points is all that is needed.

Hastily prepared literature can quickly become major impedimenta. A few years back, Tim Woodcock, a very bright and well-regarded attorney and former Bangor mayor, was running in the Republican primary for Congress in the Second District. The *Bangor Daily News* endorsed him with a glowing editorial, stating he was "a big picture thinker." Naturally, he wanted to reproduce the editorial and give it as wide a distribution as possible.

The campaign sent it to the printer, and the new literature was quickly produced, ready to mail or hand out throughout northern Maine. The problem, however, was the new-fangled software used to scan the printed newspaper editorial and convert it back into computer text. This is called OCR, or *optical character recognition* technology, and even today it's not perfect. Sometimes the scanner doesn't get it just right due to smudges, creases, or dust. So "*big picture thinker*" was translated as "*big picture drinker*." Within an hour or so of the literature drop, the phone began to ring, and shortly thereafter his opponent's campaign manager thoughtfully dropped by with a six-pack of beer.

Of course, if the piece had been carefully proofread, the error would have been caught. But what could go wrong if you simply reprint an exact copy of the editorial? But that's not what happened. Major impedimenta!

Pat Eltman comes to the rescue with her tale of a massive sign effort on behalf of the Carter for President campaign. "It was the largest lit drop in Maine history: fifty thousand pieces showed up. Four SUVs with walkie talkies—that unfortunately didn't work. No matter, the flyers that showed up were in Spanish. We did the largest lit drop in history at the Westbrook landfill."

Also think about this. When it comes to the most important aspect of a campaign, it is time. The candidate's time is invaluable and can never be recovered once wasted or spent foolishly. That is a cardinal rule of campaign management.

But it is also true for the consultant's time. As Kay Rand suggested, consultants always want to get paid and paid on time. You don't want them stewing about their pay when they should be focused on the campaign. Clear their minds so they can focus on what matters. Don't let them get bogged down in the minutia and impedimenta of the campaign.

And if some impedimenta are of only marginal value in candidate campaigns, and never worth the time and trouble they exhaust, what about in ballot measures?

The good news, for those of you planning to mount your own ballot measure or referendum, is that you don't have to worry about union bugs, bumper strips, campaign buttons, or even a great deal of literature. The state of Maine is simply too big and too spread out to have these items of any use and in 90 percent of the campaigns you will not have the grassroots organization to distribute them anyway.

Thus, you are free to go—and win—on your own fine self and lots of GRPs of statewide television.

It can be very liberating.

You are now free to focus on what truly matters, the quality and volume of your television advertising. Its "quality" times its "weight" is what matters.

Go for TV (and most regrettably now, all the multitude of social media) with a singular focus.

Think of Jeb Stuart. Leave all the impedimenta behind. Let the cavalry come post-haste. Bring your best to the battle and as soon and as consistently as you can. Press your real advantages, and don't dilute or impede their impacts.

Come to Gettysburg as fast as you can and turn the tide of the battle.

Leave the impedimenta behind.

AXIOM #13

"Celebrate the Others" with Dave Emery

Once the game is over, the king and the pawn go back into the same box.
—JOHN BOYS

Over the years, I have been as guilty as anyone of highlighting the Maine greats. I've given innumerable lectures on "the magic of Margaret Chase Smith," the "revolution of Ed Muskie" and his national contributions, "the counterrevolution of Bill Cohen" and his national contributions, and finally of George Mitchell's phoenix-like rise to national prominence and his national contributions. Angus King, Olympia Snowe, Susan Collins have all gotten coverage enough to sink a ship or even two.

This chapter is but a small effort to redress the imbalance, to show readers how others deserve some attention. There are many, many of them if truth be told. But with the help of Dave Emery, we include here a few I hope will stimulate you to think again of the legions who have participated in Maine politics without getting the attention they deserve.

The following potpourri will hopefully remind us of the many and varied contributions to Maine's political life they have made and to stimulate readers to think about all those who graced Maine politics without becoming well known beyond a cycle or even within one.

THE UNSUNG INCUBATOR

I start with Clyde Smith, who gave Margaret her last name and her start in politics. "Clyde the Glide," as he became known to students of Maine politics, is worthy of a fresh look. By all accounts he was a smooth operator and something of a dandy, but he was a hell of a campaigner. I think he won forty-nine elections without a loss. Can you imagine that? Forty-nine. Almost unbelievable. Surely an indoor and outdoor record.

Certainly, I know of nobody else in Maine history with that kind of electoral punch.

Let Paul Mills, Maine's unofficial political historian, provide some much-needed background and insights in this section.

Clyde was born in June 1876 and died in April 1940. In between those two dates he won forty-nine elections, never losing one. Think of that incredible total with the breadth of experience that went with it. In rough chronological order, he ran for and was elected as superintendent of Schools of Hartland (this was an elective position back then) at age twenty; state representative from Hartland at age twenty-one; sheriff of Somerset County at age twenty-eight (when he moved to Skowhegan); Skowhegan First Selectman for sixteen years; state representative for two more terms from Skowhegan, 1919–1923, then three terms in the state Senate from Somerset County, 1923–1929.

In the Maine Senate he was a notable champion of the interest of organized labor and an ardent—though at that time unsuccessful—advocate of "old age" pensions, as a forerunner of social security at the state level was called. He served on the State Highway Commission in the late 1920s and early 1930s, which was an appointive position, so probably not part of the forty-nine, the Governors Executive Council 1933–1937 (which was elected by the legislature) and finally he ran for Congress, winning in 1936 and 1938.

Clyde never lost, and he had some tough opponents and a somewhat compromised personal life, which in a small town could have been a liability. His sins did not, however, include alcoholism. He didn't drink at all. He loved chocolates instead, and when I mentioned that to Margaret Chase Smith herself one night over dinner, she added, "Yes, he liked chocolates, and he liked the ladies," and she left it at that.

Most importantly for our purposes, Clyde did a lot of things he didn't want to do. He didn't want to run for Congress; he wanted to run for governor, but the Republican kingmakers of 1936 thought him tainted by some road commissioner business and pushed him out of that race. He didn't want to go to Washington and was never happy there, whereas "Sis," as he called Margaret, loved it. She was not going back to teach in a one-room Maine schoolhouse or be a telephone operator ever again.

Clyde was also disinclined—very disinclined—to run for reelection, especially after he had a heart attack. But he was pushed into doing that anyway, primarily by Sis and the Rs in Maine. And when he died, Margaret took up his mantel and blazed her way through four elections in six months—winning them all. She loved being a congressperson, and she loved being in Washington.

But think of what Maine politics would have been like without Clyde because without Clyde, there would have been no Margaret. And without Margaret, no Bob Monks. And without Bob Monks, no Bill Cohen, and without Bill Cohen, no Dave Emery or Olympia Snowe or Jock McKernan. That's a lot of weight of responsibility for Clyde. Either way.

Let Dave Emery move this strange ball down the line, beginning with his description of the legendary Plato Truman.

THE KING OF PERSISTENCE

Plato Truman was undoubtedly the most colorful and persistent of all also-ran candidates in Maine history, running for office at least eleven times. He ran as a Democrat, as a Republican, and as an Independent. He ran for the state House of Representatives, the state Senate, for Congress, for the US Senate, for governor, and for mayor of Biddeford.

Born in Athens, Greece, in 1928 as Plato Throumoulos, he immigrated to Biddeford with his family when only a few months old, and his later forays into politics started out in a promising way when he was elected to the state House of Representatives from Biddeford in 1964, the year when Barry Goldwater's trouncing in Maine led to the first Democrat-controlled state legislature in half a century.

Two years later, he decided to run in the 1968 Democratic primary for US Senator, challenging Elmer Violette of Van Buren. A third candidate, Jack L. Smith of Sanford, was enticed into that race, some say, by none other than freshman Congressman Peter N. Kyros. Smith split the York County vote and tipped the primary narrowly to Violette, who then went on to lose badly to Margaret Chase Smith that November.

Next, Truman challenged Kyros in the Democratic primary and was crushed. But two years after that Truman was back, entering the 1970 Democratic primary against Governor Kenneth M. Curtis and surprised the pundits with a respectable 40 percent against the sitting governor. Truman had by now changed his slogan from "Two Great Names, One Great Candidate" to "Stop Curtis Taxes," and it obviously had had some impact.

His unexpected showing gave much encouragement to Republican James S. Erwin, but that November, Curtis edged Erwin by about eight hundred votes to win a second term as governor of Maine.

For all practical purposes, that was Plato Truman's last hurrah. He ran for office at least eight more times, sometimes as a Republican, sometimes as an Independent, and finally as a Democrat once again. But he never remotely approached the successes and near successes of those heady days when he was considered a credible candidate who had only narrowly lost a chance to run for the US Senate in a general election. He passed away in 2021 at the age of ninety-two, so politics obviously agreed with him.

Dave Emery recalls another memorable Independent:

AN OPPONENT WHO BECAME A SUPPORTER

There were three other Independent candidates (in addition to Plato Truman, Jim Longley, and Angus King) that I especially remember from Maine politics. The first was J. David Madigan, who ran against me as an Independent for Congress in 1978. David was a conservative who argued for cuts in spending, fiscal discipline, and smaller government. He was also pro-life. We didn't cross paths much during the campaign, but whenever we did, I found him to be cordial and very sincere in his beliefs; later he became a supporter.

His younger brother, Peter Madigan, subsequently joined my congressional staff and to this day is a valued friend. Peter stayed in Washington and became a very successful and highly regarded strategist for Fortune 100 companies and served on the Bush/Cheney transition team. He is also an adjunct lecturer in Leadership Studies at the University of Maine, Orono. I can thank his brother David for being the catalyst that brought Peter into my circle of friends and associates, and in the process, start him on his stellar career. I am very grateful to David for that.

Dave next brings us,

THE MAN OF GOD

Another memorable Independent candidate was Herman C. "Buddy" Frankland. Born in Eastport, Buddy became the pastor of the Bangor Baptist Church, and in the mid-1970s, he had built up quite a following as a prominent evangelical preacher in the manner of Jerry Falwell and Pat Robertson. He was eloquent, effective as an organizer and had grown his congregation to three thousand, by all accounts the largest fundamentalist church in all of New England.

He was politically very conservative, frequently preaching against gay rights, abortion, liberalization of drug and alcohol laws, public school curricula and, of course, sex in all its permutations. He believed he was the perfect candidate to succeed Independent businessman Jim Longley as governor. Longley had won a three-way race in 1974 by splitting off enough Franco-American voters and conservative Republicans to edge out Democrat George Mitchell and Republican Jim Erwin. Frankland believed he could do the same thing by galvanizing the conservative fundamentalists and the conservative Catholics around the principles of morality, fiscal restraint, and limited government.

The Republican candidate for governor that year was Linwood Palmer, a mainstream Republican from Nobleboro in Lincoln County, while the Democratic candidate was Attorney General Joseph Brennan of Portland. Brennan led the campaign from start to finish, but his win was assured when the *Bangor Daily News*, at that time a reliably Republican newspaper, endorsed Frankland.

Whatever chance Lin Palmer had quickly evaporated, but it wasn't nearly enough to bring Frankland a victory. The conservative Catholic strategy didn't work because Brennan was Catholic himself, and Frankland's fundamentalist views did not play well with Maine's moderate electorate. Brennan was elected with 48 percent of the vote to 34 percent for Palmer and only 18 percent for Frankland. Had Buddy Frankland not run, it seems a fair assumption that Lin Palmer would have gotten almost all his votes and might have been elected in a very close race.

This election occurred at a time when Republican prospects were waning at the state legislative level. In 1974, the GOP had lost the Maine House of Representatives for the first time since 1914, only to be regained for a single term in the first LePage election of 2010, following thirty-six years of unbroken Democratic control. A few years later, they would also lose the state Senate and enter a protracted period of palpable electoral weakness, broken only briefly by a single term with control of the state Senate in the national Republican landslide year of 1994.

The relative success of Frankland among conservative voters in 1978, and most particularly among Republican conservatives, presaged the rightward tilt of Maine Republicans generally, concomitant with a significant shift toward the Democrats in many traditionally moderate Republican towns throughout the state. Shifts and realignments occur occasionally in American politics, usually driven by significant cultural or economic issues; Frankland and the emergence of the Republican conservatives can be seen as a bellwether for the Maine political realignment that evolved during the latter part of the twentieth century.

THE CALM PROFESSIONAL

Many people in Maine often assume that most candidates run for office in order to get elected. They would probably be surprised at how many people who run for office actually don't plan to get elected, don't expect to get elected, and even don't want to get elected. These revelations are seldom taught in civics classes.

John Menario, the former Portland City Manager and campaign manager for Save Maine Yankee, came to me in 1986. He wanted to run for governor as an Independent. Although we subsequently did a poll to see what his chances were, he didn't seem to have the usual candidate's heightened interest or even ask "How am I doing?" or "What is my name recognition?" or "How can I win?"

In fact, he seemed almost uncaring about the process of polling and results of the findings. Those seemed pretty stark. With Jock McKernan looking strong and with the well-known Sherry Huber already running as an Independent, there weren't enough votes for a second Independent in any case. If I remember correctly, he had 5 or 6 percent. I thought he would probably save his time and effort and forget running for governor.

Usually, would-be candidates appreciate such straightforward advice. Some are even relieved and grateful. But John just smiled and took the information with total equanimity. He asked polite questions as to how we knew this, or why we thought he could only do so well statewide even though he was very well liked in his local area.

John also showed only modest interest in the issues we had tested, often saying "Well, I agree with that" or "No, I don't agree with that," but it all seemed very abstract, and his interest seemed to flag when we continued to chatter about "this influence vector" or "that push issue." We found a couple of good ones, but his eyes glazed over as we droned on. We assumed he had lost interest in his prospects and was going to bow out before ever going out on the stage.

Always trying to read the room perceptively, we offered "Well, now you know there's not much chance to become governor, so at least the poll saved you a lot of time and money. You can be at peace. It would be a good idea maybe some time, but not this cycle. You can try to build visibility for next time."

There was quite a silence in the room as he looked around and shrugged. "But I want to run. I know it's a long, long shot, maybe impossible, but I really want to run." Dumbfounded, I asked, "But why? You don't seem to have a burning ambition to be in politics at all costs, and you don't seem to be running for governor to get your name recognition up so you can run for Congress or something. Why run?"

Menario grinned broadly, "Well, I have a lot of ideas how to make government run better, and a lot of the people who want me to run for governor are bankers and brokers and Chamber of Commerce types, and they think people should hear about them from me. If I go out there and talk about these issues, look presentable, and make a good impression, perhaps I'll get some of these ideas adopted."

Well, that seemed so logical and sensible, and I really liked the guy. He was a first-rate human being who'd been city and campaign manager and done a great job at both. Why not try to help him do the best job he could? It certainly took a lot of the pressure out of campaigning if you wanted 15 percent instead of 50.1 percent.

It turned out to be an unusual, extremely pleasant campaign. No stress. There was enough money to get on TV a little, and the press coverage was pretty good. The candidate was very happy all through the campaign. John went all over the state sounding very calm and reasonable and presenting a fine appearance. He talked to a lot of Rotary Clubs and was outstanding in the statewide televised debates. He pressed very little flesh in the streets on purpose, although a lot of people came up to him to chat in Portland and other places.

On election night, he got 15 percent of the vote. Now normally on election night, if you have a nice candidate and you know he or she is going to lose, you always try to spend election night with them because they need support more than the winners. The winners don't need your presence. They already have hundreds of brand-new friends, some made in the last hours before the polls closed or even right afterward. You would be amazed, truly amazed, at the human flotsam and jetsam that shows up in the winner's campaign headquarters or ballroom on election night. And many of the winners are already beginning to forget they didn't get elected all on their own.

This election night was a jovial one. The candidate was very grateful to one and all. John spent the entire night thanking all the people there. He mingled with them and was very appreciative to everyone. He beamed. "I did better than I thought I would. I didn't spend as much as Sherry, and I got about as many votes. I'm very happy."

Later Menario did get to be a vice president of an important bank and spent the last ten years of his professional life doing what he wanted to do. Years afterward people would still come up and tell him what a fine campaign he'd run. He had been a class act and they appreciated it.

The irony of course is that he would have made a fine governor. He had good judgment, cared about the people of Maine, and had a proven record of delegating responsibility and getting things done. But he probably wouldn't have been able to get through a Republican or Democratic primary for governor, and in this election cycle there was already a credible Independent candidate running, Sherry Huber (she too would end up with 15 percent of the vote).

For an Independent to win as governor either the Rs or the Ds have to field a weak candidate (preferably both), and there can only be one credible Independent running. In this case, the Rs had a very strong candidate in Jock McKernan, and there was another well-funded Independent already in the race. But John completed his mission with skill and dispatch and seemed to have a very good time throughout.

THE HAPPIEST SACRIFICIAL LAMB

People often talk about "sacrificial lambs in politics," people who run when they have no objective chance of winning or who are asked by party bigwigs to sacrifice themselves because the party has written off the seat and simply puts up a candidate to fill the position but has no intention of ever doing anything serious to help them.

Many voters feel sorry for such candidates and shake their heads at their audacity, or foolishness as the case may be. Consultants, like sharks, however, almost always smell blood in the water (in the form of a paying client).

Usually it's a small amount of blood, so the consultant explains to other consultants (this consultant-to-consultant palaver being the innermost confessional circle in politics), "I'm just paying the overhead."

The other consultant invariable nods knowingly. They've been there before themselves.

But don't pity the sacrificial lamb. She or he has motives for running other than winning. They want to make a point; they want to push a cause or an issue. They want to have a platform so other people will listen to them. Some even have a big enough ego to assume people need to hear whatever it is they are saying, no matter *what* they are saying.

For some, there are more mercenary reasons: money and/or a job. Since Maine has public funding of most state campaigns, less than idealistic candidates see a free meal ticket and a chance to hire their friends and relatives. One wag hired her husband to be her campaign manager. Actually, he was pretty good at it and got her further than most had assumed, but a lot of people made quite a stink about it at the time.

Numerous candidates for office are wooed by the prospect that if and when they lose, they will be welcomed to Washington or Augusta with open arms. Because it is illegal to offer a public job for anything of value—like running for office—few of these folks have anything specific in mind. But the mind is putty when your ego is involved, and the would-be candidate thinks "They will want me if I lose."

But many simply like to talk and have an audience. Especially if their target is well known and popular, fringe candidates delight in going all in against the incumbent during debates. And after one or two statewide debates many can convince themselves that they really belong on the same plane as that US Senator or governor or congressperson.

It's a bit like wondering why some folks go on those humiliating television shows. Frequently it's as simple as "They asked me." or "They helped pay my way." These can be some of the same reasons why many political sacrificial lambs run. For once in their lives they are really the center of attention and that is all that matters. It's good old-fashioned, harmless fun for the most part.

THE LITTLE FRIEND OF ALL THE WORLD

Here is one example, my favorite, because Jasper Wyman was the happiest camper ever, the Little Friend of All the World.

The day that Jasper Wyman showed up in my office at Bowdoin to tell me he was running for the US Senate against George Mitchell in 1988 and that he had the support of Bill Cohen and the Republican Party in Maine (the latter having asked him to run!), I was a bit taken aback. I liked him and always found him to be honest and straightforward with me, even though we didn't agree on a lot of issues, so I didn't hold back.

"You'll get slaughtered," I said. "It's not even worth doing a poll." (Imagine how bad I must have thought it was!)

"I know," he smiled. "I know. But I don't care."

Mentally I quickly went through the checklist of why such a fool's errand was being contemplated and couldn't think of any. He'd been involved in a lot of edgy causes over the years as a spokesperson, "You've already made as many enemies as you need."

Wyman laughed and assured me he had absolutely no intention of running on the issues his previous group had espoused. No, in fact, he planned to gracefully slide away from some of their extreme positions as soon as he could. Wow! That was interesting. Was it revenge? Was it disenchantment? "No," he offered, "not at all." He liked the people he worked for and liked many of their causes. He just didn't want to promote them anymore, and he wanted a new image before moving on in life. "I want to move in new directions," he offered finally.

Since Jasper was of very modest means, and we knew he could raise no money, the whole thing was very mysterious and somewhat dubious. It turned out the state Republican Party had indeed sought him out to run. Not only that, if he passed muster, the national Republican Party said it would raise $250,000 nationally for the campaign. Now that was a piddling amount to run for a major office in a high-cost TV state.

But for his purposes, it seemed like a fortune. Without embarrassment or shame, he said, "They asked me to run. I'm going to use a lot of that money to change my image. I want more people to like me. I don't want them to dislike me anymore. I'm going to run a campaign of personality and smiles. I'm not going to say anything bad about anybody, not even my opponent."

Well, when a consultant hears that kind of honesty, they are often dumfounded by it—such candor can confuse them no end. But after further discussions, it was clear he was serious. No sham. No pretense. Just take all that partisan money and make people like you. Pretty damn gratifying to confront such total honesty, I can tell you that.

The candidate was good-hearted and now genuinely wanted to be the little friend of all the world. He didn't like being the bad guy with edgy issues; he wanted to be liked.

The makeover began when the consultant's wife discovered he did not own, nor ever had worn, a button-down shirt. So off to L.L. Bean's flagship store they went. Although somewhat aghast at the money it cost, he was very pleased when he was newly outfitted. Off he went, happy as the proverbial clam, or at least as happy as Maine clams can be now what with all those green crabs around. Laughing, happy, up every day to go out around the state, Jasper went having the time of his life.

We were a little worried when he had to go down to Washington to meet with the money boys and girls, for even at this pitiful level of support, they insisted on sizing him up. "Probably best if you sound like you really want to knock off the senator. Give them your best pit bull impersonation."

Off he went.

Since we figured we would never, ever get another chance to do this, we booked him into a very expensive suite at the Willard Hotel, a room with a view of the Capitol and Washington Monument. The Willard has hosted heavy hitters and multitudes of wannabes since the Civil War and still plays that part for many.

Jasper called in nearly hourly with all the marvels that staying there entailed. Like so many others before him, he was quite impressed with the fact that there was even a phone in the bathroom. Power city. The only rough patch for him came when he returned from his dinner meeting with the national money chaps. They had seemed impressed with his speech about "attacking and bringing the senator down to size." "You go for it," the head honcho had replied.

By the time he returned to his suite, however, Jasper found a lovely maid asking him politely if he wanted his bed turned down. Panicked and thinking we had sent a hooker to his room, he ran away and called us from a pay-phone. We calmed him down with some Biblical passages and got him to return to his room where he found, not a naked lady, but a couple of chocolates on the top of the turned-down bed. For years afterward he happily told one and all about this incident. Great fun!

From then on it was a dream campaign for everybody, especially Senator George Mitchell who couldn't believe his good fortune, although Larry Benoit had never forgotten that his candidate in 1974, Peter Kyros, took things for granted, insisted on blasting away at Jasper, even on the radio, even about weapons systems. Talk about overkill!

Regardless, Jasper had the time of his life. He paid no attention whatsoever to the Mitchell campaign. The press was initially confused, amused, and bemused, but they ended up liking the Little Friend of All the World. One reporter called me and asked obliquely if he had only months to live. "He's a different guy."

And he was.

His head got filled with lectures about nuclear weapons and theories of disarmament, and he went around sounding like the world's most strategic senator. He met with the Cohen staffers and got all sorts of useful information about nuclear weapons—a far cry from the latest research on fetal tissue. He soon stunned people and reporters with his concepts of "throw weight" and Bill Cohen's elegant "build down nuclear disarmament" plan. "Who knew he was this smart?" asked one reporter. Not once did he get angry or attack anybody. He looked like a serious senatorial candidate but more humorous. He sounded like one. People were impressed. "He seems like a statesman—what happened?" Jasper had a ball day after day after day.

There was one heart-stopping moment on the campaign trail, however. Because of his low budget, he had only enough money to hire a driver, so any field workers would have to be volunteers. Of course, you have to have someone to guide and direct those volunteers, and there was no money for that, either. So he was always on the lookout for anybody willing to help.

He was campaigning with his driver in a major mill town with high unemployment, and quite a few people turned out to hear him give his sunny message of "We are all God's children." The driver called after lunch to report that the candidate was really pumped up because he'd rounded up a volunteer coordinator, a man who offered to work for him full time, for no money, to organize the state's schools for his campaign.

This seemed odd. And was.

It turned out that "the new volunteer coordinator wannabe" had already done two spells in the slammer accused of child molestation, and we had to caution the Little Friend of All the World that, although forgiveness was the true purview of the Lord's, it probably wouldn't play all that well in a political campaign.

That was apparently the only hiccup in the campaign.

The candidate went here and there. Happy, smiling, sounding erudite and charming one and all. Jasper studied hard for the debates and came across on statewide TV as a thoughtful, knowledgeable person with impressive positions.

Of course, at the end of the day, Wyman did get slaughtered, and George Mitchell actually racked up a statewide record of 81 percent. How to explain this? In part because many of the people who had liked his edgy, hard-right stands on the earlier issues now assumed he had gone insane and refused to vote for him as a protest. And of course, many, many others were not going to abandon the very popular George Mitchell for any reason.

But no matter. Jasper was the happiest camper ever on the campaign trail and certainly the happiest camper who'd ever gotten massacred like that. The size of the defeat meant nothing. Now the election was over, and he had, however briefly, been "a major player." The press and editorial writers praised him for such a positive, issue-oriented campaign. Jasper was in seventh heaven when all was said and done.

He left the state shortly thereafter, getting a fine job in Connecticut on the strength of his personality and his courage in tackling Goliath, not with a sling and stone, but with a smile and a fine sense of humor.

And a good time was had by all, especially the junior senator who set the state record. If I remember right, amid the landside, junior Senator Mitchell tied 16–16 in Hersey in Aroostook County and only lost the Washington County Town of Talmadge 18–12. So George being George, and Larry being Larry, the day after the election, he was up there, showing the flag in those hamlets and his fine sense of humor on display. And no doubt asking his staff and the locals what had gone wrong in those tiny hamlets!

What a victory lap for the all-time champion.

So, whatever you do, don't feel sorry for sacrificial lambs and their like. They are enjoying being on stage and having at least a semi-captive audience. Many find that its own reward!

In fact, if you get bored in your daily life, go for it. A lot of people have gone before you. Albeit not with the panache of the Little Friend of All the World.

There is a life lesson here: sometimes you can have more fun losing than trying to win. And sometimes you should undertake hopeless tasks in order to achieve other goals. In short, satisfy your pleasure while your soul is smiling and don't worry about having to "win" everything.

LOYAL SOLDIER

Growing up, coming to Maine for Christmas was the high point of my year. I loved the snow and the trips to L.L. Bean to see the trappers and hunters. My cousin Charlie, who was a year older than me and was my most intimate friend, lived in Portland. He was my guide to Maine, the study of history, World War II, and toy soldiers.

He went into the army after high school and served with distinction as an MP in Germany before going to Bowdoin. But his life was not easy after that. The day he was due to arrive at Bowdoin, his father died, and he ended up commuting to classes from his home on Baxter Boulevard in Portland. With his father gone so suddenly, there was no money for college, and he relied on scholarships and working every day to pay the bills, and he lived at home with his widowed mother.

As soon as classes were over, Charlie went to work in a shoe factory in Fort Andross, Brunswick, before finally heading back to Portland for the night. Then just when he was adjusted to college life, during his junior year at Bowdoin, he was diagnosed with testicular cancer and underwent a major operation and massive doses of radiation and chemotherapy.

Despite all this, Charlie graduated with highest honors in history from Bowdoin and went on to get his Ph.D. in military history. While at Bowdoin, he met and later married his wife, Marlene, and adopted her four children. He was just beginning to get his feet on the ground, teaching at Wilton High School in Connecticut, when he was again stricken with cancer and underwent a second major operation on his other side and the same massive doses of radiation and chemotherapy. This bout left him permanently crippled with a massive fluid buildup in his legs.

Lifelong Republicans, Charlie and Marlene started out as activists in party politics with Bill Cohen and his campaign for Congress in 1972. They supported him early in the Republican primary when Cohen defeated the better known and more experienced Abbott Greene.

The Petersens came on board early and worked tirelessly as volunteers for Cohen, and in the summer of 1972 became field personnel for Bill in Oxford and Androscoggin counties, the two most important counties in our game plan. Normally Republican candidates had been coming out of the Androscoggin valley down 23,000 votes. Bill Cohen was to lose the two by only 6,000, a net pickup of 15,000 votes in their counties.

The Petersens were with Cohen the first day as well when he began his six-hundred-mile walk across the state from Gilead to Fort Kent. I have always been amused that Bill Cohen, eventually Secretary of Defense and subsequently leader of several million service men and women, started out with such a small band of followers. The first day of the walk certainly tried the patience of the candidate and those accompanying him. Charles and Marlene walked with Bill that very first day, which was almost the last day of the effort.

That first day was horrible. It was hot and still as only rural Maine can be hot and still in July. The candidate had yet to hit his stride navigating the shoulders of rural roads and had several narrow escapes from speeding cars.

And oh, what cars. There were streams and streams of them. Often the traffic was bumper to bumper in long lines coming from north to south.

Initially we were very excited about the traffic flow and all the people who were driving by and waving wildly. Excited, that is, until Charlie pointed out that most of the cars had Canadian plates; they were summer visitors from Quebec.

"Not many voters here," said the candidate ruefully.

On and on we trudged, sweltering, frustrated, and very soon, very sore and very tired. Even then Charlie's body had been weakened by his first and second bouts with cancer and the concomitant radiation and chemotherapy, and his leg swelled up alarmingly. But as the rest of us complained, Charlie strode on, never complaining, never asking for a break.

Both Bill and I were challenged by his perseverance.

For many years, he and Marlene were also well known on the Republican political trail. They were party stalwarts who supported Republican candidates whenever they could. Marlene became a political operative in her own right, running for the Maine House in a largely Democratic district and coming quite close to victory.

Both Charles and Marlene were more than just individuals who followed Maine politics. They both represent the small—and often dwindling—number of party supporters who are the true activists on the Maine political scene. Too often we overlook their contributions to the political process, focusing on the candidates, their media firms, pollsters, and other high-priced consultants associated with campaigns. But it is often the little-known workers who provide the foot soldiers for campaigns. They show up at airports and downtown rallies. They speak out for their candidates and their causes.

They are the worker bees who make politics work. Their tasks are legion.

They get out and put up signs at election time. They work stuffing envelopes and help organize volunteers. They go door to door distributing leaflets. They man phone banks. They copy telephone numbers down on voter lists. They keep up the spirits of the candidates, often cheering them when no one else will. They serve on the city, town, county, and state committees for their parties.

Sometimes they are paid, especially if they work as field personnel, traveling from one end of the state to the other. But most often they are not. They do their political activity because they like it and consider it their civic duty. They like being a part of the Maine political scene and having a say in how things turn out at election time.

They follow the political process closely, knowing who the players are and what are the issues that interest people. They are always listening to what others say and bring important information to candidates and their staff. They are the foot soldiers in the small armies that make up political campaigns, be they candidate or ballot measure.

Charles William Petersen was a profile in courage. And a poignant example of a political worker bee par excellence. He is very missed.

THE PROMISE KEEPER

I want to close with a brief story about Duke Dutremble. I think highly of Duke. He was a fine state senator from Biddeford and later a very good president of the Senate. When he ran for Congress in 1994, I was happy to be asked to help him out in the primary. I thought he would make a good congressman, too. He was my first real Democratic candidate in Maine, and his primary election night in June was one of my happiest memories of politics.

When he came to Bowdoin and asked me to help him, many Democratic operatives were upset. Some disliked me personally, some didn't think I would be of any use in a Democratic primary, and some just didn't like the idea of a Democratic candidate using a tainted Republican. Let alone Dr. Demento from Bowdoin College.

But Duke wanted me, and I tried to help out when and where I could. He was running against three other candidates, all very worthy opponents—Bill Troubh, Bonnie Titcomb, and Bill Diamond—but he had the best media firm of that cycle, and Mike Shea provided a truly outstanding biographical spot. His telling of Duke's backstory was one of the best I'd ever seen. Greg Nadeau was a very able campaign manager and Dan Paradis did yeoman service in telling Duke's story in the press. Plus, Biddeford was the best organized city I'd ever encountered.

The day of the primary hit ninety degrees, and I went to Biddeford in the middle of the day. I was so excited. Peter Burr was doing exit polling for us that day, and he was quite confident after getting the early cuts. But driving around in the 1st CD, I was apprehensive, at least until I got to Duke's Senate district and saw not only the flood of his signs, but the GOTV efforts, which were truly heroic. Two of the best GOTV people ever—Pat Eltman and Joy O'Brien—were working for Duke. The Democratic Party should put up statues to these women. Whether working on presidential campaigns or local races, they were masters of GOTV as well as its strategy.

I subsequently worked on a number of political and corporate campaigns with Pat and was always impressed by her work ethic and her take-no-prisoners attitude. She can do it all—and leave you laughing at her skill and dispatch and activities. Everybody inside Maine politics has a Pat story. Here is one of mine.

On Land for Maine's Future campaign we were working together. The Nature Conservancy and the campaign team met at Bowdoin for lunch. Kent Womack announced there was only a certain amount of money available, and it would be divided between TV and GOTV. There weren't enough GRPs in the budget, so I went into full Dr. Demento mode and blurted out, "Let's be honest, you might as well take all that GOTV money and throw it in the Androscoggin River for all the good it will do you if we don't do enough statewide TV."

The entire table swiveled toward Pat. She gave a little half smile at me as Kent asked, "How does that make you feel, Pat?"

"How does it make me feel? How does it make me feel? It makes me feel like I've been raped. *Raped!*" she exclaimed in her booming voice, causing many, if not most, in the dining hall to look at her, their mouths gaping wide.

"Rape" is a powerful word in any context, but in a college dining room of today, it is incendiary. People stopped eating and stared and listened in. I thought The Nature Conservancy people would faint.

They quickly huddled and said, "We'll find the money for both."

Later, after the meeting, Pat said, "How did you like that, White Boy?"

I had to admit it was pure genius. They broke the mold of tough political cookies after they made Patricia.

But back to the Duke primary.

That night remains mythic in my mind.

There was a huge turnout for the candidate wherever we were in Biddeford, and a little after 6 P.M., Peter Burr called and said, "It's over," even though the polls would be open for two more hours. I was higher than a kite. After all the self-imposed responsibility I'd put on my shoulders, I felt very relieved. As Dave Emery says in chapter 8, Peter knew as much about York County as he did about the back of his hand and the label on the Pepsi cans he drank like water 24/7.

I remember Duke introducing me to Jim Gratello, mayor of Biddeford, at some point. He said he would have the results soon after the polls closed. I was so excited; I began to act even crazier than usual. I fancifully blurted out to the mayor, "Now when the returns come in, don't release them. We don't want those bully boys in Portland stealing this one." Troubh was from Portland, and we'd been firing up the voters far and wide with a lot of urban rivalry.

So, when the returns started coming in, I was quite confident. But first, as I remember, Bonnie Titcomb was ahead, then Bill Diamond, and briefly

Bill Troubh when Portland checked in. Duke was running third. I remember Pat Callahan on air saying to Jan Fox or Cindy Williams, "It doesn't look good for Duke." I was panicking and felt faint. What a fiasco this would be. For Duke. And for me. Just then, I spotted the mayor. "Did you send the results in?" "No," he replied, "you told me not to."

"This would be a good time," I said, awash with relief. What a rush to see the numbers flip on the TV screen as soon as he called them in and soon after when the networks called it for Duke. I was so joyous. Usually on election night, I just want to go home and go to sleep, but this night I didn't want it to end. I stayed and stayed, and even after the headquarters began to shut down, I went out onto the streets of Biddeford that hot night and walked around with my poor, tired, bored wife, Sandy, waking up homeless people and saying, "Duke won. Duke won."

Duke ended up with 33 percent of the vote, Bonnie Titcomb and Bill Diamond each got 24 percent, and Bill Troubh got 19 percent.

After the primary, the national Democrats pretty much took over the general election campaign. The national Democratic congressional operatives who came to Maine to help Duke were insistent he would win. That summer and fall, the Republicans were surging nationally, but Jim Longley Jr., son of the former governor, had won the Republican primary and was Duke's opponent. The Democrats assumed he would lose ignominiously. But this was the cycle of Newt Gingrich's Contract with America (which the Democrats kept writing off as the Contract *on* America), which resonated widely. And some in the district thought Jr. actually *was* his father.

I remember being worried because Pat Elman was worried, and Duke's campaign manager, Greg Nadeau, was worried. We had all been stunned when Duke and Longley debated at Bowdoin in front of a large crowd, and the student audience vote actually went for Longley. Jim's father, Jim Sr., was a graduate of Bowdoin College but not a celebrated one like Bill Cohen or George Mitchell.

The next Democratic Party poll showed Duke trailing by about four points, so it was clear Duke *was* in trouble. I was stupefied by the internals.

A very distraught Mike Shea called me afterward, "Duke's going to lose. We have to go negative on Longley. Now. We have to straighten out this mess." Shea had seen this many times in Massachusetts where rough-and-tumble negative ads were the coin of the realm.

But there was a problem, a big one.

Duke had given his word that he wouldn't go negative in a well-publicized joint statement with Longley. Moreover, the major newspapers, including the

Portland Press Herald, the *Waterville Morning Sentinel*, and the *Augusta Kennebec Journal* had all endorsed Duke and had cited his pledge.

I remember many late-night calls from Shea. He'd prepared a dynamite commercial contrasting the two men and their positions and had an energetic buy to hit females in the home and drive-time radio for the females who worked outside the home.

He said Duke wouldn't budge, wouldn't run the spot.

Finally, Shea sent the commercial to my house, and Sandy and I had Duke and his wife, Dot, over and showed it to them. I said as strongly as I could, "If you don't run this ad, you're going to lose. You have to run it. Otherwise, you're not going to Congress."

Duke shook his head. "I gave my word. I won't break it."

"But the Rs are already breaking it; they went negative ten days ago," I answered.

I think I had tears in my eyes as I said it. Maybe Duke did too, but he wouldn't budge. "I don't care what they did. I gave my word. I'm not going to break it."

I was sad and frustrated, but at the same time I was also proud of Duke. And I am proud of him to this day. It was a rare moment in politics. Shea would call the next morning and get the news. Incredulous after all his years in Boston and Massachusetts politics, he said, "I've never heard of anything like this. Ever." I never had either, but my esteem for Duke as a person has never diminished. He lost the election, but he kept his word. He kept his promise. He chose honor over office.

He proved there is a lot we can learn from the "Others." Don't summarily write them off.

*"Appreciate the Agony of 'The Hunt Blew Up'
and the Joys of 'It's Over'"*

The ending decides what the title will be.
—GOETHE

In the Great North Woods of Maine, there is a hunting expression, "the hunt blew up," which is used to describe a situation that started out promising but then inexplicably ended up with nothing to show for the effort. And often, there is no truly definitive explanation as to why.

In the pursuit of varying hares or snowshoe hares, for example, you can hear it happen. When hunting them with dogs, the beagles and their kin will range through the woods quite silently until they "cut" or come across a hare's track. The best scenting snow is when it is a little moist and the scent lingers for a long time, so it is tantalizingly present when the dogs encounter it.

Once the dogs catch the scent, they begin to bark, first one dog, then another, then another as they follow the hare through the woods. This barking, which to the unappreciative ear can sound like a cacophony of disparate mismatched instruments, sounds wonderful to the hunter. Magical almost. Called "the music," it can be the very reason the hunter or hunters are afield. Many go into the woods with dogs not simply (or even) to shoot the hare for the pot but to create and listen to "the music." Note to the reader: equating political consultants and candidates with hunters will help you get into the spirit of this chapter!

Among Maine hunters it is considered bad form to simply try to kill as many hares as possible, unlike in Australia where, I believe, jackrabbits are such a nuisance that people are encouraged to shoot them at all times and in all places year-round.

It is also considered bad form to shoot any random hares other than the primary one which is causing the dogs to create their music. Usually, the dogs will stay on the track of the primary hare they are pursuing and not get distracted by other scents when they are chasing around in the woods after a particular hare. The resulting commotion will sometimes scatter other hares, and some of them may blunder into the path of the waiting hunter. Shooting such "a spare" is considered in many circles of rabbit hunters as piggish and unsportsmanlike, although, of course, some hunters don't follow this code.

The hare, interestingly, hears the noise of the barking dogs and knows something is after it, but instead of rushing blindly though the woods non-stop, it will run a bit and then stop and listen to see if the dogs are getting close or not or have actually been chasing another hare.

Also, the hare doesn't run in a straight line until it escapes or gets caught. Rather, it circles around, eventually coming back more or less to the territory where it started. But the hare doesn't run a perfect circle; otherwise the hunters would always have a pretty good shot on the return run. Instead, the roughly elliptical path brings the hare back to the vicinity from where it started but not exactly to the same spot. Also, if the hare continues to be pursued, it will continue on or around until it loses the dogs.

So here is the scene set for you. In the middle of the deep woods, the hemlocks and spruce trees and juniper bushes all around and with lots of snow in the thickets and even on the woods roads, the sounds of the beagles chasing the hare is quite exciting as the hunt develops. The dogs begin to bark differently when they are hot on the trail of the hare than when they are way behind it or confused as to the turn it may have taken through some particularly heavy brush. The music can be very varied and quite lovely, indeed.

In the ideal hunt, the hunter has positioned him or herself in a position where the rabbit will come by and offer a quick shot. In that situation, the hunter will have the option of shooting or not shooting, stopping, or letting the hunt run on.

But sometimes, just when things are going well and the music says the dogs are close behind the hare and anticipation runs high, sometimes all of a sudden, the barking will peter out or stop with only one dog, and then none, barking.

"The hunt's blown up" will be the message passed from hunter to hunter, and there will be a lot of shaking of heads and musing as to what went wrong. "Betty's nose ain't so good since she had that cold" or "That damn hare must have crossed the brook and lost them" or even "Son of a gun, that's one smart bunny."

But of course there is sometimes no true explanation—it just happened. Every one of the hunters in the party will have an idea, and many will express their hypothesis quite vehemently, but the truth is, sometimes nobody really knows why this particular hunt "blew up" and another did not.

It was unexpected. It was sudden. It was over in a flash. This is true in hunting. It is true in love.

And it is true in politics as well.

I have always felt it was better to be lucky than good—in love, in politics, and in hunting—but that's just my personal opinion.

Sometimes in political campaigns, things are going well, you are either raising good amounts of money, have good commercials on TV, your candidate is getting out and about and getting good free media, and then something happens in "the woods" of politics. The sounds of an approaching victory fade suddenly and inexplicably, and you can only conclude "the hunt blew up."

The campaign, like the hare, is gone—and cannot be revived.

Take, for example, the ballot measure of a wildlife bond in 1990 that included $19 million for public access to land and replacement of the Churchill Dam in Piscataquis County on the Allagash. I was sailing along the road from Channel 8 WMTW about midnight. It was a beautiful moonlit night, and I had just finished up a TV performance there on election night, giving my unvarnished opinions on a variety of subjects and feeling good about announcing that our land bond issue had passed. According to our polling and Election Day exit polling projections, we had delivered a predicted win.

Imagine then my surprise—and chagrin—and terror—when I heard the calm radio voice of Mal Leary announcing to the world that it was official, the land bond had lost. Not only had we lost, but it also wasn't even close: 58 percent NO, 42 percent YES.

Talk about a hunt blowing up—this one had just blown up in my face after I'd told one and all that the hare was already in the back of my pickup truck.

I was mortified and embarrassed. I almost drove off the road.

The next day I apologized to the news team at Channel 8 and the principal client, the Nature Conservancy, and told the latter I would do a follow-up poll at my expense to determine what had happened. I did, and the subsequent polling produced a lot of soft data that showed surprisingly strong opposition to the part of the bond pertaining to the Churchill Dam that we had not picked up earlier, and it turned out that many environmentalists all across the state opposed its refurbishment.

This example could also be entitled "Nothing fails like success." We had guided a substantial number of land and wildlife bonds across the country for TNC in Minnesota, Nevada, New Mexico, Florida, and other states, including the 1987 bond in Maine. The Land for Maine's Future program would win subsequent bonds in 1999, 2005, 2007, 2010 and 2012.

These bonds were very important for hunters, as Edie Smith notes that her brother, George Smith, wrote in one of his popular newspaper columns: "When Angus King was governor, he insisted on inserting language into a new LMF bond issue to require all land purchased with LMF money to be open to hunting, trapping, and fishing. His top aide, Kay Rand, and I wrote that language. And it's been included in all future LMF bond proposals."

So, we were cocky, obviously too cocky on this one, and should have done more nightly tracking—and thrown more GRPs behind our ad. But we were careless, overconfident, and truly stunned when that hunt blew up—painfully in our faces, but doubly so in mine.

Another example of a hunt that blew up most surprisingly was Dan Wathen's campaign for governor in 2001. Wathen was a highly respected Maine jurist. James Longley had appointed him to the Maine Superior Court in 1977, Joe Brennan had appointed him associate justice of the Maine Supreme Court in 1981, and Jock McKernan had appointed him chief justice of the Supreme Court in 1992.

HERE COMES THE JUDGE

Out of the political nowhere and to the delight of many, Chief Justice of the Maine Supreme Court, Dan Wathen, announced that he was running in the Republican primary for governor.

As his announcement proceeded, I was truly intrigued and delighted. Why my delight? Because I love time travel. Ever since I was a kid, I have enjoyed science fiction, especially stories about time travel. The writings of Ray Bradbury, Poul Anderson, and Brian Aldiss captured my imagination and held it. It's always exciting to go back in time and see the past come to light and experience a bygone age.

Now that's what Judge Wathen's campaign initially brought me—a political time capsule. In one fell swoop at his announcement—from his home—the Judge provided us with a campaign right out of 1950. "No polling," he said, "no consultants, no media firms." That's the way people campaigned in 1950 in Maine. That's the way the political process worked so long ago. It's exciting to look back and see the way things were done fifty years ago. And I applauded him for bringing us, however momentarily, a glimpse of this Christmas past.

And it certainly worked for the Judge initially. An incredibly sycophantic press corps trooped up to his house in Augusta—not just at his announcement but afterward as well. Eager reporters, even those with jaded reputations, wrote down his every word. The *Portland Press Herald* even ran two pictures of the little devil, one of which showed him indeed sitting on his porch as if it really were 1950.

Or 1896 and he was William McKinley for that matter, sitting on his porch and letting the political world come to him as he ran for president. I loved it!

But of course the problem with time travel is that it brings with it paradoxes and conundrums galore. Although some of my good political friends— John Christie, Alex Ray, George Smith, and Mike Healey—believed he was just what the party needed, I thought that unless the laws of political gravity have been suspended for this race, he's already made a huge, fatal mistake. His statement about doing this race without professional political assistance was an echo from the very distant past. Unworkable now.

In 1950, candidates, especially Republican candidates, didn't need pollsters or consultants or media firms. All they needed to do was be themselves—successful Republican types. After all, in the decade of the 1940s, Republicans won every single governorship, every single Senate race, and every single House race that was up for grabs. That's right, every single one.

But by 2001, however, "No polling, no consultants, no media firm" meant something very different. In 2001, "No polling, no consultants, no media firm" equaled "No chance."

The last old-style campaign waged by as significant a figure as Judge Wathen was Margaret Chase Smith's reelection campaign of 1972. A towering and historical figure in Maine politics, she should have won comfortably in an otherwise Republican year, but she lost to Congressman Bill Hathaway 53–47 percent. Hathaway ran a modern campaign featuring very effective TV ads; but "Margaret," as she was affectionately known, only mailed postcards to her network of known supporters, reminding them to vote. She had no radio, no TV, no targeted direct mail campaign, and no statewide GOTV effort of her own. And consequently, she lost. Badly.

I thought Judge Wathen, too, would lose and lose ignominiously, or he would have to change his viewpoint radically. He'd have to alter his campaign strategy dramatically and hire a pollster and consultants and a media firm or he would lose.

You simply cannot campaign in the twenty-first century the way you did fifty years ago, even if the Maine press is incredibly sympathetic toward you.

Although I had to admit I've never seen the Maine press corps so mesmerized by a political figure in forty years of following politics. They worshiped this guy and gave him passes on just about everything; and the free publicity they gave him was more than they gave all the other candidates that cycle put together.

Part of the misperception about campaigns and how they are waged may be due to the illusion that the two Independent governors, Longley in 1974 and King in 1994, did it on their own. In fact, of course, without the brilliance of Jack Havey and Beryl Ann Johnson of Ad Media, and Jim McGregor, Longley would not have made it to the Blaine House. And Angus King had one of the strongest all-around campaign teams ever assembled in his 1994 venture.

You can't do it alone. You can't do it with your wife's cellphone. You can't just jump into the political realm and wander around any old way you feel like.

I also remembered the incredibly enduring truth of the 1970s film with Robert Redford called *The Candidate*. Redford says he will be the candidate, but "I want to go where I want and say what I want and do what I want." His astute campaign manager, speaking for all political professionals, writes his reply on the back of a matchbook. "You lose." Folksy loners make good copy and can hold the press attention for a while, but ultimately, believing in that self-image is a fatal flaw.

Over time, I thought, the Judge is too smart to believe in his own image and will act accordingly. I said he would have to do a major flip-flop and sign up a highly professional campaign team with pollsters and media consultants and a campaign staff. The Judge would have to change his mind and get with the twenty-first century.

Sure enough. It was fun. Like shooting fish in a barrel. No contest. Within weeks Dan Wathen, candidate for the Republican nomination for governor, went out and hired the political consulting firm Savvy, Inc. led by Dennis Bailey and the polling firm of Critical Insights.

I love predictions that come true—especially when I make them! There goes the Judge.

But no sooner was the ink dry on those consultant contracts when the Judge decided he'd had enough of politics and dropped out of the race. True to the off-handed way he entered the race, the Judge dropped out precipitously and somewhat gratuitously, leaving behind a wide range of supporters high and dry. Many were incredulous.

The hunt blew up just as it was getting started!

Apparently, the Judge had not been sleeping well and had lost twenty-five pounds and didn't like the person he was becoming on the campaign trail as a "politician." Fair enough, for the campaign trail isn't for everyone. In fact, I'd hate to have to do what the Judge and other candidates have to go through to get elected. I decided fifty years ago when *I* wanted to run for governor that while I love politics, I would hate being a candidate. So I have considerable sympathy for the Judge and those reasons for dropping out.

Unfortunately, the Judge didn't leave it there.

Now I don't fault him for not laying out another obvious reason he dropped out: his failure to arouse any significant interest on the part of those Republicans who would actually be voting in the primary.

But I do fault him for gratuitously holding up "politicians" as something he never wanted to be. That rang somewhat false to me. By his own admission, nobody asked the Judge to become "a politician." He decided that all on his own. In fact, had he asked anybody they probably would have told him to run as an Independent and run as a so-called Clean Elections candidate so that he wouldn't have to ask ordinary people for cash, but instead, just belly up to the public trough and dive right in.

Mostly, however, I found the Judge's remarks about politicians somewhat insulting. He sounded as if he had suddenly just found himself in a leper colony and wanted no part of them and feared whatever they had would rub off on him if he stayed! I thought that was a cheap shot. I have known hundreds of "politicians" in Maine, and for the most part they all deserve our thanks for taking time out from their daily lives to undergo the grueling and taxing political process.

The Judge was, as many who knew him agreed, intelligent and witty. I enjoyed meeting him at our Bowdoin candidate fair where he did a good job, finishing second, as I remember, to Mike Michaud, who stole the show. Later he and I shared a delightful luncheon, and I found him smart, well-meaning, and sincere.

Out of the political arena, he seemed a classy guy. And he would have a stellar future career doing good work on many fronts and getting further nominations for many important positions in the Pine Tree State: Paul LePage would later appoint him co-chair of the Maine Unemployment Investigation Commission. He was clearly a man of integrity and purpose, and bipartisan appeal.

In the political arena, however, he seemed totally at sea, or at least a fish out of water. But the truth of the matter is this: Maine is chock full of bright, witty, classy, public-spirited people. But they don't all make good candidates.

Being a politician, especially running for a major office, takes a ton of effort, perseverance, and a willingness to put in long, often thankless hours. Those who get off their duffs and out into the public arena and take their shots without whining and whimpering about how tough it is deserve our acclaim, not our disapproval.

As for the press, the Judge apparently found them too harsh and demanding. All I can say about that is in fifty years of following politics in Maine, I've never seen the press corps so mesmerized by a candidacy. Or so gentle to that candidate. Most of the working press treated the Judge with a deference they never accord others. It was a strange business and yet the Judge thought they were being tough on him!

When it comes to being a politician and running for major office in Maine, it takes guts and drive and a true sense of inner worth to slog it out day by day with the voters. It takes humility to put up with reporters' self-fulfilling prophecies and (usually justifiable) disdain for one's press releases. It takes a tough inner core to put up with all the bullshit of politics. It's not for everybody. It's certainly not for elitists who expect to be elected by acclamation.

Dennis Bailey, who was with the rogue hunters that fine year, offers another very candid assessment of this hunt and also the broader implication of life skills applied to the political arena:

Another thing candidates (and the news media) don't often understand is, if you *really* want to be governor—or senator, congressperson, or whatever—you really have to want it. I mean really want it, with every fiber of your being. That means being willing to undergo the indignities of a long campaign, the rough and tumble, the constant criticism, the cynical press, begging your friends and family for money, all of it. It's not for everybody. As Dan Wathen could tell you.

In early October 2001, Dan Wathen showed up unexpectedly at the Blaine House one morning and asked to speak to Governor Angus King. At the time, Wathen was the chief justice of the Maine Supreme Judicial Court, an intelligent, affable, and accomplished native of Aroostook County. After retiring to the living room, Dan pulled out an envelope and handed it to Angus, who immediately said, "Oh no, you're resigning?" Dan smiled and said, "It's worse than that."

The letter said Wathen was indeed resigning from the Maine Supreme Court . . . to run for governor. It was a big surprise. Wathen had been around politics and politicians for some time, going back as far as the Ken Curtis administration. He was appointed to the Superior Court by Independent Governor Jim Longley, elevated as an associate justice of the Supreme Court by Joe Brennan, and named chief justice by Jock McKernan.

After years of being in close proximity to governors of all parties, seeing them up close, Wathen apparently thought to himself, "I could do this job." And he probably could have. With his sharp legal mind, affable charm, and deep Maine roots, he probably could have been a good governor, even a great one. But there was one thing standing in the way: the campaign.

After surprising Angus with his decision, Wathen held a news conference to announce his bid. It did not go well. For one thing, it wasn't clear what party he was going to run in. Seems he hadn't decided yet. Then a reporter asked him his position on abortion. He said he hadn't really thought about it. You couldn't blame the reporters for being a bit confused.

After the disastrous news conference, I called Dan and offered my help. I had known Dan for years, going back to my days as a reporter. I liked him and really believed at the very least he'd offer an interesting contrast to the usual lineup of governor wannabes. We met the next day in my office, and I was stunned to learn that like his party affiliation and position on abortion, everything was unclear.

He had no staff, no campaign manager, no scheduler, no fundraiser. And most important, he had done no polling to see if his candidacy made any sense. I don't think he had even bounced the idea off his friends for their reaction and advice. He had jumped into the race without giving it much thought at all about what it takes to run a real campaign.

Over the next few days, I pulled together a small crew of experienced hands to run the nuts and bolts of the campaign. I thought things were going ok, but after only a few weeks, Dan called and wanted to meet with me. He came in the next day, red in the face, looking tired, stressed, agitated. He said he wanted to quit. Stunned, I asked why? He said, "I just don't have any free time." Wow. I said, "If you don't think you have any free time now, just wait until you're governor."

I suspected the real reason went deeper than that. Dan was a judge, someone used to a fairly cloistered environment, sitting in his office thinking deeply about complex legal issues, commanding respect from his peers and everyone else wherever he went.

A political campaign is the inverse of all that. One night at some small, rural county Republican committee meeting, and you discover that a lot of people not only don't respect you, they detest you, and will tell you to your face. They aren't impressed with anything on your résumé, and don't hesitate to challenge you on everything that comes out of your mouth. Like I said, it's not for everybody, and I suspect it's especially stressful to someone like a supreme court justice.

Nevertheless, I urged him to stay in the race and told him that the early days of the campaign are always the hardest, that we'd get more staff to help schedule his time better and smooth out all the rough edges. It would get easier. I also suggested that he have dinner with Angus at his home to see what after-hours life as a governor is like. It's mostly chaos. I don't recall ever being at Angus's home in Brunswick without cell phones ringing, the fax machine humming, pagers going off. Free time? What's that?

After meeting with Angus, who also encouraged him to stay in, Dan plodded on, but only for a short time. In late November, a little more than a month after he announced his candidacy, I was in Boston at my brother's for Thanksgiving. My phone rang early Sunday morning (I was still in bed), and I saw that it was Dan calling. I knew it wouldn't be good. The conversation was short. "I can't do this," he said. "I'm out." I didn't argue. I told him I would put out a news release announcing his withdrawal.

The moral of the story is that it takes a special talent to be a governor or any elected official. And it takes a special talent to be a likable, effective candidate too. And only rarely do the two talents combine to make one great package.

Our final example of a hunt blowing up ignominiously is quite astonishing, especially considering what happened afterward. George Mitchell's gubernatorial hunt blew up, just as the political cycle's sun was setting in 1974.

Mitchell was the odds-on favorite to win after defeating Joe Brennan, Peter Kelley, and Lloyd LaFountain in the Democratic primary and had a huge lead thereafter. In the Republican primary, Harry Richardson, Wakine Tanous, and Bennett Katz lost to Jim Erwin. Erwin was a capable, honorable man but had already run and lost twice before, and the losers in the primary were not likely to be of great help.

The Independent, James Longley, was unknown and, although charismatic, didn't have a much of a base to start with; and moreover, a lot of his ideas seemed unrealistic, even off the wall. It should have been a big year for the Democrats nationally, and Mitchell would have more money, more staff, more supporters, and quite a national tailwind. He should have won easily and was expected to do so. For a satirical look at the rise of Longley, see Willis Johnson, *The Year of the Longley.*

On Election Day 1974, I went to Lewiston. I always go there to see what is going to happen, and now there were masses of voters milling around, excitement in the air. Cars taking supporters to the polls were everywhere, Democratic field people were rushing around. I loved the feeling of the circus coming to town. It looked like a huge turnout. I ran into Charlie Micoleau, a fellow Bowdoin graduate and longtime, very effective operator for Democrats, including Senator Ed Muskie. I expected him to be smiling broadly and celebrating a Mitchell win.

Instead, Charlie looked stricken.

"We can't turn off the bubble machine," he said, referring to the Democratic GOTV effort. "We are taking Longley voters to the polls. So many of them. So many."

The Francos were in play! Again.

Again deciding a Maine election.

Just not in the way the Democrats had hoped.

I was stunned. Just like that, his hunt had blown up. Suddenly and irrevocably, the rabbit was away, and the dogs were running around aimlessly and fruitlessly and displaying every pernicious habit. Conventional wisdom had been turned on its head—for the first time in Maine history an Independent had beaten the Republican *and* the Democratic candidate for governor. The rabbit had turned around, and the dogs were running the other way, to continue our overworked metaphor.

The hunt had really blown up!

I don't care what the pundits and insiders say now—or what they say they said at the time, 90 percent of them, including me, did not predict that George Mitchell's 1974 campaign would blow up in such spectacular fashion. Only a rare few, like the *BDN*'s political reporter John Day and Auburn Mayor John Linnell correctly predicted a Longley victory in my hearing. I know because I firmly and confidently predicted to one and all that Longley would finish second. As the last part of this chapter will show, not everybody can declare "It's over" and be right.

I did think Erwin would finish last. Sent to Augusta the week before on some Cohen errand, I found Paul Hawthorne, the campaign manager for Erwin, looking at a huge wall-sized map of Maine, calmly moving around pins representing GOTV efforts town by town. I was pretty sure a lot of those units no longer existed or had already gone over to the enemy.

Why did Mitchell lose? With hindsight there is clarity now that was not there immediately. He wasn't then a very good campaigner; his campaign ignored Longley and concentrated his negative attacks on Erwin even though he didn't need to. He was out of touch with many voters—for example, using billboards all over the state in an era when the environmental movement had turned on them, and generally he ran a most lackluster campaign. His media was uninspiring. Larry Benoit, who would run Mitchell's subsequently successful US Senate run in 1982, says the difference was that Mitchell is actually a likeable, humorous, friendly guy, but in 1974 he came across as too serious, unsmiling, and aloof.

In 1974, however, the hunt had blown up, but good. Not only would he lose, but Mitchell would also receive an even smaller percentage in the general election (36.3 percent) than he had in the Democratic primary (37.5 percent).

The hunt had really blown up big time, but fortunately for him, George Mitchell would get another chance at rabbit hunting, this time for an even bigger super-sized one. After being appointed US Senator by Governor Joe Brennan in 1980 when Ed Muskie became Secretary of State under President Jimmy Carter, Mitchell was in a good position to run, although he began as a serious underdog in the polls when he came up for reelection.

But in an almost perfect mirror image of his disastrous 1974 campaign, he did everything right and emerged with a substantial victory, 61–39 percent. He had reinvented a mirror image of himself as an ace campaigner as he and his team, led by Larry Benoit, ran a nearly flawless race. It was as if he had made all the mistakes in 1974 and now had forgotten how to make any at all. That election night, beaming with excitement and pleasure and sporting a huge grin, he exclaimed the immortal political line, "I've tried losing and I've tried winning and I prefer winning." Those magical words still ring true in political circles. Not only was he a US Senator on his own, but he would also, as he proclaimed that night, no longer have to be known as "Swisher's little brother."

He was now a bone fide, fully elected US Senator, and as we saw in the sacrificial lambs chapter, he would go on to became the Senate majority leader and defeat his next Republican rival in 1988 by the largest margin of victory in the history of US Senate elections in Maine.

IT'S OVER

From the point of view of consultants and their clients, a much, much more desirable end game lament than "The Hunt Blew Up" is the exultant declaration, "It's Over."

I first heard the phrase in June 1972 when the votes had been cast in the Republican primary for Maine's 2nd CD between Bill Cohen and Abbott Greene. Mike Harkins, the national campaign consultant from Delaware, and president of the firm "The Agency," had been with us from the start and he was a veteran hand when it came to election nights.

Bill Cohen was ahead, especially after the Bangor results were in. He had been a popular mayor there, so it wasn't actually a bellwether for the Republican voters in the smaller towns north and east. I was very nervous because there was so much riding on the election for Bill and me and for our families. On Election Day, I am always spooked anyway, looking to the sky for "signs" as the geese are flying north, or flying upside down. It often gets worse after the polls finally close, and you know you can't do anything else to help the campaign succeed.

Anyway, even though Bill was ahead, and my head told me we were going to win, my emotions were asking how I'd feel when we lost. Lousy, I knew. So it was poignantly reassuring when Harkins, waving around some fragments of returns, announced confidently, "It's over. There aren't enough votes left out there, Billy, to catch you."

Thereafter, I've always been listening to hear those words myself. You'd think after all these years I would be able to say them myself with equanimity, but I've never felt comfortable saying them, even in cases where I thought they were warranted. To say them is to break a taboo, much as I like to hear others say, "It's over."

The same feeling washed over me during election night in 1980 when my first ballot measure was being counted. We hoped to win and thought we were going to win the Maine Yankee Shutdown referendum. But initially that night, the TV stations were all showing the YES side winning, first by hundreds, then thousands of votes.

"Where are those votes coming from?" a concerned Chuck Winner asked, beginning to wonder what we local yokels had gotten him into and maybe wishing he was in Los Angeles if things were going bad. "Just the back to the land crowd in Waldo County, the flat-earth people," responded Peter Burr, who was checking on some of the key precincts across the state. "No problem. Wait for the Franco votes. We're going to hit 60–40. No sweat. It's over."

"It's over," he said again for emphasis. I relaxed at once, though for Chuck it took a little longer.

Over time, Burr's "It's over" became widely known to consultants and campaigns as he worked for Republicans, Democrats, and Independents and was never shy about getting out front in predicting the outcome ahead of other pundits, the networks, the candidates, and the relevant campaigns.

Sometimes his early calls bordered on the seemingly insanely small amount of data.

For example, he called Bill Cohen's US Senate race in 1978 very early on election night based on only the results from Mohegan Island ("His worst town, he wouldn't go there for the Fourth of July") and two precincts from Presque Isle ("Always the predictor of predictors for a Republican statewide").

The night in 1994 when Angus King beat Joe Brennan in a very, very close race, Burr called in his projections from exit polling to the campaign headquarters at Cook's Corner at 5 P.M., announcing to one and all, "It's over.

Angus is our next governor. But don't tell him, I want him out there campaigning until 8 P.M." Kay and Dennis and I looked at each other and smiled.

The campaign staff was already having a good laugh that day as a $5,000 check from one of Maine's top businessmen arrived by courier just prior to Peter's phone call. Since said businessman had already donated $5,000 to Collins and $5,000 to Brennan, it seemed a welcome straw in the wind.

Perhaps the most humorous of his election night antics occurred in 1995 when the Gay Rights referendum was very close. Even though he had no official role in the campaign at all, Peter was bound and determined to declare victory that night in the Portland ballroom. He had to be physically restrained by people like Amy Pritchard who were actually running the campaign. Said operatives thought it premature to announce victory at 9 P.M. as he rushed the stage—especially since they were running a thousand votes behind at the time.

Of course, he was subsequently proven exactly right, but had to be content that evening with venting in an elevator to the legendary reporter turned columnist, Al "The Little Friend of Nobody" Diamon in an elevator, giving young Al his next whole column free of charge.

Great fun.

Another time Peter also proved annoying to some was in 1982 Republican primary for governor. Charlie Cragin almost drove off the road on his primary election night in June when he heard Herr Burr on the radio announcing Cragin's victory either before the polls had even closed, or shortly thereafter. Four others were running for the Republican nominations for governor that cycle.

"It's over," Peter declared across the state's airways to one and all, but not to that Cragin fellow himself.

Cragin often admitted to being chagrined that night. But perhaps he should have remembered the old Maine saying, "Never look a gift horse in the mouth," because looking back, he should have just taken the news at face value and counted his lucky stars.

Because in November of that year, there was Peter Burr again declaring early and often to one an all, "It's over." But this time he was announcing the news that Joe Brennan was trouncing Young Charles. This time Cragin was losing 62–38 percent. At least he got the bad news early.

The *worst* is waiting up all election night to discover that, in fact, your hunt *is* really over at 2 A.M. Just like it's better to lose by a huge amount than a fractional one (think second-guessing this and that minutiae for *years*!). It's always better to know you lost early, give your concession speech, and have a few drinks. It *is* over. This is very important! Think how much better off our beloved country would be if Donald Trump drank or conceded, or both.

Actually Burr had an anti-"It's over" approach as well if he didn't like the client or was just feeling frisky. In 1981 some Masters of the Universe types—I think they were from Congoleum or were their bankers, or both—showed up in Augusta on election night. Bath Iron Works had somehow convinced the legislature to put a bond issue on the ballot with money in it for the state to pay for the creation of a BIW drydock and ship repair facility in Portland.

Jack Havey of Ad Media, along with his fine team of John Christie and Beryl Ann Johnson, did strong commercials to sell the project to the voting public and on election night, four or five top executives flew up from New York or Milwaukee to watch the returns at the Ad Media headquarters with other major players in the effort, Bob Turner and Bill Haggett. The Congoleum executives had obviously been told to bring home a victory.

But by the time I arrived, Peter had taken it into his head to torture the visitors a little. Perhaps he agreed with Maine Common Cause, which had opposed the project, saying Congoleum was rich enough to pay for the new drydock without taxpayer assistance. Perhaps he didn't like the sense of entitlement he got from the visitors. In any case, he took umbrage at their presence and refused to play "It's over" with his usual verve and alacrity.

Luckily, the Ad Media facility was set up for self-sufficiency with a kitchen, editing suite, workout facility, and conference room. Peter thrived on junk food, consuming vast quantities of Pepsi and Cheetos as he sat hunched over his computer. "Boy, early returns look poor," he announced. The executives clustered around him and his jazzed-up computer projection screen as he threw precincts up onto the screen willy nilly.

"That's not good," he would mutter from time to time. Near panic prevailed as the executives saw streams of selected negative data. "Get me a Pepsi," he would call out, and one of the head honchos would run and get one, or "I could use some more Cheetos," and another would go off to find some. The Masters of the Universe had met their match. On the TV, Maine stations were showing the bond passing. "Don't pay any attention to the networks. They don't know anything," he insisted.

On and on it went for a couple of hours. Really quite amusing.

I had to leave the room several times to keep from laughing out loud when Peter took some tiny township result ("That's Cow Shit Corner up in Lincoln County, very important"), and shook his head glumly and demanded more Cheetos and more Pepsi. Jack Havey grinned as well at inappropriate moments, loving the byplay, his checks from Congoleum, like those of all good media consultants, already safely cashed well in advance. Gradually Peter fed in some other precincts, and ever so gradually things "improved" bit by bit on his private screen. As the running extrapolations finally went over 50 percent and then 55 percent, the boys from *away* got more and more excited. "I sure hope we can break 60 percent. That would be a convincing win," said one of the Masters of the Universe about midnight. Without missing a beat Peter responded, "Well, in order for me to get these numbers to finish above 60 percent, you guys would have to abstain from sexual intercourse tonight."

At that point, the executives seemed happy to settle for his final projection of 57.5 percent and trooped off into the night. I smiled all the way home in the moonlight, enjoying the convincing win and all the fun that went with it. Jack had even wondered what, if anything, the Masters of the Universe had on their waiting aircraft that night.

Thus, Dear Reader, on this happy note ends this chronicle of what odd things Maine people do for fun, profit, their causes, and our public offices in our GREAT STATE of MAINE.

Just think of what all the consultants mentioned in this volume did to make Maine history turn out the way it ultimately did.

Or happen in spite of them.

"You pays your money, you makes your pick," as they say up Cow Shit Corner way.

Let us close with those immortal words from earlier in this chapter, for they can be applied to virtually all consultants as much as they apply to candidates and causes:

"I've tried losing and I've tried winning and I prefer winning."

In their heart of hearts, all consultants agree.

In that regard, we all are truly Swisher's little brother.

BOWDOIN STUDENT AXIOMS

The sons (and now daughters!) of Portland families went to Bowdoin not to satisfy social customs, but to gain a serious education. —Barbara Tuchman, *The Proud Tower*

What fun it has been to explore politics with them! I learned as much from them as they did from me. Maybe more.

1. "Political wisdom isn't knowing what you're doing; it's knowing what to do next." (Kala Hardacker)
2. "It's hard to win without money, and easy to lose with money." (Elizabeth McCaffery)
3. "In ballot measures, keep your enemies close and your friends closer." (Chris Donnelly)
4. "You get on the back of a good horse and hold on." (Casey Tibbs)
5. "In politics, it's more blessed to receive than to give."(Cory Ferguson)
6. "If you can't be open to changing yourself, then you'll never change politics." (Hannah Colburn)
7. "It's not the size of the dog in the fight but the size of the fight in the dog." (Evan Fensterstock)
8. "Never underestimate the importance of hard work." (Andrew O'Brien)
9. "Washington is surely worth the walk." (Luke Wilson)
10. "Gone in 30 Seconds." (John Koperniak)
11. "In Maine, tradition is more than just a nine-letter word." (Nick Lawler)
12. "When challenging an incumbent, recognize the importance of name recognition." (Dylan Brix)
13. "Don't get trapped out of your frame or trapped in theirs." (Charlie Ticotsky)
14. "A lily pad has a maximum occupancy of one." (Megan MacLennan)
15. "In Maine politics, Mother Nature dominates." (Mike Karrat)
16. "Your opponent's weaknesses are not necessarily your strengths." (Melissa Davis)
17. "The enemy of my enemy is my friend." (Team Mitchell)
18. "Define yourself or be defined by others." (Mike Buckley)

19. "A winning politician finds opportunity in every mistake; a losing politician finds a mistake in every opportunity." (Brook Schafer)
20. "When it comes to media, identify your authority figures, or give authority to your opponent." (Aurora Kurland)
21. "Referendums, like children, need TV and authority figures." (Pat Driscoll)
22. "Hunting in Maine, a tradition unlike any other." (Paul Evans)
23. "Maine, the way politics should be!" (Ryan Turgeon)
24. "In Maine politics, if they lose their guns, you lose their votes." (Karen Reni)
25. "In Maine politics, it is how you play the game that determines whether you win or lose." (Peter Wadden)
26. "There are mainstream issues, and then there are Maine's stream issues." (Patrick Duchette)
27. "In politics, perception can be more important than reality." (Tim Colton)
28. "Seven days without Maine politics makes one *weak*." (K. J. Kozens)
29. "In Maine politics, it's important to think outside of the "big box." (Ingrid Anid)
30. "In Maine politics, the Independent candidate is only as strong as the major party candidates are weak." (Rich Hall)
31. "In Maine politics, the path from top to bottom is very short." (Brandon Mazer)
32. "In campaigns, taking the middle road makes all the difference." (Alex von Grechten)
33. "When in doubt, go negative!" (Jack Lynch)
34. "In politics, candidates are only as strong as their opponents allow them to be." (Greg McConnell)
35. "When running a campaign in Maine, be sure to respect your elders." (Greg Racioppe)
36. "In Maine politics, don't talk the talk if you're not willing to make the walk." (Tim Lane)
37. "Uncle S.A.M. wants YOU to vote for tradition." (Katie Gundersen)
38. "When campaigning for the future, it is important to learn from the past." (Team Anti-Same Day Registration)
39. "Maine, where elephants are jackasses and donkeys have long trunks." (Josh King)
40. "When campaigning in Maine, an ounce of small business will earn a gallon of Huguenot blood." (Ian Merry)

41. "Maine voters are like bottles of wine: the older they get, the more valuable they become." (Joanne Jacquet)
42. "Cross the aisles, walk the miles." (Team Pro Snowe)
43. "Behind every good candidate is a better team." (Team Anti-Casino)
44. "Never explain, never complain. Just learn the rules of *This Splendid Game.*" (Steve Robinson)
45. "In Maine, politicians must love the outdoors, or they will be kicked out the door." (Team Scontras)
46. "If you are riding a horse and it dies, get off it." (Peter Carter)
47. "The number-one priority of all politicians is to get elected. And the number-two priority is to stay elected." (Malcolm Gauld)

INDEX

MAJOR CONTRIBUTORS

Chris Potholm taught about Maine politics at Bowdoin for fifty years and is the author of eight previous books on the Pine Tree State: *Just Do It!*, *An Insider's Guide to Maine Politics*, *This Splendid Game*, *Maine: the Dynamics of Political Change*, *The Delights of Democracy*, *Maine: An Annotated Bibliography*, *Tall Tales from the Tall Pines*, and *Bill Cohen's 1972 Campaign for Congress*.

He has served as senior strategist for Bill Cohen, Angus King, and John Baldacci, and was involved in numerous ballot measures, including Widening the Maine Turnpike, Sunday Sales, Land for Maine's Future bonds, Save Maine Yankee, Elected Public Utilities Commission, Physician-Assisted Suicide, various anti-tax caps, school consolidation, bear hunting, moose hunting, forest practices, gay rights, and gay marriage, among others.

Dennis Bailey is a native of Livermore Falls, Maine. He received a BA in journalism from the University of Maine and worked as a reporter for the *Lewiston Daily Sun*, the *Maine Times*, and the *Portland Press Herald*. Dennis worked on the congressional campaign of Democratic state Senator Tom Andrews and became his communications director in the US House and reelection campaign. In 1994, Dennis joined the Tom Allen for Governor campaign as press advisor, and following the June primary was asked by Independent Angus King to join his campaign for governor. "When he joined my campaign," King said, "he added instant credibility to what had been often viewed by the media as a lark on the part of a neophyte Independent." Dennis served six years as Governor King's communications director.

In 2000, he launched Savvy, Inc., a public relations firm in Portland that represented businesses, law firms, political candidates, and state and local referendum campaigns. He served as Casinos *NO!* public spokesperson and strategic advisor in 2003 and went on to serve as a consultant on anti-casino efforts nationwide. He has a master's degree in strategic public relations from George Washington University. Now living in Portugal as a digital nomad, Dennis continues to advise clients and campaigns.

David Emery is a native of Rockland, Maine. He served as a state representative, US Congressman from Maine's First District, chief deputy Republican whip of the US House of Representatives, and as the deputy director of the United States Arms Control and Disarmament Agency, appointed by President Reagan, during which time he was acting ambassador to the UN Committee on Disarmament. After returning home to Maine, Dave served as interim president of Thomas College in Waterville, Maine.

He founded *Scientific Marketing & Analysis* to provide public opinion research and analysis. In that capacity, he provided polling and analytical services for a range of ballot measures, including Widening the Maine Turnpike, Land for Maine's Future bonds, bear hunting, and several Forest Practices campaigns, among many other Maine candidate and ballot measures. He also provided polling services for Maine media, businesses, and municipalities, and was the Republican consultant for the reapportionment of Maine legislative and congressional districts over four cycles.

Erik Potholm grew up in Harpswell and is the managing partner at SRCP media in Alexandria, Virginia. He received his master's degree from George Washington University and his bachelor's degree from Colby College. For the last twenty-five years he's created, directed, and produced award-winning advertising for candidates, referenda and initiatives, corporations, and trade associations. His recent clients include Texas Governor Greg Abbott, Ohio Governor Mike DeWine, the Republican Governors Association, the US Chamber of Commerce, and the major super PAC supporting US Senator Susan Collins.

Erik has also created advertising campaigns for over thirty successful statewide ballot measures around the country. In Maine, those initiatives include the Maine Turnpike widening, bear hunting, healthcare and vaccines, gaming, research and development, forestry regulations, transportation, and education.

Kay Rand, a native of Ashland, served as an intern to Senator Bill Hathaway and earned a BA in political science from the University of Southern Maine. She worked for the Maine Municipal Association and now serves on several boards and manages her consulting firm, Kay Rand LLC.

In 1994, Rand managed Angus King's startling upset victory for governor and served as his chief of staff in Washington, later becoming managing director of Bernstein Shur Government Solutions, the consulting arm of the law firm where she had a wide array of experiences dealing with public, non-profit, and business clients. She then managed King's successful campaign for the US Senate in 2012 and served as his chief of staff in Washington from 2013 to 2019. In 2018, on the floor of the US Senate, Senator King said,

"Kay reflects all the important aspects of good leadership: vision, teamwork, empathy, management, communication, optimism, decisive homework, integrity, and character."

Edie Smith is a native of Winthrop and a graduate of Bowdoin College. Her campaign experience is truly extraordinary. She has done signature gathering, fundraising, GOTV, and campaign management. She has also worked for numerous candidates (including Dave Emery, Angus King, and Les Otten). She continues to serve as a key staffer for Senator King, specializing in northern Maine.

Edie was involved in a host of ballot measures, ranging from Sunday Sales, Save Big Bird, and fish and wildlife bonds, and served as campaign manager for three of the most highly contested referenda in Maine history: Casinos *NO!*, assisted suicide, and bear hunting I. For her ballot prowess, she is known as "Queen of the South—and North."

She also did tours of duty at Eaton Peabody Consulting Group, the Maine Funeral Directors Association, Maine's Fish & Wildlife Conservation Council, the Coalition to Grow and Preserve Northern Maine, and the Maine Department of Inland Fisheries and Wildlife.